AF659196

Strategic Hospitality Management

STRATEGIC HOSPITALITY MANAGEMENT

Ajay Kaul

CENTRUM PRESS
NEW DELHI-110002 (INDIA)

CENTRUM PRESS

H.O.: 4360/4, Ansari Road, Daryaganj,
New Delhi-110002 (India)
Tel: 23278000, 23261597, 23255577, 23286875

B.O.: No. 1015, Ist Main Road, BSK IIIrd Stage,
IIIrd Phase, IIIrd Block, Bengaluru-560085 (INDIA)
Tel: 080-41723429

Email: centrumpress@gmail.com
Visit us at: www.centrumpress.com

Strategic Hospitality Management

© Reserved

First Edition, 2013

ISBN 978-93-81460-09-2

PRINTED IN INDIA

Printed at Balaji Offset, Delhi.

Contents

Preface

The most successful hospitality managers and leaders are able to see their properties or companies from a strategic perspective. They use this skill to differentiate themselves from their competition and create value for their customers and for the organization. Successful hospitality managers and leaders have a thorough understanding of the process of creating value and the role of the value proposition in developing the best strategy to create a unique, sustainable competitive advantage.

Strategy can be explored from a variety of different perspectives and there are many definitions of what strategy is. It is important to understand these different strategic perspectives so as to gain an holistic understanding of strategy formulation and implementation. It is often the case that the opening chapter of any generic strategy textbook will include an initial definition and interpretation of strategy. An analysis of the macro environment is crucial in determining the factors which have a direct impact and/or might influence the strategic direction of an organisation. A number of different concepts can be used to analyse the external macro environment in an attempt to identify those factors, which might have an impact upon the organisation, both in terms of being a threat or an opportunity. The analysis of the immediate competitive environment is important for understanding the strengths and weaknesses of the competition and the organisation's relative position in the industry. It is upon this basis that the organisation can then go on to formulate strategies that enable a strategic advantage to be gained over competitors. An understanding of stakeholder needs and expectations are paramount in the development, implementation and success of an organisation's strategy. It is therefore important to analyse the power and interest stakeholders may have over an organisation. The formulation of the organisational vision, mission, aims and objectives are crucial for the firm in having a clear strategic direction. However, the composition and content of the vision, mission, aims and objectives is open to interpretation. In contrast to analysing the external micro and macro environment, the resource-based view (RBV) seeks to explore the internal resources of an organisation and how these can be leveraged to gain a competitive advantage. An analysis of an organisation's resources can include its financial, physical, human, intellectual and reputational resources. In the deployment of these resources, it is also important to understand the competences and core competences of an organisation. Once an organisation has been through the process of analysing the external macro and micro environment and has conducted a rigorous analysis of its internal resources and culture, then the organisation is in a position to formulate strategies in pursuit of a competitive advantage. In order to fulfil a strategic direction an organisation will need to consider various strategic methods. This may include the formation of an alliance and merger with, or the acquisition of, another organisation. Alternatively the organisation may decide to achieve its selected strategy alone by growing organically. The evaluation and implementation of a strategy is important for understanding future strategy formulation. There are many alternative perspectives on how a strategy can be evaluated but it is not unusual for this to be broadly classified under the headings of suitability, acceptability and feasibility.

This book offers a comprehensive analysis of modern trends in hospitality industry. Every care has been taken to include material in accordance with the course contents of the students at various level of their studies.

—Author

1

Service Facility in Hospitality Industry

This chapter helps a housekeeping professional appreciate the role of various divisions and departments of a hotel and their contributions to operations. They will especially learn their needs from the Housekeeping Department. For example, most departments rely on the Public Area section of the Housekeeping Department for their cleaning requirements. First, let us see how the hotel is organisationally structured.

Large Hotel Organisation Structure

First let us understand some terms:

1. Organisation Structure: A framework that assigns responsibilities and channels of communications
2. Organisation Chart: A schematic depiction of relationships between jobs
3. A Division: A grouping of related departments,
4. Department: An independent activity that contributes to business.

The Housekeeping Department is clubbed under the Accommodations Division. There are essentially two major divisions: *Accommodations* and *Food and Beverage,* both supported by Staff Departments.

Food and Beverage Division

The Food and Beverage Division has a set of departments responsible for the sale of food and beverage.

These departments are:

- Restaurants
- Kitchens
- Kitchen Stewarding
- Bars
- Room Service
- Banquets
- Delicatessen
- Pastry Shop
- Human Resources.

Staff Departments

Staff departments are nonrevenue departments that create and support sales.

- Sales and Marketing Advertising, promotion, marketing and selling
- Finance and Accounting Financial management, accounting, F&B controls, purchasing, receiving, storing, MIS and audit.
- Information Technology Installation of hardware, software, main frame servers, cabling, net-working and troubleshooting
- Security Guest, employee, hotel security, fire prevention and fire sighting.

Small Hotel Organisation Structure

Smaller hotels have similar functions as larger hotels, executed by fewer people with multiple skills. For example:

1. The General Manager takes on the roles of human resources manager and sales manager in addition to the operations responsibilities.
2. The Front Office Supervisor overseas the front desk operations as well as lobby activities.
3. The Dining Room Supervisor oversees the dining room

operations and bar. Small operations would have limited restaurant options, possibly only a dining room that serves at all meal times. It is possible that the dining room has a dispensing bar to provide drinks eliminating the need for a formal bar.

4. The Housekeeper takes on the roles of the floor supervisors or the housekeeping control desk supervisor.
5. The Accountant takes over the income and payable responsibilities in addition to producing the statutory requirements such as Profit and Loss Statements and Balance Sheets.
6. The Purchase Clerk also performs the receiving and store functions. Though this is strictly not ideal in terms of food and beverage control, the operations are small enough for direct supervision and control of the General Manager.
7. The Food and Beverage Cost Clerk does all the costing functions.
8. The Engineering Supervisor is multi-skilled to troubleshoot engineering problems. However, an) operation requires specialists like airconditioning and heating mechanics and plumbers.
9. Most other services such as laundry, horticulture, civil works, etc. are outsourced.

The Front Office Department has the following functions:

- To reserve rooms
- To register guests into the hotel
- To provide information to guests during their stay
- To maintain their master bills.

Their prime responsibility is to sell rooms achieving budgeted revenue targets. The principal job positions are:

Front Office Manager: Oversees the front office and lobby. He translates company policies and procedures in practice in the department.

Front Office Supervisor: Oversees a shift in twenty-four hour front office operation.

Registration Agent: The person who registers guests into the hotel and allots rooms to them. *Reservation Agent:* Makes room reservations and controls the supply of rooms for sale.

Front Office Cashier: Maintains the guest folios (bills) and receives payment when guests check out. He functionally comes under the Accounts Department, but administratively coordinates closely with the front office.

Uniformed Services

The front office is supported by the uniformed services based in the lobby. Their main functions are:

- To provide porter services to handle guest baggage.
- To provide a lobby manager's desk for round the clock management contact.
- To provide transportation services.
- To provide concierge assistance for external facilitation.
- To provide valet-parking services.
- To administer a left-luggage facility.

The principal job positions are:

Lobby Manager: Oversees lobby operations and guest coordination services in a shift.

Concierge: Provides information and facilitation to in-house guests and visitors; handles guest and hotel mail; and provides the messaging services.

Senior Bell Captain: Responsible for all guest baggage handling services through bell captains.

Bell Captain: Oversees guest baggage services in a shift through a team of bell boys.

Bell Boys: Primarily handle guest baggage.

Transportation Supervisor.. Responsible for all hotel owned transport and services provided by drivers.

These include airport transfers, staff pick-up and city tours.

Doorman: Receives guests at the main portal and provides security information to Security Department. He also ensures traffic control in the hotel porch.

Valets: Provide car parking services to the visitors of the hotel.

Note: The Housekeeping coordinates closely with the Front Office for the preparation of guest rooms for sale through teams of floor supervisors and room attendants. The public area section cleans all front office and lobby areas while the florist provides floral arrangements. Details are given in subsequent lessons.

Business Centre

The business centre is a viable revenue generating operation nowadays, in a business hotel. It is considered a minor operating department under the accommodations division. They lease office space to visiting business persons on a daily basis. The business centre provides the following services:

- Office space on hire
- Reception services,
- Secretarial services,
- Office automation
- Meeting rooms, and board rooms.
- Broadband computer connections and telecommunication services.

The typical staff would include:

Business Centre Executive: Responsible for business development and Centre coordination.

Receptionist: Books offices, handles appointments and handles the billing.

Secretaries: They provide the secretarial services to visiting business persons.

Note: *Business executives who live on executive floors of the hotel have free access to a business lounge which has an exclusive ambience. The hotel provides special food and beverage service at these lounges. Housekeeping cleans both the business centre and business lounge.*

Housekeeping

This department is responsible for the cleanliness, maintenance and the aesthetic standard of the hotel. Its primary functions are:

- To clean guest rooms for sale

- To clean public areas
- To maintain and provide laundered employee uniforms,
- To maintain and provide laundered guest room and restaurant linen
- To decorate the hotel with fresh and dried flower arrangements
- To maintain the landscapes and gardens
- To administer the lost and found articles of guests.

Health Club

A health club is responsible for all health and recreational activities. These include:

1. Swimming pool
2. Children's pool
3. Gymnasium for men and women
4. Massage rooms
5. Turkish baths
6. Saunas and Jacuzzis
7. Spas
8. Yoga rooms
9. Aerobic rooms.

Sometimes, the operations are so large that health and recreation are segregated-the health club is under a Health Club manager, while recreation is supervised by a Recreation Supervisor. Typical jobs include:

Health Club Manager: Responsible for the organisation and control of all health club activities.

Masseurs and Masseuses: For massage of men and women.

There are variations in massages such as Thai massages, Kerala Massages, etc.

Yoga Instructors: Qualified to give yogic instructions. *Life Guards:* For swimming pool safety.

Gym Instructor: Supervises and maintains the gym independently for men and women, and gives specialist counsel on muscle building and weight loss.

Aerobic Instructor.-One who provides aerobic instruction for health and fitness to guests. *Receptionist-cum-Cashier:* Who registers guests and raises bills for the use of facilities. She would perhaps also maintain membership cards if the facility is open to the local populace.

Note: *While the poolside is cleaned by the Housekeeping, the swimming pool itself is maintained and cleaned* by the Engineering department. Health club areas are cleaned by the Housekeeping.

Recreation

Recreational. facilities in a hotel can include:

1. Squash courts
2. Tennis courts
3. Badminton courts
4. Para-sailing
5. Jet skis
6. Motorboats
7. Paddle boats
8. Surfing.

Typical Jobs Include

Recreation Supervisor: Manages/Oversees all recreational activities including the purchase of sports equipment, its safe storage, maintenance and repair of courts and revenue generation campaigns. *Coaches:* There may be separate coaches for tennis, squash, badminton, etc. There are separate coaches for water sports like parasailing, jet skis and surfing.

Life Guards: Provides safety at water sport centres like beaches, lakes, rivers and waterfalls.

Receptionist-cum-Cashier: Generates billing records and ensure due payment. Controls all memberships. Note: *The cleaning of beach fronts is a challenge which requires different skills including the ability to word* in and tackle sand..

Beauty Salon

A beauty salon has become increasingly essential in most of the superior hotels. This is because of the emergence of women travellers as a significant market segment. Women have pervaded all professions especially business. Hotels often lease space to beauticians who run the business. Many hotels want to ensure standards and have their captive beauty facility. Beauty salon personnel include:

Beautician: She is qualified in the subject and also supervises operations. *Hairstylists.* Specialists on hair cuts, perms, trims, styles, etc.

Manicurists: Experts on maintaining good hand and feet nails. *Waxing specialists:* These are experts in unwanted hair removal.

Cashier: Raises bills and receives payments.

Barber Shop

An extension to the beauty salon for women, is the barber shop for men. Men nowadays have become very fashion conscious and are influenced by superstars and the television. The barber is a stylist, and is as accomplished as the beautician. A large hotel can earn well from such a facility. The people that are found in the barber shop are:

Hairstylists: Crops and style the hair to latest fashions.

Manicurists: Attends to fingernails and toe nails.

Flower Shop

This minor revenue outlet falls under the purview of housekeeping. A hotel with plenty of landscaped gardens, nurseries and greenhouses use this source for additional revenue. Resident guests require well assembled bouquets for various occasions. The flower shop is manned by:

- Florist: Organises the flower shop. She also decorates the hotel with dried and fresh flower arrangements
- Assistant: Supports the florist in flower arrangements by cutting and pruning flower arrangements.
- Gardeners: Grow the flowers.

Engineering and Maintenance

This department is responsible for the following services:

- Airconditioning (or heating)

- Exhaust systems
- Boilers for providing hot water (and steam where applicable) for guests rooms, kitchens, and laundries.
- Lighting including the use of solar energy and biogas.
- Mechanical works including maintenance of mechanical equipment.
- Electrical works including managing the electicity substation.
- Carpentry.
- Electronic systems which includes sound systems and channel music, electronic panels, etc.
- Civil works including water supply, construction, masonary work, and painting, waste management.
- Plumbing
- Fire fighting system including water reservoirs, fire alarm systems, and fire fighting systems. They conduct fire drills periodically.

Chief Engineer: A man qualified and experienced to lead a team of engineers.

Mechanical Engineer: Responsible for all mechanical works like elevators, escalators, mechanical equipment, etc. He has a workshop where mechanics repair and maintain things.

Civil Engineer: Responsible for all building and allied services. In addition to carpentry, masonry, and plumbing, he is also responsible for all water treatment and sewage systems.

Electrical Engineer: Responsible for all electrical systems like power and lighting fed by substations to the building. He has the responsibility for the airconditioning and refrigeration.

Electronics Engineer: Responsible for all electronic equipment including networked personal computers, electronic engineering control panels, security systems, fire alarm systems, audiovisual systems, etc.

Note: *The Engineering Department maintains the housekeeping equipment, furniture and fixtures used in housekeeping operations. It also provides the central heating or air conditioning as well as lighting systems of the department.*

Staff Departments

Staff departments are those that support revenue generating activity of the hotel.

Finance and Accounts

The Finance and Accounts Department is responsible for two major activities:

1. Finance-responsible for raising funds and multiplying profits through innovative investments. It is because of this that the traditional accountant has been retitled as the Financial Controller.
2. Accounts-monitors the revenues and expenditures of the hotel. They ensure that cash flows are available for daily operations through the General Cashier. The Accounts Section prepares the statutory Balance Sheets and Profit and Loss Statements for the hotel investors. The Accounts Section has the following important professionals:

- *Financial Controller:* Creates the finance and accounting policies and procedures and ensures that they are followed.
- *Financial Analysts:* Manages funds.
- *The Income Accountant.*-Monitors all the cash and credit receivables from guests.
- *City ledger clerk:* Monitors all credit receivables.
- *Accounts Payable Clerk:* Pays all creditors including contractors and suppliers.
- *Salaries and Wages Clerk:* Computes monthly staff salaries and deductions.
- *Food the Beverage Controller:* Costs all food and beverages consumed and food outlets. He is responsible for the inventories of all stores including the General Stores-for items like stationery & general supplies; the Food Stores-for food items with longer shelf lives like proprietary sauces, packaged peanuts, etc.; Beverage Stores-for supplies of spirits, beers and v lees (Such stores are often 'bonded' as they store imported beverages also); Perishable Stores-which are refrigerated for perishable food items

like meats, poultry and vegetables; Engineering Stores-for engineering supplies; Housekeeping Stores-for supplies of linen, uniforms and draperies.

- *Purchase Supervisor:* For all purchases of the hotel from the market.
- *Receiving Supervisor:* For accepting all in-bound purchases by contractors.

Note: *Housekeeping professionals lean on this department for the following things:*

1. Salaries and wages;
2. issue of supplies from stores;
3. approval of the annual housekeeping budget;
4. purchase of goods; and
5. audit.

This makes Finance and Accounting Department a key section of the hotel for the housekeeping operations.

Human Resources

The Human Resources Department is vital to any hotel operation as it is concerned with the very important resource-people. The department is responsible for the following:

- Recruitment and selection
- Joining formalities
- Orientation and Socialisation
- Training and Development
- Compensation and Benefits
- Labour Relations
- Career Planning
- Rewards and Recognition
- Employee Welfare.

Human Resources Department has the following professionals:

- *Human Resources Manager:* Provides the hotel with capable talent and ensures that the people hired are well trained and motivated to meet the organisational objectives.

- *Recruitment Executives:* Fill permanent and temporary vacancies.
- *Orientation and Socialisation Executives:* Orient newcomers.
- *Training Executives:* Develop skills and careers according to the standards set by the organisation.
- *Compensation and Benefits Executives:* Ensure that salaries and wages are kept competitive.
- *Labour Officer..* Manages union relations.

Note: *The Human Resources Department selects and orients housekeeping professionals into the organisation. This Department sets the compensation package and pays salaries. Human Resources Department acts as a friend, philosopher and guide" throughout the career of a person by offering professional counselling, career plans, and professional advancement. They maintain employee's records during their career at the property.*

Sales and Marketing

The Marketing Department creates the groundwork that results in sales. Its scope of activity includes:

- Advertisement in various media such as television, newspapers, trade magazines, etc.
- Sales promotions to attract guests in different seasons and festivities.
- Sales efforts to corporate houses, travel agents. —our operators and airlines for volume business.
- Coordination with the front-office to improve room occupancy.

Sales and Marketing Department has the following professionals:

Sales and Marketing Manager: Alerts the management with the external changing environment through market research and market intelligence. He converts this into marketing plans that meet the revenue targets of the hotel.

Marketing Manager. Coordinates with advertising agencies who prepare advertisement campaigns; brochures and sales kits; merchandising material for all revenue departments of the hotel;

and special promotional campaigns. He will commission market research agencies to conduct guest surveys and competition analysis.

Sales Manager: Conducts personal sales calls with his team of sales executives.

Sales Executives: Their responsibilities may be distributed in two ways: (1) by geographical regions, or (2) by specialised clients such as travel agencies, airlines, corporate houses, diplomatic missions and government.

Information Technology

Hotels are leaning towards information technology to process information quickly to make important decisions. Departments are networked to access information that is important for their operational success. Progressive hotels have software that help them in the process. The IT Department is concerned with the following:

- Procuring and maintaining hardware (the computers and servers)
- Installing software
- Troubleshoot any user problems
- Network the departments to servers with lengthy cabling systems
- Train employees.

The department is led by an IT Manager supported by specialists in hardware; software; cabling and troubleshooting.

Security

The concern for security has become very important in modern times in view of terrorist actions, fire, and theft. In most of the hotels, the Security Department reports directly to the General Manager. The security activities include:

- Surveilance
- Crowd management
- Traffic management within the hotel precincts
- Protection of hotel property

- Taking the lead in case of fire
- Intelligence work
- First Aid
- Protection of hotel employees.

The job positions in the Security Department are:

Chief Security Officer: *To* create and implement the security *policies.*

Security Officers: They are supervisors to oversee security concerns throughout the property with *a* team of security guards.

Security Guards: They are positioned at vital spots such as lobbies, guest floors, car parks, basements, entry and exit gates of the property, and staff entrances who provide safety to guests, employees, and hotel property.

Doorman: He is positioned at the hotel entrance to welcome guests. He also alerts the management *of* any suspicious or undesirable people who enter the property.

Types of Rooms

A housekeeping professional must be familiar with the rooms and should have knowledge of the rooms of the hotel avail-able for sale. Housekeeping is responsible for cleaning and maintaining guest rooms and so this knowledge is essential for a housekeeping professional.

The features in each room determine the time and guest supplies required to prepare a room for sale. Each hotel has a variety of rooms to meet the needs of guests.

A single guest would like to stay in a single room which is more cost effective for him, while a couple will find a double room more convenient.

A family may choose a suite to have more leg room for children to move around. A business executive may want a special suite to entertain privately or show off his financial status to his or her clients. Similarly, budget groups may be willing to share twin rooms, while up-market groups may prefer single rooms. Guest needs are endless and their motives for booking a type of room may be varied.

Significance of Rooms

The sale of rooms contributes approximately 50 per cent or more to the total hotel revenue. In some lodging establishments it could be the only source of revenue. A room 'sale' occurs when a room is leased for occupation for 24 hours, at a predetermined cost. A room not sold on a particular day loses its opportunity to earn revenue for that day. Hence rooms are referred to as 'perishable' commodities. The loss of sale can also result from the inefficiency of the housekeeping department to have a room ready when required. What does a room mean to a guest?

It means comfort: Hotel investors translate comfort in the following manner:

- Quality beds and mattresses
- Weather control
- Channel music
- Hot and cold water
- Attached bathrooms
- Soft linen.

It is the responsibility of housekeeping to ensure that these comforts must be regularly maintained and in functioning order.

It means security: This need is translated in the following manner:

- A single door for entry and exit
- Double locks from inside
- Peep-holes
- Door chains
- Concealed electrical wires
- Secure connection of room equipment
- Fire detection system and sprinklers provide immediate response to a fire emergency
- Fire exit route plan behind the room door in case of an emergency
- Security personnel patrolling floors

- Entry into rooms by authorised personnel only.

Housekeeping personnel should remain alert to unknown guests on a floor and contact the security in case of suspicion.

It means privacy: Privacy is provided by the following:

- Guest room windows are provided with curtains or blinds.
- Superior hotels have daylight sheer curtains and heavy curtains for the night.
- The Telephone Department and the Front Office are instructed to protect information of room numbers and guests staying in them from the external public.
- Authorised personnel that wish to enter a room have to announce themselves.

Housekeeping staff is trained to knock the door announcing themselves twice before entering the room.

It means convenience: A guest is provided with entertainment, food and beverage ervices, telephone services, etc. in the room. The housekeeping department provides the guest a house directory to access such conveniences.

It means cleanliness and hygiene: A room is the most personal area of a guest during his/her stay. The room must be clean and the bathroom made hygienic for the guest's stay. This is a major factor that makes the guest to return. Housekeeping is responsible to clean and maintain all guest rooms.

A 'Home Away from Home': A hotel room provides a residen;e and address when a guest is travelling. They expect all the comfort and security of a home and-are willing to pay for it.

Layout of the Housekeeping Department

There is no ideal or universal model for the layout of a housekeeping department. The layout differs in hotels based upon the size and the limitations of physical space. However, the layouts must respond to certain considerations:

- The number of guest rooms determines the space required to maintain inventories of room linen and supplies.
- The number of function rooms determined the amount of linen to be maintained,

- The number of public area facilities and the anticipated volume of business determine the amount of restaurant linen to be maintianed.
- Whether the hotel decided to outsource some services like landscaping, flower arrangements, tailoring, upholstery, laundry, etc. to be able to optimally utilise space.
- The number of total employees for the amount of uniform inventories that have to be maintained. Hotel space is .valuable and used mostly to gen.-rate revenue. An investor makes decisions whether to allot space to revenue generating activities areas or submit to nonrevenue activities such as housekeeping. He chooses most unattractive locations in the building for nonrevenue activities. It is for this reason that the housekeeping department is located in the basement termed as 'backhouse' areas.

Housekeeping Design Factors

There are a few considerations to be kept in mind when planning housekeeping facilities:

(a) It must be accessible to all employees of the hotel as they visit the uniform room for exchanging uniforms. Food and beverage personnel and floor supervisors visit the linen room for exchanging linen.

(b) The location must be away from guest view and traffic.

(c) The floors must be strong for heavy equipment such as laundry machines.

(d) The sound and vibration of equipment should not disturb guests.

(e) Effective climate control is necessary. Extreme temperatures ruin textiles and equipment.

(f) Housekeeping corridors must be spacious for mobile equipment and staff traffic, especially at exchange counters of the uniform and linen rooms.

(g) Adequate storage to stock volumes of linen, uniforms, cleaning detergents, operational equipment, lost and found items, toxic chemicals, etc.

(h) Utilities such as power, fuel, water and steam connections are required for housekeeping and laundry equipment. The utility connections should be easily accessible and concealed for safety.

(i) The facility design must be so that it is easy to keep the facility safe and sanitised. Cleaning crews must have access to every corner of the facility especially under heavy equipment.

(j) The layout should match the type of building construction. Skyscrapers, for instance, require efficient service elevators while chalet-type resort properties may require sturdy access roads to roll trolleys and carts.

(k) Distribution points for linen may vary. Busy hotels may have floor pantries, while chalet-type resort properties may need service huts to serve a given number of chalets.

(1) Physical fatigue is caused by too much movement, lack of climate control and carrying heavy loads. The physical layout should take productivity of staff into account while planning the facility.

(m) Lighting must be bright in linen and uniform rooms so that stains and damages can be spotted.

(n) Every government prescribes safety codes especially where people work. The codes prescribe adequate methods of waste disposal, recycling of materials like bottles, newspapers and cans, sanitation schedules, preventive maintenance schedule, etc.

Layout and Housekeeping Facilities

It is representative only. It portrays the basic facilities required by the Housekeeping Department.

Its main features are:

- It is the main administration centre for the department.
- It must be an independent cabin for silence and privacy.
- It is glass-panelled so as to give the Housekeeper a view of what is happening outside her office.

- The office is preceded by a cabin for the secretary who would control movement into the Housekeeper's office.

Control Desk Room

Its main features are:

- It is the main communication centre where relevant housekeeping information is sent and received.
- It is the nerve centre for coordination with the front office, banquets, etc.
- The room has a desk and a chair, preferably more than one telephone, and a computer terminal for information storage and control.
- It should have a large notice board to display essential information for the staff.
- The Desk Control Room is the point where all staff report for duty and check out at the end of duty. It adjoins the Housekeeper's Office.

Lost and Found Section

Its main features are:

- It is a cupboard in the Control Desk Room to store misplaced guest belongings that may be claimed later.
- It is away from thoroughfare.
- The area is secure, cool, and dry.

The Linen Room

This is where current linen is stored for issue and receipt. Its main features are:

- The room is well lit, large and airy, and free from heat and humidity.
- It has adequate shelves to stack linen and secure it from pilferage.
- The linen room has a counter for the exchange of linen.
- The linen room must adjoin the in-house laundry for smooth and speedy exchange of fresh and-r soiled linen and uniforms.
- It is accessible only to authorised persons.

The Uniform Room

This room stocks the uniforms in current circulation. It is possible that smaller hotels may choose to combine this room with the linen room as shown in the layout above. The volume of uniforms in circulation determines whether to have an independent uniform room or not. The features of a Uniform: Room are:

- Hanging racks as most uniforms are best maintained when hung.
- Shelves for regular hardy uniforms like dungarees, chefs jackets, etc.
- Cupboards for small accessories like gloves, ties, bows, caps, etc.
- Exchange counter for employees who come to collect and deposit their uniforms.
- Exchange counter with the in-house laundry
- It has only one entry/exit door for security

Housekeeping Store

The store stocks materials for linen and uniforms. Ideally, the stock maintained should be enough to replenish once all over the whole hotel. However, due to budgetary constraints the hotel may stock less. Stocks in the store are only touched when the linen or uniforms in circulation fall short due to damage or loss. The main features of the store are:

- The room should be cool and dry.
- It is provided with shelves to stock the linen and materials. Larger hotels may have an independent store for linen and another for uniforms, based on the volume of materials in circulation and the hotel's policy to stock such large numbers.
- It has only one entry/exit door for security.

Heavy Equipment Store

This is a store to stock bulky housekeeping equipment like vacuum cleaners, carpet shampoo machines, ladders for chandelier and window cleaning, etc. Its main features are:

- The room should be clean and dry.

- It is securely lock°d to prevent pilferage or theft, as they constitute substantial capital investment.
- It has only one entry/exit door for security.

Tailor Room

This room is for in-house full-time tailors who stitch and mend damaged linen and uniforms. Its features are:

- The room has sewing machines at machining stations based on the number of tailors employed.
- It has shelves and cupboards to store materials used for uniforms.
- It is accessible only to tailors and uniform room personnel.
- It is a clean and dry place.

Smaller hotels may outsource this function to reliable tailors in the city to save space and recurrent labour costs.

Upholstery and Furniture Yard

This is a space provided to store damaged upholstered furniture. Tailors specialised in re-upholstery work in this yard. Since furniture takes space, it requires adequate space, to store them.

The Floor Linen Room (Pantry)

Each guest floor has a floor linen room to keep a supply of linen, guest supplies, and cleaning supplies to service the rooms on a floor. Its features are:

- It is the housekeeping nerve centre for the floor.
- It is away from guest view situated at the end of floors or off the foyers of service elevators.
- It maintains a complete turnover of fresh linen to service all rooms on the floor.

Flower Room

This room is used by the in-house florist who prepares flower arrangements for display at various parts of the hotel. Flowers beautify rooms and public areas. They are supplied to restaurants for table decoration and buffet displays. Its features are:

- The room is air-conditioned to keep the flowers fresh.
- It has work tables to assemble the flower arrangements.
- It has a tap with running water and a sink.

Green House

This is an external facility to grow exotic plants that need special climatic conditions. Horticulture comes under the housekeeping and therefore, this facility is provided for by the housekeeper. Its features are:

- It is a an area covered in polythene or glass.
- It has a water source to water the plants.

Horticulture Equipment Store

There are a number of garden equipment such as lawn mowers, spades, rakes, pots etc. That is essential for gardening operations. These need to be stored safely. The store is an external facility easily accessible to gardeners. The size of the store increases as the area of landscaping increases.

Organisation of the Housekeeping Department

Housekeeping responsibilities embrace the entire hotel. Naturally, the largest work force of the hotel belongs to the Housekeeping Department.

Responsibilities of Housekeeping

We observe from the charts that Housekeeping has responsibility of six broad areas.

1. The cleaning of guest rooms
2. The cleaning of public areas
3. The upkeep and exchange of linen and uniforms
4. The maintenance of external landscapes and gardens as well as internal flower arrangements
5. The management of the laundry
6. Communications through the Control Desk

These areas need human resources to carry out the work. Each area needs an expert to fulfil the responsibility of tasks involved. Let's see briefly the responsibilities of each one of them.

Executive Housekeeper

- Is the head of housekeeping
- Is responsible for translating hotel policies, procedures, and standards into housekeeping operations.
- Is normally a woman's role and part of the middle-management team.
- She represents the department at the General Manager's meetings
- Ensures that all the resources made available to her are effectively utilised.

Assistant Housekeepers

- Heads a shift in a twenty-four hour housekeeping service.
- Explains the Executive Housekeeper's policies, procedures, and standards to all the housekeeping supervisors and ensures that they are actualised at the operational level.
- Substitutes the Housekeeper in her absence.
- Perform some administrative functions.

Floor Supervisors

- Direct the cleaning and maintenance of guest rooms on allotted floors.
- Controls the resources on the floor which include room attendants and housemen; bed and bath linen; guest and room amenities; and cleaning equipment and detergents.
- Responsible for the cleaning and maintenance of guest rooms as per policies, procedures, and standards of the establishment.
- Supervise the exchange of floor linen with the laundry.
- Ensure their proper storage of linen in floor pantries.
- Ensure the supplies are readily at hand and requisition them from stores in case of any shortfalls.
- Give feedback to the front office on the occupancy status of guest rooms in each shift as a measure of controlling room sales and availability.

Control Desk Supervisor

- Coordinates communication with housekeeping personnel spread to all parts of the hotel.
- Coordinates with the Maintenance Department to ensure that all maintenance requests are attended to.
- Coordinates with the Front Office to take over departure rooms for cleaning and to release cleaned rooms.
- The Control Desk is manned in all shifts as it is the lifeline for all housekeeping staff.
- Controls lost and found procedures.
- Performs some administrative functions.

Room Attendant

This is a common title for both men and women. Women room attendants are also called chambermaids, housemaids, or room maids.

- They are responsible for cleaning and maintaining allotted guest rooms as per set procedures and standards.
- They are the eyes and ears of the security team to report any untoward incidents.
- They ensure the privacy of guests at all times.
- They alert the concerned department of any maintenance and engineering requirements in the room.

Housemen

They are male cleaning personnel allotted to rooms and public areas to manage heavy cleaning duties. [heir duties include

- moving heavy furniture
- vacuuming long corridors of carpet
- helping in the exchange of linen from floors because the sheer volume requires strong hands
- cleaning public area spaces and furniture
- cleaning windows.

Linen Room Supervisor

- Coordinates the exchange of soiled linen for fresh ones with a team of linen attendants.
- Is the custodian of the linen asset and ensures their security.
- Maintains proper storage conditions to minimise minimise loss due to damage and theft.
- Works closely with the Laundry for the supply of clean linen.

Uniform Room Supervisor

- Is responsible for keeping uniforms in safe storage conditions.
- Issues laundered uniforms to hotel staff against soiled ones.
- Is assisted by with a team of Uniform Room attendants and tailors.
- Coordinates closely with the Laundry for washing and dry-cleaning schedules to keep constant supply of fresh uniforms.

Tailors/Upholsterers

They mend uniforms, linen and upholstery to give them longer life. Some hotels may have the tailors stitch uniforms in-house. Smaller properties may outsource this activity.

Public Area Supervisor

He ensures the cleanliness, maintenance and aesthetic upkeep of all public areas like lobbies, restaurants, banquets space, etc. with a team of housemen.

His area of control is *very* large and he has to be energetic to give close supervision to every public area.

Horticulturist

He is responsible for the upkeep of all landscapes and gardens with a team of gardeners based on the area. The task becomes more challenging when landscapes include waterways, fountains, waterfalls, rockeries, etc.

Florist

He is responsible for all internal flower arrangements for guest rooms, public areas, banquet, buffets, etc. He may be given an additional charge of maintaining a florist for sale of flowers and bouquets to resident guests and the public.

Gardener

He is responsible for the upkeep of an allotted area of a landscape. He may be required to maintain internal plants and roof gardens also, where required.

Laundry Manager

Normally a male, has a large brigade of washer men, drycleaners, ironers, etc. (discussed in detail in Part 10, "Laundry Services").

Competencies of a Housekeeping Professional

Competencies are a set of behavioural traits and technical abilities that are suitable for a job. While new technical abilities are covered extensively in the section of "Introduction" titled "The New Housekeeping Professional" (readers are urged to read it along with this lesson), we shall look at behavioural sets required. To fulfil them, certain behaviour traits are essential to complement knowledge and skills. Behaviour competencies traits translate into competencies. Recruiters give importance to competencies when hiring housekeeping professionals. Here are few competencies of which some are age old and some new in keeping with the times.

Competencies —-Smile!

Many of us may have forgotten how we look when we smile. Many have even forgotten to smile! Yet it is the most enduring competency required of hotel professionals. As simple as it may seem, it is the most effective way of dealing with guests. A smile gets a smile in response. It immediately breaks down barriers of fatigue, low spirits, doubt, anxiety, etc. Recruiters look for this competency at the time of interview. It is recommended that housekeeping professionals smile in front of the mirror and assess their competency in it. Keeping a smile, while speaking on the telephone, is a powerful way to convey tone and intention to guests and colleagues who judge the caller by the voice. We must not forget that housekeeping personnel are in direct contact with guests in guest rooms, on the floor and in public areas. While care is taken to be as unobtrusive to guests as possible, contact with them is inevitable.

Grooming and Hygiene

Grooming is an important feature of a hotel professional. The room attendant, floor supervisor, houseman, public area personnel and cloak room attendants have face-to-face contact with guests of the hotel.

He, therefore, carries with himself the image of the property. A well-groomed housekeeping member represents qualities of hygiene, professionalism, management style, reliability, etc. Some Tips for a Male Housekeeping Professional:

1. Hair should be cut close.
2. The uniform should be spotless and well ironed. A tight or oversized uniform should be avoided as it gives a sloppy appearance.
3. Nails should be well manicured and hands absolutely clean. This is important especially since housekeeping personnel deal with the most intimate part of the guest's stay-the room.
4. Staff must guard against body odours or cheap perfumes. The market has some wonderful antiperspirants.
5. Shoes should always be polished, and of a conservative style.
6. A close shave is necessary before starting duty. Stubbles of a beard or moustache should be avoided as they could look uncomely.
7. Bad breath could be nauseating to a guest since a houseman could speak to the guest at close proximity.
8. Uniforms must be crisply ironed and clean.

Some Tips for a Female Housekeeping Professional

1. The elastic hair band should always be clean.
2. High heels could be physically strenuous to the women

as they have to be on their feet for a complete shift. Flat shoes with sturdy heels are advisable.

3. Stockings should be clean.
4. It is preferred for them to wear a light make-up to project a professional working image.
5. Excessive jewellery should be avoided.
6. A very strong perfume could leave its presence in a room. Some guests could feel nauseated. Fresh light cologne is preferable.
7. Uniforms must be crisply ironed and clean.

Basic Etiquettes

The hotel business is a social business. All front/line personnel are required to have the ability to communicate effectively with certain manners and etiquettes associated to a good host.

The basic etiquettes that a housekeeping member should exhibit are to:

1. Smile and attend to guests as soon as they approach them. Acknowledge their presence by wishing them the time of the day.
2. Recognise guests-Recognition is a powerful tool to use for regular guests. The use of their name gives them importance and a feeling of belonging.
3. Be polite to guests by frequently using terms such as "Thank you", "Please", "May I help you?", "Excuse me", "Pardon me", etc.
4. Avoid mannerisms such as touching the hair, scratching oneself, picking the nose, etc. 5. Stand erect at all times.
6. Listen carefully to guest needs. Note down their requests and room number.
7. Assist guests wherever possible especially in providing them information about hotel services. This requires thorough knowledge of hotel services. Take action on the request immediately.
8. Talk softly.

9. Avoid arguing with service staffand guests on the floors and public areas.
10. Carry pencils in the pockets and not behind ears or clipped in front of the uniform. 11. Desist from chewing gum or beetle nut.
12. Enter and leave the floor through the service door only.
13. Shut the doors quietly.

Orderliness

Guests evaluate a property by how orderly the hotel personnel are. They observe whether the maid's carts are kept clean and in an orderly fashion. Corridors must be kept clean and free from litter.

1. Keep all linen and supplies in the maid's cart in an orderly manner.
2. Ensure that flower displays in rooms and floor foyers are fresh and properly arranged. Contact the florist if necessary.
3. Keep the access door to the service landings closed at all times. Most properties install a swing door with a peep window.
4. Floor foyer telephone tables must be kept clean at all times. A handy duster is helpful to keep the counter tops clean and polished.
5. Ensure that cigarette urns in the foyer are cleared of cigarette butts regularly.
6. Garbage hampers are essential features of maid's carts and garbage chutes are important in service landings.

Teamwork

Teams have become the cornerstones of service operations. A poor team performance can severely damage the establishment's reputation, while superior team performance directly enhances it. Teamwork is one of the essential competencies at the time of recruitment. Results are the responsibility of the entire team and not the team leader alone. Team dynamics have changed over the years. Let us understand the anatomy of teamwork.

What is a Team?

A team is a small group of people, who rely on each other to achieve a common goal.

No one person can deliver any goals. It takes a team with L, complimentary skills to AA;– rults with complementary specialisations with the desire to accomplish objectives and hold themselves responsible for a success or failure.

Why should we have Teams?

Teams-can meet significant performance challenges. They have a common purpose and are able to assist when a team member is slow. They harness the complimentary skills of team members and have trust in their competency. They can be an influence on each other to be ethical, disciplined, and motivating.

Who is the Team in a Housekeeping Operation?

The direct teams are the teams of the floor supervisors with their coterie of room attendants and house-men and the team of the Public Area Supervisor with her team of housemen; and the linen/uniform supervisor with her team of attendants and helpers.

The indirect teams are the teams of the head gardener comprising gardeners; the linen/uniform supervisor with her team of attendants and helpers; maintenance personnel who rectify engineering problems; and the laundry who supplies fresh linen and uniforms; etc. The performance of indirect teams is crucial to the success of direct teams.

What is the Team Leader's Role?

The team leader's role is to build commitment to the common purpose. He or she fills gaps in competencies; delegates leadership; is himself a hands-on performer with the team; makes key decisions and manages external relationships including the management, guests, and suppliers.

What are the Team Member's Qualities?

They are all performers who find excitement in their performance. They take ownership of the task and) objectives and hold themselves accountable for success or failure. They have a sense of urgency with youthful enthusiasm and energy. They are result oriented and respect each other.

Attitude

Attitude is a buzzword in modern operations. We wear an attitude. In other words, attitudes are some-thing that we own and are responsible for.

It comes from within and can be positive or negative, based on one's experiences. Let us take an inventory of key attitudes required in housekeeping operations:

1. The joy of serving people-The benefits of service are many. People are giving business to those who have better service. A good service gets better paychecks and tips. It ensures repeat customers. Service is the cutting edge.
2. A cheerful attitude-It is infectious and spreads cheer and goodwill to others. It fosters a pleasant and tension-free workplace.
3. Cooperation is vital in team performances. Unless you do not cooperate with others, they will not cooperate with you.
4. Pride in one's work-This brings excellence. There is a difference between doing routine work and doing work with an aim to make a difference. Service can be done with showmanship, sincerity and enthusiasm. Initiative-This is a valued competency in today's world. The only way to beat competition is to innovate and bring in new ideas. Each housekeeping professional must always look for new ideas and introduce them. Some may have the benefit of directly introducing new ideas, while others will need to seek the approval of superiors. Continuous improvement or "Kaizen" is a science introduced in by the Japanese, which has made them economic giant.
6. Salesmanship-This is a vital job requirement to motivate the guest to spend that extra dollar.
7. Honesty-This is a precious attribute. There are many temptations in a service operation. There are opportunities for theft of property and guest belongings; misleading

guests with information; giving secrets to competitors; etc. Organisations value and reward employees who are upright and truthful.

Self-Discipline

Discipline is the hallmark of a good housekeeping professional. This is because the temptations in a hotel are many. Discipline is of two types *physical,* where grooming and physical conduct play a role; and *mental,* which demands sincerity, honesty and perseverance. Here are some tips for the housekeepers and supervisors to prevent indiscipline:

1. Update continuously with the house rules and regulations.
2. Make disciplined behaviour bring reputation, recognition, better rewards.
3. Act professionally at work by being businesslike in actions and conversation.
4. Amend mistakes immediately.
5. Always air grievances in privacy.
6. Be an example to others.
7. Improve skills by training to avoid mistakes that may be viewed as indiscipline.

Courtesy

It is the hallmark of a Hotel professional. Courtesy must be shown not only towards guests, but also towards colleagues.

Courtesy should be inherent in one's nature and a sign of one's desire to please those with whom one comes in contact with. Courtesy should not be a "technique" but a spontaneous and genuine manner.

Being courteous not only makes the operations smooth, but also ensures better relationships.

Examples of courtesy are:

(a) Each approaching guest must be attended to with a smile and a cheery greeting.

(b) If the staff member knows the guest's name, it is advisable to address him or her by the name as this gives the guest recognition. Do not mispronounce names or call them by somebody else's name!

(c) If rooms are not ready when a resident guest arrives, ask them if you should return later. If they permit you to continue, complete the task quietly and quickly.

(d) When a guest is seeking assistance on the floor use the word 'assist', e.g. "May I assist you" or "May I be of assistance".

(e) When listening to guest requests or complaints, show empathy and tell them what you will do to meet that need or resolve the complaint. Then do it. A guest must not need to remind housekeeping about the issue again.

(f) After completing any transaction say, "Thank you, have a pleasant day", It should be said with utmost sincerity.

Intrapreneurship

Intrapreneurship means "internal entrepreneurship." Housekeeping professionals must think like businesspersons by constantly evaluating one's performance and find ways to improve productivity and quality. They should be also resourceful to meet emergency situations. The housekeeping thinks dollars and how to give the owner a return on investment.

Continuous Education

Housekeeping professionals will be required to upgrade themselves constantly. They should not wait for the organisation to improve their knowledge and skills, but take initiative for self-development.

This they can do by reading relevant trade magazines, learning through websites, attending seminars, joining professional bodies that advance knowledge, or going back to hotel schools to learn or read textbooks of hotel schools.

Organisations expect the true professional to convert new ideas into business opportunities for the hotel and are willing to reward such enterprise. A follow-up on learning is certification. Professionals show physical proof of their learning. The effort of the future professional must be to get more technical qualifications.

Customer Orientation

The customer is the king. Unless a hotel makes the customer as their main focus, the business is likely to decline. Customer focus means putting all thoughts and actions towards creating positive customer experiences. This is achieved through empathy and proverbially described as "putting yourself in the guest's shoes." It requires sensitivity to guest needs and responding to them in a timely manner. If a lady guest requires a hairdryer at the middle of the night, she must have it! Excuses for inaction are many, but going that extra mile to provide the guest needs makes the difference between one hotel and another.

Physical Fitness

The television has rightly exposed the public to health and fitness. A housekeeping professional must be physically fit to manage rigorous hours on his/her feet. There is a saying that "a healthy body makes a healthy mind." It is very true. If a person is physically fit it translates into energy, enthusiasm, ability to cope, lightness, youth and joy. Housekeeping professionals must bring in physical fitness regimen into their personal lives. It may be just an hour's walk in one's neighbourhood or a workout in a gymnasium.

Eye for Detail

Housekeepers worldwide have been known for their eye for detail. This term means that the person has a sharp eye to detect things that are not quite right. It is in view of this competency that women are selected as housekeepers, and it is presumed that women acquire a greater eye for detail from their roles at home. However, men have also come into housekeeping and have shown this competency over the years. This competency appears repeatedly in all housekeeping job descriptions.

1. Grooming reflects on the image of the property.
2. The hotel business is the alchemy of showmanship, tact and sociability.
3. Housekeeping personnel can use the guest elector to reach the floors.
4. Recognition gives a guest the feeling of belonging.

5. Guest requests may be actioned the next day.
6. A team consists of people with complementary skills.
7. A team leader's role is to build commitment to a common purpose.
8. Always air grievances in public.
9. A reason for indiscipline is to attract attention.
10. Housekeeping personnel must upgrade themselves constantly.

Housekeeping Administrative Duties

There are certain routine tasks that a housekeeper does on a daily basis. These are essential to keep the operations smooth.

Routine Tasks of the Housekeeper

Taking Attendance

Attendance is taken in every shift as it affects salaries and wages. Some workers are paid hourly wages while others are paid a monthly salary. Salary is related to attendance or the person's presence at work.

The Executive Housekeeper must maintain three attendance registers:

(a) One which has all the names of housekeeping personnel listed on a single page.

(b) One which devotes a page to each housekeeping member, recording the number of hours each has worked, along with their days off, overtime statistics and special duties.

(c) One register that records the hours put in by daily wagers or hourly based-employees.

Modern technology has introduced the timecard system that does away with tedious registers. The moment an employee is hired, the Human Resource Department issues a time card that is maintained at the time office located at the employee entrance at the back of the hotel. This is a single door through which all employees enter and exit the building. The time office (as the name suggests) is where employees register their time-in and time-out. It is located at the employee entrance. The time office is manned 24 hours of the day by timekeepers in three shifts. The system consists of specially designed cards that have columns for the dates, time-in and time-out, which are maintained in racks at the time office.

The timekeeper punches the time through a time punch machine each time an employee enters or exits the hotel. This is a foolproof method as machines do not lie. Modern technology has introduced electronic time punch machines that send the data directly to terminals in the Accounts Department, Human Resources Department and the Housekeeping Control Desk. Each can monitor when an employee has clocked in and out.

The registers or time cards are legal documents maintained as per labour laws. controlled while registers are used for a year, time cards are issued each month. The payroll section, located either in the Human Resources Department or the Accounts Department, as per policy, calculates the salaries and wages given at the end of each month. Some establishments may pay salaries every fortnight to help their employees maintain their personal cash flows. Salary payment schedules are also determined by the labour law. The Executive Housekeeper must ensure some norms while maintaining the attendance of staff-

- Staff coming late must be marked late because late-coming is taboo in the service industry. Service is provided by "warm bodies", and late-coming can seriously jeopardise the quality of service. The Human Resources Department can incur legal penalties on the staff through wage deductions to emphasise the importance of attendance.
- The Executive Housekeeper must mark the attendance with a pen to prevent any malpractice. Any additions or deletions must be countersigned by the housekeeper and employee in acknowledgement of amendments.
- The Executive Housekeeper must counsel habitual latecomers and absentees before taking action. Late-coming and absenteeism are punishable offences and can even lead to dismissal of the employee.
- The Executive Housekeeper and Supervisors must always emphasise the importance of attendance in all briefings.

Briefing

Briefing is the process at the beginning of a work shift provided by management to facilitate a two-way communication between management and staff. It takes place one time at the beginning of a shift when the housekeeping staff are together to share information and feelings before they disperse for work.

This is after the employees have formally clocked into the hotel at the time office and have collected their fresh uniforms which they change in the locker rooms, provided separately for men and women. All employees are required to report for briefing properly attired and before the scheduled commencement of the shift.

In the Housekeeping Department, briefing is conducted at the Housekeeping Control Desk room. Ideally, the Executive Housekeeper must conduct the briefing. However, she may delegate this responsibility to the Assistant Housekeeper, if she is busy. Given below are the issues covered in a briefing that takes about 15 minutes:

Grooming

This has been discussed in detail in Lesson 8, "Competencies of a Housekeeping Professional".

Allotment of Duties

At a briefing, personnel are allotted their duties. Some housekeepers rotate staff on floors and public areas while others may assign dedicated floors and areas on the belief that this brings about ownership of those set of rooms and areas resulting in fierce pride of their domain. Supervisors are assigned to floors. The Public Area Supervisor receives special instructions about public areas that need more attention in a given day. Her duties would also include periodic preventive maintenance schedules like chandelier cleaning, carpet shampooing, wall cleaning, etc.

Policies and Procedures

The briefing is the opportunity for re-emphasising existing policies and procedures of the property especially those that have an impact on housekeeping staff. It is the time to introduce new policies and give receive queries and clarifications about them.

VIPs in the House

The Housekeeper gives the names and room numbers of VIPs in the house. Each room attendant will check those numbers which are in his responsibility. VIP rooms will receive special attention and amenities. The VIP list is further displayed on the communications notice board of the Desk Control room.

Feedback from Staff

Briefing time is the best opportunity to handle professional grievances that impact the productivity of the staff. (Personal grievances are handled in privacy on a one-to-one basis and not in a public forum like a briefing.) It is beneficial to productivity and morale if grievances are resolved immediately and not allowed to fester. Feedback is valuable in the quest for continuous improvement. Frontline personnel know best how guest experiences can be enhanced by giving suggestions.

Training

Briefing is the time to coach staff in minor tasks. Staff is trained in the standards of performance. Standards are re-emphasised daily. The Housekeeper gives feedback of supervisor reports on standards and ascertains those that need training or disciplinary action.

Recognition and Praise

Briefing is the best opportunity to praise those who have performed well. It is taught in good management to praise in public and discipline in private.

Guest Complaints

In spite of the best intentions, guest complaints continue to occur as each guest perceives service in his/her own special way. Such complaints are logged by the guest with the (a) Control Desk Supervisor, (b) Guest Relations Executive, (c) Lobby Manager, (d) Guest Comment Forms, (d) General Manager, (e) Floor Supervisor and (f) Room Attendant. Complaints must be looked upon as gifts by the guest to improve services. A guest who does not voice a complaint is dangerous because he would not come again and definitely speak about the bad experience to others. It is best to tackle complaints immediately and encourage suggestions from the housekeeping staff on how to rectify the same.

Other Information

It is important to give information of a general nature. The housekeeping staff must be integrated with the rest of the hotel so that they see "the larger picture" of operations rather than being cocooned in their own small world. Some additional information that should be shared is:

1. Performance of the hotel
2. New policies and practices
3. Functions in the house
4. New management and staff joined in other departments
5. Inspections by government authorities in the house
6. Special food promotions in restaurants
7. Groups and crews expected
8. Special requests by guests regarding amenities in the room
9. Assignment of baby sitting services.

Managing Discipline

Discipline is the hallmark of a good hotelier. Discipline is required for many reasons:

(a) Guests like to see staff in professional outfit doing their duties with clockwork precision.

(b) Indiscipline reflects on the image of the property, which can be ruined through the word-of-mouth.

(c) A lack of discipline severely affects the final quality of service-Imagine a room attendant who forgets to log a request for baby sitting services by a guest or when a room attendant forgets to leave water tumblers in the room.

(d) It reflects badly on the hygiene and sanitation standards of the property if employees are not well groomed and hygienically unclean-imagine room attendants with soiled uniforms.

(e) There is discipline in the way employees communicate

with guests. A lack of courtesy, etiquettes and manners can spoil the entire experience for a guest.

(f) Following systems and procedures to avoid chaos during busy operations. Shortcuts to service invariably affect standards.

(g) Coordination with other departments and fellow-members is necessary to get their cooperation. If the kitchen decides to slow down its service, the restaurant brigade will be faced with the wrath of the guests as they are in the frontline.

(h) Discipline in the punctuality and attendance. If there are no "warm bodies", the department cannot give the desired standards of service.

Indiscipline happens for several reasons as seen in the previous lesson. While the above are some reasons for indiscipline and how to deal with them, the following are some general guidelines to maintain a disciplined team:

1. Ensure that there are written house rules and code of conduct. These must be distributed to each employee and reinforced at briefings.
2. Motivate staff to follow rules and maintain discipline and how it can benefit them in terms of advancement, better tips and cooperation from team members.
3. A fault committed must be checked at once. 4. Always discipline in private.
5. Set an example by being self-disciplined. Staff must see their housekeeper or superviscr as their role model.
6. Check the Labour laws regarding disciplinary proceedings. Normally two warnings are given in writine before formal charees can he made.
7. Take the help of the Human Resources Department who are trained and qualified to han disciplinary proceedings within the law.

Cost Control

A measure of increasing the profits of a housekeeping operation is by reducing costs. While this is responsibility of the entire brigade, the accountability for cost control lies with the Executi Housekeeper. Here are some tips to reduce costs:

1. Check that quantity standards are strictly maintained. The guest amenities in a room must number those that are prescribed. The amount of detergents used must be in the correct quantities,
2. Staff must be trained to handle equipment correctly. Proper usage gives equipment a longer life
3. Linen is expensive and constitutes a major investment by the owner. It should not be used wiping tables or floors. Dusters are of cheaper material and used for cleaning purposes.
4. Expensive stationery must not be used as rough pads for dawdling.
5. Employees must be trained to meet productivity standards. Labour costs consume a large porno of the budget.
6. Inspections are important to ensure that correct procedures are followed.
7. Staff scheduling must ensure that there is the best utilisation of human resources in any given day,
8. Send timely maintenance orders to the maintenance staff. Items fixed on time will avoid highs costs when bigger breakdowns take place.
9. Recycle reusable items like flower arrangements, soaps, discarded linen, newspapers, bottles and cans.
10. The staff must be trained to complete their tasks correctly the first time round. Repeating a task takes valuable human resource time.
11. Florists must raise checks for flower arrangements ordered by guests. Similarly babysitting services, special laundry charges must be meticulously accounted for.
12. The housekeeper must be hawk-eyed for pilferage by staff.
13. Ensure the daily cleaning of the premises to keep assets fresh.

14. Ensure that the staff strength is optimum to meet business demands. Excess staff is a cost.

Employee Scheduling

The scheduling of employees of the Housekeeping Department is very demanding and critical as it has a large workforce and the greatest proportion of employee hours to cover. Moreover, unlike the restaurant and bar, which generate revenues that cover employee costs, housekeeping is a cost centre. Revenue centres can afford to add employees as the potential for revenue increases. Housekeeping does not have this flexibility. Each employee added has to justify the cost of such addition. The Housekeeping Department is very visible to guests and any deficiency in standards of housekeeping is immediately noticed. The Executive Housekeeper is challenged to ensure the right mix of employees that uphold the tasks of keeping a clean house to the highest standards.

The housekeeping department has an elaborate employee structure depending on the size of hotel.

Employee scheduling ensures employee presence and satisfies the following requirements:

1. The type of hotel and guest, e.g. business people require quicker and closer attention than people on holiday.
2. The number of guests staying in the hotel. Fortunately, most people book ahead and the expected occupancy is known. Scheduling ensures that the demands during the business hours are met.
3. It provides a human face.
4. It takes into account employee leaves and the weekly off-day, without affecting service.
5. It rotates employees equitably through shifts and holidays. Hotel business is a 24 x 7 business and not all employees can get leave on the same day. Guests occupy rooms even on weekends and national holidays. Staff have to be on duty to give the guests their service.
6. It distributes off days fairly as given in the schedule below.

7. It is planned in advance before it becomes effective to enable employees to plan their personal commitments.

Considerations while Scheduling

Employee scheduling is not that simple in large busy hotels. The following considerations are shown when scheduling employees:

1. Occupancy of the hotel. The numbers change appreciably during peak season and off season.
2. Productivity standards and whether the staff can meet them. For example, the guest room cleaning standard is 16 rooms to a room attendant in a shift.
3. Hotel's age. Scheduling for an existing hotel is easier as past records exist as a guide. New hotels rely on data from competing hotels.
4. Software makes scheduling easier. However, they are expensive.
5. Employee vacations have to be factored in. This is controlled by an annual leave plan.
6. Staff turnover affects scheduling. The responsibilities of an employee who has left has to be distributed among others. Past records are a useful guideline.
7. Absenteeism, sickness, and holidays.
8. Training days of employees is essential to be built into a schedule as continuous education and training is now a way of life.
9. Work practice improvements affect productivity and the number of people required. 10. **Job rotation** to develop employees and reduce boredom through routine.
   - (i) Polishing brassware
   - (ii) Exchanging linen
   - (iii) Collecting supplies from stores
   - (iv) Preparing the Housekeeping Report
   - (v) Checking fire prevention systems
   - (vi) Providing babysitting services (after work hours)

(vii) Manning the Control Desk

(viii) Cleaning the floor pantry

11. Equitable workloads so that everyone gets exactly the right number of hours of work at the least cost to the hotel.
12. Assignment of duties must be fair and equitable. No employee must be over burdened to an extent that his or her productivity is affected.

Preparing a Room Report

The Room Report is a document that confirms the occupancy of rooms in a given shift. The procedure to prepare a room report is followed in every shift as a check on unauthorised room occupancies or inadvertent mistakes in recording room occupancies by the front office.

The Floor Supervisor is the best person to physically confirm room occupancy as she has access to guest rooms on her allotted floor. She performs this task to enable the front office staff tally her findings with their room rack, which lists registered guests by room number. In case of a discrepancy, the receptionist sends a bell boy to make another physical verification to re confirm the room status.

The Room Report

The floor supervisor prepares the Room Report in triplicate. The original is meant for the front office, the duplicate for the auditor who calculates expected revenues, and the triplicate for the housekeeping records. The Floor Supervisor may delegate this task to a room attendant. She then sends the report to the Housekeeping Control Desk Supervisor who compiles a consolidated list of all floors.

The Room Report is basically a list of room numbers against which the floor supervisor indicates the occupancy status by prescribed occupancy codes. The codes may vary in each hotel but the basic information and intention is the same. The Floor Supervisor physically enters each room on the floor with her master key following the entry procedure discussed later. Once in the room she ascertains the number of guests by three methods: (1) by noticing the number of beds used; (2) by seeing the number of bath towels used; and *(3) by* observing the types of guest clothes hung in the wardrobe. The first check normally confirms occupancy. She will obviously not enter rooms with a 'Do-not-Disturb' sign.

Occupancy Codes

An explanation of the codes will be useful here:

Occupied: This status shows that a guest has checked into the room and is staying in the hotel.

The signs of occupancy are beds that have been used, baggage on the baggage rack, clothes in the wardrobe, room service trays that are not cleared, bath towels that have been used and personal effects in the room and bathroom.

Vacant: This room is empty and ready for sale.

DND: This is a sign displayed either by a door knob card or a lit DND light beside the door. Obviously the guest cannot be disturbed.

Luggage in Room but not Used: This code may seem odd. There are guests who may lease a room but stay with friends and relatives in the city. The luggage is not opened and the bed is not used. The danger is that the guest may have skipped without paying the room bill and has left the baggage as a decoy.

Under Repair: Indicates that the room is declared unsuitable for occupancy till repairs in the room are set right. This is a temporary situation where the room can be released in a short time.

Occupied, but no Luggage: These rooms show that the beds and bath linen have been used in spite of no guest luggage. There are several possibilities in such rooms:

1. It is a departure room.
2. The night manager may have used the room to rest.
3. Staff may have used the room without permission.
4. A guest with light luggage may have checked out without paying the bill.

Scanty Baggage: A room with light luggage. This can be a potential skipper (a person who *may* depart without paying the bill).

Occupancy Codes

Out-of-Order: A room on a long-term maintenance requirement and therefore, unsuitable for sale.

Double Lock: A double lock is a security feature that cannot be opened with a master key. The room certainly shows occupancy but not the number of people inside.

Other Duties

In addition to routine functions explained in the earlier lesson, the Floor Supervisor has other periodic duties to accomplish. This may be done once a weekly, monthly, or biannually.

Periodic Duties of a Floor Supervisor

Weekly Cleaning Procedure

The Floor Supervisor rotates room attendants and housemen to accomplish daily certain cleaning chores that are time-consuming and labour intensive:

1. Polishing brassware in rooms
2. Scrubbing bathroom tiles that have stubborn stains
3. Pest control
4. Unhooking translucent day curtains that may gather dust over time and sending them for laundering. The curtains brought down will require a replacement to be hooked on
5. Scrubbing shower curtains that have stubborn stains
6. Cleaning window panes-A special crew will clean window panes from outside on a biannual or annual basis
7. Scrubbing balconies and terraces
8. Vacuuming carpets under heavy furniture
9. Changing paper underliners in guest closets and drawers 10. Recycling potted plants with those in the nursery
11. Grouting bathroom tiles

Rooms Under Repair

The Executive Housekeeper has a preventive maintenance cycle for all rooms such as painting, masonry work etc. executed by the Maintenance Depart-ment. The Floor Supervisor follows certain procedures as follows:

1. Inform the Housekeeping Control Desk to advice front office not to sell rooms taken under major repair.
2. Call the tailor from the linen room to dismantle the curtains and send them for storage at the linen room.
3. Send lamp shades, bed covers, skirting, linen, guest supplies, etc. to the floor linen room for storage.
4. Cover the telephone instrument/s with polythene and disconnect it. 5. Close inlet valves of taps and water closets.
6. Call the audiovisual technician to disconnect the televisions/radios/music systems and store them in the music room.
7. Send upholstered furniture to the upholstery yard for mending or shampoo.
8. Call the horticulturist to collect indoor plants for storage at the nursery. 9. Remove all dresser and wardrobe drawers and store them in the floor linen room.
10. Roll up carpets and send them to the ',piiolstery yard for shampooing.
11. Cover remaining furniture and fixtures with polythene sheets or condemned bed sheets.

Note: All items must be labelled with the room number for identification when it is time to replace then Guest Loan Items

The Floor Supervisor will periodically loan items to guests on request, as the extra service provided by the hotel. Some hotels may charge for these items. Such items are hand iron, hair dryer, ironing board, cribs, sewing kits, rollaway beds, voltage adaptors, hot water bottles, extra pillows, orthopedic mattress, extra blankets, vanity sets, etc.

These items need to be controlled carefully as they cost and the supervisor will be held accountable for them. Each Floor Supervisor is issued a stock of these items stored in the floor linen room. The par stock is based on historical demand for these items. The hazards associated with loaning these items are:

- Theft
- Damage
- Misplacement
- Misuse.

The Floor Supervisor will maintain a Guest Loan Register as a control measure.

The supervisor controls the movement of these items and ensures their recovery before she ends her shift. The control features in the register has the date, guest name and the root, number. The call and delivery times are there to ascertain how promptly the guest request was serviced.

The persons receiving and recovering the items are held responsible for the safe return the item to the floor linen room. The last column "Comments" gives the status of the item. If dam the floor supervisor can advise the Control Desk who may charge the damage to the guest folio.

Fa hotels who charge for this service, the period of usage delivery is informed to the front office cashia who will enter the charge in the guest folio. Some hotels charge by the hour and some levy a fu charge. These services require close coordination with the Control Desk who advises the front officers of such charges.

Inventory of Guest Supplies

Another important concern for a floor supervisor is the control of guest supplies. Every guest room ha a standard number of items and therefore, it is *easy* to calculate the demand for such items on a daily basis.

The variable element is occupancy. The supervisor will need to establish a par stock of each item based on historical occupancy in various seasons. Peak seasons will need higher par stocks while low seasons will need less. The supervisor may realise that some items like ashtrays, room service menus, do-not-disturb signs, directories, etc. have a longer room life than other consumables. She must maintain appropriate par stocks in the floor linen room and a par on each maid's cart. She would know exactly the consumption of each cart on a daily basis. She maintains these records in a Guest Supplies Consumption Register.

Layout of a Guest Room

The purpose of a hotel, since the early inns, is to provide accommodation to travellers, or as cliched saying states, a hotel is "a home away from home". It is important that a future house-keeping professional is thoroughly familiar with the guest room as its maintenance and cleanliness is one of his/her major responsibilities. Guest rooms generate over 50 per cent revenue for the hotel, and in some cases, it is the only source of revenue for the hotel without food and beverage operations.

Investors, therefore, put in a great deal of money into creating rooms. The common belief is that the more rooms are there in a hotel, the better it is for business economics. It is for this reason that we find some hotels that have over 5000 rooms. The future indicates mega hotels with thousands of rooms.

Types of Guest Room

We have seen the different types of rooms in hotels and available to the traveller in Lesson 4, "Types of Rooms." The most sensible type of rooms are the twin rooms (having two single beds), because the two rooms can be used as single, double or triple rooms with an additional roll-away bed. Luxury hotels prefer to provide two queen-sized double beds. It however, does not give the flexibility to be used as two single beds for two unrelated travellers in a group. Luxury hotels provide two queen-sized beds to make each person's stay comfortable.

Features in a Typical Room

Beds

As shown in the schematic diagram below (not drawn to scale but representative only), a typical room will have a bed or beds that have two elements:

(i) Separate 1" to 4" mattresses depending on the type of luxury the hotel wishes to provide.

(ii) The cot which is the form on which mattresses set. This gives the room attendant flexibility to move the bed around especially when preparing it and cleaning beneath it. It is prudent to fix the headboard to the wall enabling the room attendant to reach the head side of the bed as well as the headboard for cleaning purposes. The owner of the hotel can change the headboard during major renovations without having to change the bed.

Bedside Table

The bedside table has a table lamp for reading; a bedside telephone; a shelf which has a copy of Bible, Koran or Gita; a bedstead lamp; directories; and other features like alarms-clocks, etc.

The bedside table becomes a console when electrical connections lead to it to control all the lights in a room and the power to the television set. Modern technology has provided electronic remote controls doing away with electrical connection to the console, leaving this piece of furniture as bedside tables only.

Lighting System

It is important at this stage to be familiar with the lighting system in a typical room. The room will have an entrance light in the passage as one enters the room; table lamps on either side of the bed, (wall or headboard mounted behind the bed); one standing lamp at the corner of the room; mirror light for the dresser; wall mounted lights especially in large rooms and suites; and floor night lamps for those who do not like to sleep in the dark.

The standard bulb power for bedside tables is 60 watts while the standard lamp and dresser light has a bulb of 100 watts. Bathrooms have a neon mirror light and a ceiling spot light with a normal bulb.

Luggage Rack

The luggage rack comes in two types. The fixed wooden feature that has brass strips so as not to damage the wood, and the foldable rack that can be stored in the wardrobe when not in use. The wooden rack is sturdier and preferred by hotels that have international travellers with heavy baggage. The housekeeping can keep a few foldable ones in the floor linen room in case a guest requires additional storage.

Wardrobe

The wardrobe is usually found at the entrance passage way. The wardrobe is the prime storage space in the room for guest belongings, and additional blankets and pillows. It has a section to hang long clothes like dresses and gowns; shelves for extra pillows and blankets and drawers for clothing accessories. Superior hotels provide room safety boxes that are installed in the wardrobe for additional security. The wardrobe normally has a full length mirror for guests to use just as they leave the room. The guest will find the following amenities inside the wardrobe: laundry lists; bath slippers, shoeshine tag, hangers; bathrobe, extra pillows and blankets. Some wardrobes have internal lighting so that the articles in the cupboardcan be seen clearly.

Dresser

The dresser is a multipurpose piece of furniture. It has a base that acts as a dresser as well as the writing desk. Above it is mounted a mirror or a three-panelled one. The dresser has drawers where the guest will find guest stationary an sewing kits. On the top, the dresser will display menu cards, guest comment forms and other into advertisement material.

Coffee Table and Chairs

The room is complete with a coffee table and two chairs. This is where magazines are displayed and where the guest can eat his meals ordered from the room service. It is the place where the guest can entertain his/her visitors.

Garden Furniture

Many hotels have balconies, terrace gardens and patios. They provide garden furniture for these areas that can resist external temperatures. A room attendant will have to maintain them as well. Chalet type of structures may provide verandas that will have seating appropriate for outdoor purposes. In hotels, with this feature, guests may want to eat their room service meals outdoors and enjoy the views and ambience that is provided.

Bathroom

The room attendant has to be familiar with the bathroom as

it is an intimate part of a guest room. The bathroom will be normally found off the entrance passageway. A typical bathroom of a luxury hotel will have a bath tub with a shower curtain; counter where the sink is mounted that serves the place to display vanity sets, guest toiletries, merchandising material and perhaps a flower arrangement; a water closet; and rods for bath towels, face towels and hand towels. Deluxe hotels may provide shower trays as well, while economy hotels will do away with bath tubs due to space restrictions and provide shower trays instead. Some budget hotels may just provide a shower with a shower curtain.

At this point it is important for the room attendant to know the difference between various terms used for bathing: a "bath" provides a bath tub to immerse the body, whereas a "shower" is an alcove where a person bathes standing under a shower fountain. A **"shower** tray " is an enclosed cubicle with a shower fountain. This completes the guest room which is a composite of a bedroom and bathroom with perhaps balconies, patios, terraces and verandas based on the design of the property. A shower tray is also the responsibility of the room attendant.

Guest Amenities

Now that we know the facilities which should there in a guest room, let's glance at the complete checklists of guest amenities, equipment and supplies required for a room:

Guest Supplies in a Room

- Stationery with Pen
- Sewing Kit
- Bible/Koran/Gita
- Telephone Directory
- Service Directory
- Ashtrays
- Bedside Telephone Notepad with Pen
- Clothes Hangers
- Laundry Bags
- "Do Not Disturb" Cards

- Breakfast Card
- Laundry Forms & Bags
- Guest Comment Forms
- Room Service Menu & Tent Cards.

Guest Supplies in a Bathroom

- Shoe Mitts
- Soaps/Soap Dish
- Toilet Rolls
- Toilet Tissues
- Blade dispenser
- Shower Cap
- Disposal Bags.

Rules on a Guest Floor

Room attendants must follow some floor rules that project professionalism and efficiency ensuring least inconvenience to guests. The floor and rooms are quite private and personal for guests and so they are concerned about the people who frequent these places. The guests trust the room attendants who are pity to their rooms and belongings. The room attendant is issued the master keys by the Desk Control Supervisor. He/She signs for this facility and therefore, becomes responsible for its safekeeping. The issuing of the master key to the room attendant also signifies the fact that trust has been placed on him/her by both the management and guest to access guest floors and rooms.

Rules on a Guest Floor

To uphold this trust, the following rules must be strictly observed on the floor:

1. Room Attendants must always be in uniform and should appear properly groomed when entering the floor as this reflects on the image of the property.
2. They should reach the floor by the service elevator and enter the floor through the service entrance. The guest elevators are meant for guests only.

3. Speech among the floor staff must be restricted to the minimum. In case communication is necessary, this must be done in low tones even when guests are not in sight.
4. Unnecessary movements like running or jumping should be avoided. Such movements can disturb guests in the room.
5. The passageway must be kept free of equipment, trays or trolleys.
6. Room attendants may enter only those rooms that are allotted to them. They are not permitted to enter other rooms as a precaution towards security and accountability.
7. Guest room doors must be kept wide open when servicing a room. This notifies the supervisor as to which room is being cleaned and where to find the room attendant. It is also a protection of the room attendant from undesirable guests.
8. When speaking to a guest in the room for any reason, the room attendant should stand at the doorway and not inside the room, which is viewed as an infringement of the guest's privacy.
9. The floor telephone must be attended to promptly. Continuous ringing of a phone can beirksome to guests in the neighbouring rooms.
10. Room attendants must greet all guests with a smile, according to the time of the day. It is a professional courtesy and creates a friendly environment on the floor.
11. Staff must be helpful and should readily give information about hotel services, when requested. Misinformation can lead to dissatisfaction of the guests.
12. Alertness about the movements of the guests necessary so that if any suspicious movement is spotted, it can be immediately reported to the supervisor and ultimately the security.
13. Remember that the guest is always right. Arguing with a guest is prohibited. Unreasonable guests may be referred to the floor supervisor.

14. It is prohibited to enter rooms with a "Do-not-Disturb" sign. The DND feature;,s provided by the hotels worldwide to permit guests to rest without disturbance. Guests may have checked in late or getting over jet lag. This particularly applies to airline crews who check in at odd hours especially when they have been on international flights.
15. If a DND sign is on for a long time, this may be reported to the floor supervisor who will take further decisions and actions. Long DND signs, especially those that span over two shifts, are unusual. A guest could be sick and in need of medical help. There have been many cases of death.
16. If the guest returns when the room is being cleaned, the room attendant may ask the guest if he/She can continue or come later.
17. In spite of following the room entry procedure, if the guest is found asleep or awake, one should apologise and quickly withdraw and shut the door softly. Sometimes the room attendant may hear the sound of the shower in the bathroom indicating the reason for the guest not attending to the door knock.
18. Attendants must always follow the procedure of entering a room even if the room is declared vacant. The procedure includes knocking the door and announcing "Housekeeping" which is to be repeated after 15 seconds if there is no reply. This is required, especially in busy hotels that have frequent check-ins. The status of an arrival is known to the room attendant much later
19. Attendants must always accompany the room service staff when they are clearing trays, and maintenance staff when they are attending to repairs in the room. The room attendant is the custodian of the rooms allotted to him/her and that he/she will be held accountable for any property of the guest or hotel missing from the room.
20. Attendants should not open the room for any unauthorised personnel. Resident guests are expected to have their own keys. Other guests should not enter at any cost.

21. It is important to report any suspicious articles like arms and drugs to the floor supervisor who may call the security for further inspection.
22. Housekeeping personnel cannot make external calls from guest rooms or the floor telephone.
23. Maid carts are kept along the walls to give freedom of movement along the corridors to guests and other personnel.
24. It is important for security reasons for the room attendants to try and familiarise themselves with the faces of resident guests as a control measure. While this may always not be possible, it is a good practice.
25. Garbage and soiled linen must be dumped in the designated hampers of the maid cart. Such items must be away from the guest view.
26. Caution guests of wet floors in the corridors (if uncarpeted) or in the room. The correct practice is to put 'Wet Floor' signs as a precaution.
27. Guest belongings found in departure rooms should be immediately reported to the floor supervisor. He/She will check if the guests have checked out or are still paying their bills with the front office cashier. If the guests have checked out, then the floor supervisor will follow the lost and found procedure.
28. The room attendant must return the master key to the Desk Control Supervisor at the end of the shift.

The Maid's Cart

The maid's cart is a trolley meant to stock a given number of linen, supplies and equipment to service an allotted number of rooms. Each maid, after receiving her room assignment, should check her supplies against a standard checklist to avoid needless trips. The maid is responsible for the condition, cleanliness and appearance of her cart.

Design of a Maid's Cart

The lower shelf of the cart is used to carry heavier items like mattress protectors, bed sheets and night spreads. The middle and top shelves stock pillow slips and bath linen.

In addition, the maid's cart stores the following cleaning equipment placed below the trash bag of the cart:

- Feather Brush
- Dustpan
- Mop
- Sponges
- Duster Clothes
- Carpet Brushes
- Vacuum Cleaner
- Clean Scrub Bucket
- Scrub Brush.

Following cleaning agents are kept on the top tray for easy access:

- Disinfectants
- Dettol
- Deodoriser
- Room Freshener
- Vim
- Sanifresh
- Liquid Soap
- Naphthalene Balls
- Anol.

These supplies are procured by the room attendant from the floor linen room. After stocking that cart, the room attendant proceeds to the section of rooms on the floor that are assigned to her. Maid' carts are placed along the wall of the corridor on the side of the room to be serviced. The cart shout be positioned so as to service a minimum number of two rooms without much movement of the room attendant. This would minimise trips of the room attendant to the cart thereby reducing the fatigue factor.

When selecting maid's carts, consideration is given to it being lightweight to ensure easy mobility by the maid. Heavy carts also pucker corridor carpets. The wheels of the cart must be of sturdy construction and should be oiled well periodically to ensure smooth movement. The diagram below gives some of the considerations shown by the designers to make the room attendant's job easier.

Cleaning a Room

Prior to reporting on a floor, the room attendant already knows the status of the rooms assigned to him on the floor. This is given to him at the time of briefing by the floor supervisor. The room attendant can prioritise the rooms according to the status of the occupancy.

He can attend to departure rooms first to prepare them for sale. Next he can attend to rooms with the tag "Clean my Room" left by resident guests when they leave the room for the day. Lastly, he can attend to the occupied rooms. He must avoid the moms with a "Do-not-Disturb" sign displayed.

Procedure for Checking a Room

Given below is a step-by-step procedure for checking a room:

Entering the Room

1. Knock the door announcing "Housekeeping."
2. If there is no answer, after fifteen seconds knock the door again the second time announcing "Housekeeping."
3. If there is still no answer, use the master key to open the door announcing "Housekeeping" and knocking the door when ajar. When relatively sure that there is no occupant, open the door wide. 4. Switch off the room airconditioner or heating. Draw all curtains and open all windows to air the room.

Guest Belonging Check

1. Check departure rooms for guest lost and found items and report them immediately to the control desk.
2. Pick guest clothes and hang them in the wardrobe in occupied rooms.

3. Empty all ash trays into a waste paper basket in the room. Collect other loose trash on tables and floors and throw them in the waste paper basket checking for guest belongings.
4. Check waste paper baskets for guest's belongings before emptying them into the trash bag of maid's cart.
5. Collect all loose papers and magazines and stack them neatly on the desk.

Making the Bed

Bed making requires technical expertise in a hotel because of the sheer volume of beds to be made in a given shift. If a room attendant has to prepare 16 rooms, as per the prevalent standards, in a shift, he has potentially 32 beds to make. This is in addition to cleaning the rooms and bathrooms. It is here that his productivity is determined. Given below are the detailed steps for making a bed:

1. Pull the bed away from the headboard by tugging the bed from the foot of the bed. All the beds in hotels are mounted on wheels for easy maneuverability
2. Remove all soiled linen from the bed. Shake them out for any guest articles that may be misplaced in the folds.
3. Deposit the soiled linen in the linen hamper of the maid's cart.
4. Invert mattresses over-side and end-to-end to ensure even use, every alternate day. Adjust the skirting so that they fall evenly to the floor.
5. Shake out the mattress protector and relay it on the mattress. Change the protector if soiled or smelling.
6. Clean the headboard with a feather duster.
7. Open out a fresh lower sheet and tuck it securely at the head, sides and at the foot of the bed.
8. Miter the corners following the sequence shown in the pictures above.
9. Open out the fresh top sheet and distribute it evenly on the lower sheet. Ensure that the laundry crease is in the

same line as the inner sheet for even distribution. The sheet hem must be evenly pulled up to the headboard. Tuck this sheet at the footboard.

10. Open out the blanket and distribute it evenly on the top sheet using the crease as described earlier for even distribution. Ensure that the blanket labels are at the foot of the bed. Pull the blanket eight inches from the headboard to position the pillows and create a fold for the guest to slide in.
11. Fold the top sheet at the head of the bed, over the blanket and fold the blanket and top sheet once again.
12. The blanket and the top sheet are tucked uniformly under the mattress on both sides and the corners at the foot of the bed are mitered.
13. Fold the corner of the blanket and top sheet as shown in the picture for the guest to easily slide into the bed.
14. Cover the pillows with fresh pillow covers. Fluff the pillow and even out pillow covers to look full, neat and tidy. Since pillow slips are usually larger than the pillow, the excess slip should be neatly folded downward. The side of the pillow which has the fold should be away from guest view. In the turn/down service, a breakfast knob is placed on the pillow.
15. Cover the completed bed with a bed spread ensuring it is right side up and falling evenly all around the bed to look appealing. The bed spread corners must fall to the floor in an aesthetic manner.
16. Tuck the bed spread under the pillows to complete the bed.
17. Push the bed back towards the headboard ensuring that it is aligned.
18. Put spare blankets (upon guest's request) in plastic covers and store in the top shelf or lower shelf of the wardrobe in the guest room. The blankets are folded in a manner where the hotel logo is at the top.

2

Positioning and Objectives of Hotel Management

Introduction

Tourism and hospitality is the fastest growing industry in the world with over 72.4 million jobs within the industry. Through the growth of e-commerce and globalization, a wide variety of career opportunities have emerged in the meeting and convention, attractions, event planning, travel, gaming, transportations, airline, recreation and food and beverage fields.

Many modern words readily associated with hospitality are evolved from the same hypothetical Proto-Indo-European root ghosti (1) meaning: stranger, guest, host: properly 'someone with whom one has reciprocal duties of hospitality' (American Heritage Dictionary, 2001). The word guest came from the Middle English gest, evolved from Old Norse gestor, and from Old High German gast, both come from Germanic gastiz. Ghosti also evolved to the Latin root hostis, meaning enemy, army, and where host (multitude) and hostile find their origin; and the Latin root hostia, meaning sacrifice, host (Eucharistic). The combination of ghosti and another Proto-Indo-European root poti powerful, gave the compound root ghospot, ghospod-, which evolved to the Latin hospes and eventually into hospice, hospitable, hospital, hospitality, host (giver of hospitality), hostage and hostel. The Greek languages also evolved from the same Proto-Indo-European base; ghosti gave the Greek xenos which has the interchangeable meaning guest, host or stranger. Hospitality, then, 'represents a kind of guarantee of reciprocity—one protects the stranger in order to be protected from him'.

Grecian Hospitality Mythology

In Ancient Greece, it was not known if the stranger knocking at the door was going to be hostile or hospitable, whether they were a god disguised, or watching from above and passing judgment. This was not considered important for 'it is hard for mortals to see divinity'. Hospitality was a way of honouring the gods, which was so essential, so fundamental to civilized life, that its patron was the god of gods. In true hospitality, it doesn't matter who the guest is, nor their apparent status in life. Generous hospitality freely given to a stranger was the same as that given to a god. Reese (1993) in his analysis of the writings attributed to Homer identifies 18 'hospitality' scenes. It is clear from these scenes in the Homeric writings that hospitality brought expectations. As the traveller would not usually be wandering without cause from their home into the dangers of the world.

Hospitality management is the academic study of the hospitality industry. A degree in Hospitality management is often conferred from either a university college dedicated to the studies of hospitality management or a business school with a department in hospitality management studies. Hospitality management is the academic study of the hospitality industry. A degree in Hospitality management is often conferred from either a university college dedicated to the studies of hospitality management or a business school with a department in hospitality management studies.

Hospitality and Tourism Management

In America, Hospitality and Tourism Management (HTM) can be a business major in either a Bachelors of Science, Bachelors of Commerce or a Bachelors of Arts.

Graduate students graduate with a Masters of Business Administration, a Masters or Science, or a Doctorate of Philosophy in Hospitality and Tourism Management.

It is a focus that is studied by individuals that are intending to work in the Hospitality Industry, examples of which are; Hotels,

Resorts, Casinos, Restaurants, and Events. Within the HTM concentration there is generally:

- Food Management and Operations (Examples: Food Science, Food Selection and Preparation, Food and Beverage Operations)
- Lodging Operations (Examples: Hotel Operations, Resort Management, Lodging Management, Financial Management and Cost Control for Hospitality Organizations)
- Global Tourism (Examples: Travel and Tourism Management, Tourism Analysis, Hospitality and Research Methods)
- Sustainable Tourism (Examples: Natural Destination Management, Responsible Tourism, Green Tourism and Eco-Tourism, Alternative and more Environmentally friendly ways of working within the whole Tourism industry)
- Tourist Attractions Management (Examples: Heritage Attractions, Arts and Cultural Attractions, Industrial Attractions, City Based Attractions, Retail Attractions, Natural Attractions)
- Entertainment Management (Examples: Theme Park Management, Theatre Management, Cinema Management, Museology, Live Music and Music Festival Management).
- Event Management (Examples: Hospitality Sales, Catering Management, Hospitality Marketing Management).

Several large corporations such as Marriott, IHG, Hyatt, Starwood, Wyndham and Hilton Hotels have summer internships in training programs for students majoring in Hospitality and Tourism Management, to help students get valuable work experience.

Hospitality and Tourism Management

In America, Hospitality and Tourism Management (HTM) can be a business major in either a Bachelors of Science, Bachelors of Commerce or a Bachelors of Arts.

Graduate students graduate with a Masters of Business Administration, a Masters or Science, or a Doctorate of Philosophy in Hospitality and Tourism Management.

It is a focus that is studied by individuals that are intending to work in the Hospitality Industry, examples of which are; Hotels, Resorts, Casinos, Restaurants, and Events.

Within the HTM concentration there is generally:

- Food Management and Operations (Examples: Food Science, Food Selection and Preparation, Food and Beverage Operations)
- Lodging Operations (Examples: Hotel Operations, Resort Management, Lodging Management, Financial Management and Cost Control for Hospitality Organizations)
- Global Tourism (Examples: Travel and Tourism Management, Tourism Analysis, Hospitality and Research Methods)
- Sustainable Tourism (Examples: Natural Destination Management, Responsible Tourism, Green Tourism and Eco-Tourism, Alternative and more Environmentally friendly ways of working within the whole Tourism industry)
- Tourist Attractions Management (Examples: Heritage Attractions, Arts and Cultural Attractions, Industrial Attractions, City Based Attractions, Retail Attractions, Natural Attractions)
- Entertainment Management (Examples: Theme Park Management, Theatre Management, Cinema Management, Museology, Live Music and Music Festival Management).
- Event Management (Examples: Hospitality Sales, Catering Management, Hospitality Marketing Management).

Several large corporations such as Marriott, IHG, Hyatt, Starwood, Wyndham and Hilton Hotels have summer internships in training programs for students majoring in Hospitality and Tourism Management, to help students get valuable work experience.

Hospitality Industry

The hospitality industry consists of broad category of fields within the service industry that includes lodging, restaurants, event planning, theme parks, transportation, cruise line, and additional fields within the tourism industry. The hospitality industry is a several billion dollar industry that mostly depends on the availability of leisure time and disposable income. A hospitality unit such as a restaurant, hotel, or even an amusement park consists of multiple groups such as facility maintenance, direct operations (servers, housekeepers, porters, kitchen workers, bartenders, etc.), management, marketing, and human resources.

Usage rate is an important variable for the hospitality industry. Just as a factory owner would wish to have his or her productive asset in use as much as possible (as opposed to having to pay fixed costs while the factory isn't producing), so do restaurants, hotels, and theme parks seek to maximize the number of customers they "process".

In viewing various industries, "barriers to entry" by newcomers and competitive advantages between current players are very important. Among other things, hospitality industry players find advantage in old classics (location), initial and ongoing investment support (reflected in the material upkeep of facilities and the luxuries located therein), and particular themes adopted by the marketing arm of the organization in question (such as a restaurant called the 51st fighter group that has a WW2 theme in music and other environmental aspects). Very important is also the characteristics of the personnel working in direct contact with the customers. The authenticity, professionalism, and actual concern for the happiness and well-being of the customers that is communicated by successful organizations is a clear competitive advantage.

Accommodations

- Destination spas
- Floatels
- Hostels
- Hotels

- Inns
- Motels.

Restaurants & Bars

- Cafes
- Nightclubs
- Public houses
- Pubs
- Restaurants.

Travel and Tourism

- Airline Cabin Staff
- Travel agents.

Hotel

A hotel is an establishment that provides paid lodging on a short-term basis. The provision of basic accommodation, in times past, consisting only of a room with a bed, a cupboard, a small table and a washstand has largely been replaced by rooms with modern facilities, including en-suite bathrooms and air conditioning or climate control. Additional common features found in hotel rooms are a telephone, an alarm clock, a television, and Internet connectivity; snack foods and drinks may be supplied in a mini-bar, and facilities for making hot drinks. Larger hotels may provide a number of additional guest facilities such as a restaurant, a swimming pool or childcare, and have conference and social function services. Hotels rooms are usually numbered to allow guests identify their room.

Some hotels offer meals as part of a room and board arrangement. In the United Kingdom, a hotel is required by law to serve food and drinks to all guests within certain stated hours; to avoid this requirement it is not uncommon to come across *private hotels* which are not subject to this requirement. In Japan, capsule hotels provide a minimized amount of room space and shared facilities.

In the United Kingdom, Australia, Canada and Ireland (and rarely in some parts of the United States), the word may also refer to a pub or bar and might not offer accommodation. In India and Bangladesh, the word may also refer to a restaurant.

Etymology

The word *hotel* is derived from the French *hotel* (coming from *hotel* meaning *host*), which referred to a French version of a townhouse or any other building seeing frequent visitors, rather than a place offering accommodation. In contemporary French usage, *hôtel* now has the same meaning as the English term, and *hôtel particulier* is used for the old meaning. The French spelling, with the circumflex, was also used in English, but is now rare. The circumflex replaces the 's' found in the earlier *hostel* spelling, which over time took on a new, but closely related meaning. Grammatically, hotels usually take the definite article-hence "The Astoria Hotel" or simply "The Astoria".

Classification

The cost and quality of hotels are usually indicative of the range and type of services available. Due to the enormous increase in tourism worldwide during the last decades of the 20th century, standards, especially those of smaller establishments, have improved considerably. For the sake of greater comparability, rating systems have been introduced, with the one to five stars classification being most common and with higher star ratings indicating more luxury. Hotels are independently assessed in traditional systems and these rely heavily on the facilities provided. Some consider this disadvantageous to smaller hotels whose quality of accommodation could fall into one class but the lack of an item such as an elevator would prevent it from reaching a higher categorization. In some countries, there is an official body with standard criteria for classifying hotels, but in many others there is none.

There have been attempts at unifying the classification system so that it becomes an internationally recognized and reliable standard but large differences exist in the quality of the accommodation and the food within one category of hotel, sometimes even in the same country. The American Automobile Association (AAA) and their affiliated bodies use diamonds instead of stars to express hotel and restaurant ratings levels.

Hotels are also classified by service type ranging for all-inclusive full-service resorts that cater to vacationers to small limited service hotels that cater to transient business travellers. The main categories of hotels are as follows;

- Full Service Upscale :
    - o *Examples include Conrad Hotels, Ritz Carlton, Four Seasons Hotels, and JW Marriott.*
- Full Service :
    - o *Examples include Hilton, Marriott, Doubletree, and Hyatt.*
- Select Service :
    - o *Examples include Courtyard by Marriott and Hilton Garden Inn.*
- Limited Service :
    - o *Examples include Hampton Inn, Fairfield Inn, Days Inn, and La Quinta Inn.*
- Extended Stay :
    - o *Examples include Homewood Suites by Hilton, Residence Inn by Marriott, and Extended Stay Hotels.*
- Timeshare :
    - o *Examples include Marriott Vacation Club, Westgate Resorts, and Disney Vacation Club.*
- Destination Club.

Historic Hotels

Some hotels have gained their renown through tradition, by hosting significant events or persons, such as Schloss Cecilienhof in Potsdam, Germany, which derives its fame from the Potsdam Conference of the World War II allies Winston Churchill, Harry Truman and Joseph Stalin in 1945.

The Taj Mahal Palace & Tower in Mumbai is one of India's most famous and historic hotels because of its association with the Indian independence movement. Some establishments have given name to a particular meal or beverage, as is the case with the Waldorf Astoria in New York City, United States where the Waldorf Salad was first created or the Hotel Sacher in Vienna, Austria, home of the Sachertorte. Others have achieved fame by association with dishes or cocktails created on their premises, such as the Hotel de Paris where the crepe Suzette was invented or the Raffles Hotel in Singapore, where the Singapore Sling cocktail was devised.

A number of hotels have entered the public consciousness through popular culture, such as the Ritz Hotel in London, United Kingdom, through its association with Irving Berlin's song, 'Puttin' on the Ritz'. The Algonquin Hotel in New York City is famed as the meeting place of the literary group, the Algonquin Round Table, and Hotel Chelsea, also in New York City, has been the subject of a number of songs and the scene of the stabbing of Nancy Spungen (allegedly by her boyfriend Sid Vicious). The Waldorf Astoria and Statler hotels in New York City are also immortalized in the names of Muppets Statler and Waldorf.

The luxurious Grand Hotel Europe in Saint Petersburg, Russia achieved fame with its inclusion in the James Bond film GoldenEye.

Unusual Hotels

Many hotels can be considered destinations in themselves, by dint of unusual features of the lodging or its immediate environment:

Treehouse Hotels

Some hotels are built with living trees as structural elements, for example the Costa Rica Tree House in the Gandoca-Manzanillo Wildlife Refuge, Costa Rica; the Treetops Hotel in Aberdare National Park, Kenya; the Ariau Towers near Manaus, Brazil, on the Rio Negro in the Amazon; and Bayram's Tree Houses in Olympos, Turkey.

Bunker Hotels

The Null Stern Hotel in Teufen, Appenzellerland, Switzerland and the Concrete Mushrooms in Albania are former nuclear bunkers transformed into hotels.

Cave Hotels

Desert Cave Hotel in Coober Pedy, South Australia and the Cuevas Pedro Antonio de Alarcon (named after the author) in Guadix, Spain, as well as several hotels in Cappadocia, Turkey, are notable for being built into natural cave formations, some with rooms underground.

Capsule Hotels

Capsule hotels are a type of economical hotel that are found in Japan, where people sleep in stacks of rectangular containers.

Ice and Snow Hotels

The Ice Hotel in Jukkasjarvi, Sweden, and the Hotel de Glace in Duschenay, Canada, melt every spring and are rebuilt each winter; the Mammut Snow Hotel in Finland is located within the walls of the Kemi snow castle; and the Lainio Snow Hotel is part of a snow village near Yllas, Finland.

Garden Hotels

Garden hotels, famous for their gardens before they became hotels, include Gravetye Manor, the home of garden designer William Robinson, and Cliveden, designed by Charles Barry with a rose garden by Geoffrey Jellicoe.

Underwater Hotels

Some hotels have accommodation underwater, such as Utter Inn in Lake Malaren, Sweden. Hydropolis, project cancelled 2004 in Dubai, would have had suites on the bottom of the Persian Gulf, and Jules Undersea Lodge in Key Largo, Florida requires scuba diving to access its rooms.

Other Unusual Hotels

- The Library Hotel in New York City, is unique in that each of its ten floors is assigned one category from the Dewey Decimal System.
- The Burj al-Arab hotel in Dubai, United Arab Emirates, built on an artificial island, is structured in the shape of a boat's sail.
- The Jailhotel Löwengraben in Lucerne, Switzerland is a converted prison now used as a hotel.
- The Luxor, a hotel and casino on the Las Vegas Strip in Paradise, Nevada, United States due to its pyramidal structure.

- The Liberty Hotel in Boston, used to be the Charles Street Jail.
- Built in Scotland and completed in 1936, The former ocean liner RMS *Queen Mary* in Long Beach, California, United States uses its first-class staterooms as a hotel, after retiring in 1967 from Transatlantic service.

Resort Hotels

Some hotels are built specifically to create a captive trade, example at casinos and holiday resorts. Though of course hotels have always been built in popular desinations, the defining characteristic of a resort hotel is that it exists purely to serve another attraction, the two having the same owners. In Las Vegas there is a tradition of one-upmanship with luxurious and extravagant hotels in a concentrated area known as the Las Vegas Strip. This trend now has extended to other resorts worldwide, but the concentration in Las Vegas is still the world's highest: nineteen of the world's twenty-five largest hotels by room count are on the Strip, with a total of over 67,000 rooms. In Europe Centre Parcs might be considered a chain of resort hotels, since the sites are largely man-made (though set in natural surroundings such as country parks) with captive trade, whereas holiday camps such as Butlins and Pontin's are probably not considered as resort hotels, since they are set at traditional holiday destinations which existed before the camps.

Railway Hotels

Frequently, expanding railway companies built grand hotels at their termini, such as the Midland Hotel, Manchester next to the former Manchester Central Station and in London the ones above St Pancras railway station and Charing Cross railway station also in London is the Chiltern Court Hotel above Baker Street tube station and Canada's grand railway hotels. They are or were mostly, but not exclusively, used by those travelling by rail.

Motels

A motel (Motor Hotel) is a hotel which is for a short stay, usually for a night, for motorists on long journeys. It has direct access from the room to the vehicle (for example a central parking lot around which the buildings are set), and is built conveniently close to major roads and intersections.

World Record Setting Hotels

Largest

In 2006, Guinness World Records listed the First World Hotel in Genting Highlands, Malaysia as the world's largest hotel with a total of 6,118 rooms.

Oldest

According to the Guinness Book of World Records, the oldest hotel still in operation is the Hoshi Ryokan, in the Awazu Onsen area of Komatsu, Japan which opened in 718.

Tallest

Burj Al Arab in United Arab Emirates is the tallest building used exclusively as a hotel. However, the Rose Tower, also in Dubai, which has already topped Burj Al Arab's height at 333 m (1,093 ft.), will take away this title upon its opening.

Hotel Rooms as an Investment

Some hotels sell individual rooms to investors. The buyer is allowed to stay in the room without charge or at a reduced rate for a given number of days each year. The investor is paid a share of the takings for the room. Rooms can be sold on a leasehold basis, sometimes on a 999 year lease. Room owners are free to sell at any time.

Living in Hotels

A number of public figures have notably chosen to take up semipermanent or permanent residence in hotels.

Actor Richard Harris lived at the Savoy Hotel while in London. Hotel archivist Susan Scott recounts an anecdote that when he was being taken out of the building on a stretcher shortly before his death he raised his hand and told the diners "it was the food".

Fictitious Hotels

Hotels have been used as the settings for television programmes such as the British situation comedies Fawlty Towers and I'm Alan

Partridge, the British soap opera Crossroads, and in films such as the Bates Motel in Hitchcock's 1960 film Psycho.

Hospitality Service

The concept of Hospitality Exchange, also known as "accommodation sharing", "hospitality services" (short "hospex"), and "home stay networks", refers to centrally organized social networks of individuals, generally travellers, who offer or seek accommodation without monetary exchange. Generally, these services connect users via the internet.

History

In 1949, Bob Luitweiler founded the first hospitality service called Servas Open Doors as a cross national, nonprofit, volunteer run organization advocating interracial and international peace. In 1965, John Wilcock set up the Traveller's Directory as a listing of his friends willing to host each other when travelling. In 1988, Joy Lily rescued the organization from imminent shutdown, forming Hospitality Exchange. In 2000, Veit Kuhne founded Hospitality Club, the first Internet-based service. In 2004, Casey Fenton started CouchSurfing, now the largest hospitality exchange organization.

How they Work

Generally, after registering, members have the option of providing very detailed information and pictures of themselves and of the sleeping accommodation being offered, if any. The more information provided by a member improves the chances that someone will find the member trustworthy enough to be their host or guest. Names and addresses may be verified by volunteers. Members looking for accommodation can search for hosts using several parameters such as age, location, sex, and activity level. Home stays are entirely consensual between the host and guest, and the duration, nature, and terms of the guest's stay are generally worked out in advance to the convenience of both parties. No monetary exchange takes place except under certain circumstances (e.g. the guest may compensate the host for food). After using the service, members can leave a noticeable reference about their host or guest.

Instead of or in addition to accommodation, members also offer to provide guide services or travel-related advice. The websites of the networks also provide editable travel guides and forums where members may seek travel partners or advice. Many such organizations are also focused on "social networking" and members organize activities such as camping trips, bar crawls, meetings, and sporting events.

Some networks cater to specific niche markets such as students, activists, religious pilgrims, and even occupational groups like police officers.

Benefits

Monetary Savings

As these networks provide accommodation at no charge, monetary savings can be significant.

Local Contact

Hospitality exchange gives travellers the chance to experience what life is like for people living in other places. In addition, making interpersonal connections and fostering understanding of different cultures may in the long run also be important to international relations. During hospitality exchanges, hosts may show off their local knowledge and exciting places "off the tourist map". Not only may travellers get a distinct experience, but they will also get a feel for the everyday lives of local residents.

Reciprocity

These systems foster richer and more convenient travel experiences not so much on the premise of altruism, but on the basis of social exchange theory. Implicit in the agreement to host travellers is the ability to ask to be hosted by them in the future. If one enjoys having interesting guests in their home, this works out well for both parties.

It works comparatively better if you are visited by travellers from a locale you find particularly attractive. Thus, hosting someone from New York City in Gainesville, Florida seems to be an unbelievable opportunity. Moreover, if you are a Westerner visiting someone in a developing country, your stay might be the only way that this individual or family could afford a trip to a rich nation. This may mean more than just a relaxing vacation for such disadvantaged parties.

Drawbacks

Lack of Guarantee

There is no contractual agreement between users in these systems. Reservations are made, but if they are for some reason broken, there is no higher authority to which one could plead for a refund or other compensation.

The only repercussion will be the poor rating you give that user and your only consolation will be that your warning will deter others from visiting or hosting them. For those who feel insecure unless their travel arrangements are written in stone before departure, this system will not be comforting.

Potential Interpersonal Conflict or Awkwardness

There is a chance that guest and host will not get along. Perhaps there will be scheduling or ideological conflicts. Maybe you will find that hosts or visitors have misrepresented themselves. Perhaps the experience will not live up to your expectations. Intense interpersonal communications in advance and a flexibility once you have arrived is your best bet.

These experiences require additional planning and courtesy towards the demands of your host. Thus, your living conditions, length of stay, and overall experience will be circumscribed by the living conditions you enter into.

Digital Divide and Demographic Segregation

As use of these services generally requires access to the internet and knowledge of the English language, the sample population found in searches of these databases is really much less diverse than a geographical representation of worldwide users might suggest.

Security

Staying in someone's house, or inviting people into your house leaves open the possibility of being taken advantage of.

Example Networks

There are countless websites that serve the idea of hospitality service, with new ones appearing as this phenomenon becomes more popular. While this page is not intended to be a directory listing, here is a small sample of the well-established and long-standing networks:

- CouchSurfing-A very active network with over 1.3 million members in more than 200 countries
- Hospitality Club-A very active network with over 550,000 members in more than 200 countries
- Servas International-human rights and global peace oriented since 1949. A relatively small network now with over 15,000 members(?) with a very long history.
- BeWelcome.

Hilton Hotels Corporation Announces Global Sustainability Goals

Hilton Hotels Corporation recently announced short and long term goals and objectives towards building sustainability into the core fabric of its businesses worldwide. Christopher J. Nassetta, President & CEO, outlined directional targets for improvement in the company's sustainability performance throughout the next five years within systemwide hotels globally. By 2014, goals for the Hilton Family of Hotels are to:

- Reduce energy consumption from direct operations by 20%
- Reduce Co2 emissions by 20%
- Reduce output of waste by 20% and
- Reduce water consumption by 10%.

"Upon becoming a truly global company with the acquisition of Hilton International and following the acquisition of our company by Blackstone late last year, we are in an ideal position to lay down a framework for sustainability within our global hotels and corporate offices," said Nassetta.

As a global business serving more than a quarter billion guests a year in more than 3000 hotels across 74 countries, the Hilton family of Hotels, including Hilton, Conrad Hotels & Resorts, Doubletree, Embassy Suites Hotels, Hampton Inn and Suites, Hilton Garden Inn, Hilton Grand Vacations, Homewood Suites by Hilton and The Waldorf=Astoria Collection, are well-positioned to make a difference environmentally, socially, culturally and economically.

"Population growth and global industrialization are accelerating the depletion of our natural resources. Around the world, demand for energy continues to grow and fresh water scarcity is becoming a global reality. How we respond to these challenges will determine the sustainability of our future lifestyles, the sustainability of our communities as we know them, and ultimately the sustainability of our planet.

"To meet the growing demand of increased travel around the world, we must be able to do so in a sustainable fashion while still delivering unsurpassed levels of hospitality, including a better night's sleep, an enhanced dining experience and a more productive meeting," Nassetta continued. "We must operate our business in ways that provide for our current needs while allowing future generations to meet their own needs. This is the essence of sustainability and the path we must follow. Not only is it the right thing to do as responsible global citizens, it's the right thing to do for our business."

Long-Term, High-Impact Goals

In addition to the stated measurable short-term targets, the company also has committed to focus on several high-impact areas that offer significant long-term benefits. Sustainable buildings and operations, including the advancement of sustainable design and construction, operations, chemical management and purchasing will be one key area. The company is also committed to the advancement of renewable energy as a source of power for its operations, not only to reduce its carbon footprint but to develop a viable commercial infrastructure for powering hotels and corporate offices.

External Assessment by Leading Consulting Group

In the past year, Hilton Hotels Corporation conducted a thorough assessment of its global operations with the goal of identifying current impacts, and creating a strategy to define, galvanize and build sustainability into the business. To lead this effort, HHC brought in Blu Skye Sustainability Consulting, led by company founder and CEO Jib Ellison. Blu Skye visited a cross-section of Hilton Family hotels, interviewed various business units and analyzed the company's operating procedures. As a result of these efforts, corporate and brand management teams, together with Blu Skye, were able to identify specific areas of focus to build the company's sustainability framework focusing on short and long term value creation. "Hilton is building on its strong history of environmental stewardship by launching these ambitious goals," said Ellison. "Their comprehensive sustainability strategy has put them on a path to leadership in the hospitality industry."

Support Strategy

Under the direction of a newly appointed vice president – global sustainability Christopher Corpuel, HHC will build out a team to develop and implement its sustainability strategy. This team will support all of HHC's core businesses and work closely with hotel ownership and management groups to achieve its stated goals.

In addition, Hilton Hotels Corporation is supporting its portfolio of commitments in a number of ways, by:

- Building out educational and engagement programs for all brands and team members, including online learning, centralized web content, and various training modules.
- Measuring and reporting on our progress. The internal environmental management tool used within company-managed hotels will be extended to all properties, allowing us to track and report on our commitments and design processes and programs that identify areas of opportunity to drive innovation and efficiencies.
- Revising brand operational, and design and construction standards for 2009 to ensure both internal and external best practices are shared, adopted and transparent around the globe.
- Evaluating all current and future purchasing policies and practices across the brands to ensure that the range of products placed in hotels not only enhance the guest

experience but drive value for owners while supporting the company's overall sustainability efforts.

Current Practices

Hilton Hotels Corporation has demonstrated its commitment to sustainability with several projects that currently are underway. In the European region, energy and water consumption already have been reduced by 10% during the last two years. In the U.K. and Ireland, the introduction of carbon-free electricity has reduced CO2 emissions in participating Hilton hotels by more than 64,000 tons, or 56% of our carbon footprint. In the United States, Hilton was the first in the industry to complete the installation of a commercial fuel cell power system, atop the Hilton New York, delivering one of the cleanest power generating technologies available today.

Galvanizing the spirit demonstrated by its recent and past successes together with its current commitments, Hilton Hotels Corporation has created a Mission Statement that will carry forward throughout its business practices.

Mission Statement

The Hilton Family of Hotels will manage our business through a lens of sustainability to benefit this generation and those that follow. Through action and innovation, we will lead our industry in products and programs that:

- Enhance the guest experience
- Engage our employees
- Improve operational efficiency
- Advance building design
- Strengthen our partnerships
- Serve our communities
- Protect our global environment
- Enrich our Family of Brands.

Summary

"If we can use the lens of sustainability and find ways to enhance our leadership position in the industry, I am confident we will not only drive business value in the short and long term, but innovate our products and offerings in ways we never imagined," said Nassetta. "We can create better experiences for our guests, better business opportunities for our partners and investors, better work facilities for our colleagues, and better serve our communities, giving back in ways that actually restore resources instead of removing them, and improving the well-being of all involved. The platform for change we create now is one that will serve us for many years to come and support our goal of being the world's preeminent hospitality company."

About the Hilton Hotels Corporation

Hilton Hotels Corporation is the leading global hospitality company, with more than 3,000 hotels and 500,000 rooms in 74 countries, with more than 135,000 team members worldwide. The company owns, manages or franchises some of the best known and highly regarded hotel brands including Hilton®, Conrad® Hotels & Resorts, Doubletree®, Embassy Suites Hotels®, Hampton Inn®, Hampton Inn & Suites®, Hilton Garden Inn®, Hilton Grand Vacations™, Homewood Suites by Hilton® and The Waldorf=Astoria Collection™.

Hilton Hotels Corporation is an Official Sponsor of the U.S. Olympic Team, which will extend through the 2010 Olympic and Paralympic Winter Games in Vancouver, the 2012 Olympic and Paralympic Games in London, the 2010/2012 U.S. Paralympic Team and the 2011 U.S. Pan American Team.

The Hilton Family of Hotels adheres to founder Conrad Hilton's philosophy that, "It has been, and continues to be, our responsibility to fill the earth with the light and warmth of hospitality." The company put a name to its unique brand of service that has made it the best known and most highly regarded hotel company: be hospitable®. The philosophy is shared by all brands in the Hilton Family of Hotels, and is the inspiration for its overarching message of kindness and generosity.

Selecting and Attracting the Right Customers

The following case is completely against the above statement made by Ratan Tata. One day in the month of December Mr.X and his friend Mr.Y went to deposit cash in one of the leading Multi

National commercial Bank, They entered the bank premises found one of their executives attending only selective customers which they felt that it is unfair treatment but still they approached him, enquired for pay-in-slip they got it and filled it, later joined the queue with other customers towards the teller counter to deposit the cash which took more than five minutes, employee at the teller counter said "please collect the token for depositing the cash", They left the queue and went to the token machine and opted for non customer with deposit of Rupees less than 50000 and they got the token with (NW72) number and they were waiting for their turn to come and also observing the pattern of calling the customers, customers who came after them were provided priority services, in first 10-12 minutes they came to a conclusion that first preference was given to the customers of the bank itself, They immediately went to the token machine and opted for an another token as customer of the bank with deposit of Rupees less than 50000 and got the token with (CD81) number, their turn came just after fourth customer. They deposited the money and went to see the manager and put forth their complaint to him that the treatment what a non customer is getting is unreasonable and it is unfair on the part of the bank, the bank manager says that "this is a system where in non customers have been provided a separate counter and as an when their turn comes they will get the service and he was arguing with them and goes on explaining the system, procedure etc., But Mr. X & Y were not at all impressed with his justification and his indifferent comments on the problem made them felt awful, They thanked the Bank Manager and left his cabin.

This is nothing but over automation where in there is no personal touch or humane touch in their approach. This conversation have created an permanent negative image of the bank in their minds that they would never ever be a customer of such Bank or its sister concern and will never suggest any of their friends, relatives and even strangers to be a customer of that bank. Does any customer wants to hear "what are the company's systems and procedures, rules & regulations etc., As a direct or indirect customer one would never want to hear all those justifications, they just want quick service. And there is every possibility that automation of customer service will be abandoned in the frontline and induction of specialists in customer services in front office will be a future trend now which can be observed in Aviation industry. As of now few financial institutions are serving their customers in depositing money, withdrawals, financial planning and tax planning etc., at customer's premises.

The following example explains how indirectly a customer can be a valuable asset for an organization.

Eg: An individual who spends merely an average dollar amount per month with a wireless phone provider might be considered even more valuable if the wireless company knew the customer's spouse was responsible for selecting the wireless service plan for 5,000 workers at a large company.

In general there is misconception in the peoples mind that Public sector undertakings are poor at customer service, to some extent this comment may be right, but not completely true. Here are two public sector banks 'C' Bank (CB) and 'O' Bank (OB). Whose services are far better than that of Indian Multi National Bank. In the month of December Mr. X have been to CB to collect a Demand Draft, it took him more than half an hour when he asked about the time delay in issuing Demand Draft the Assistant Manager was courteous enough to say that "Sir, please wait for few minutes it will be done" and he did it in next ten minutes. Though Mr. X felt bad about the delay in issuing the draft but Mr. X was pleased by the response of the Assistant Manger. This episode haven't made him much disappointed and have not provoked him to erase completely CB from his mind; He still wanted to open an account because it is convenient for him to transact and staff's aptitude to handle customer services are better. And Mr. X still felt CB is bankable and there are better chances that he would suggest his friends to bank at CB. Unfortunately on the same day itself a situation came, where in he was forced to take one more Demand Draft, he visited OB and enquired about DD form at the counter, the employee just shown the place where they were, with a pathetic face, he took the form and his first question to the bank employee was "How much time does it take to issue a Demand Draft" there was no response from that bank employee who was sitting at the counter, suddenly there was a unexpected response which he heard from an unusual person, a middle aged woman, who is just a Peon " Sir it will just take five minutes" He was convinced with her approach of attending him, he simply paid the amount at the teller and stood near the counter, rest she took over the Job. During this time, she was doing her job simultaneously interacting with him by posing soft questions like "Are you in a hurry Sir?" Where do you come from? And other few similar questions. By the time he answered her questions, the Demand Draft was ready. It took only seven minutes as compared to official time to make a DD is twenty minutes, though it was delayed by two minutes as promised, he was extremely satisfied with that Lady's service. He felt like it would have been better if she would have placed in front office as an executive instead of Peon. Mr. X was extremely impressed by that lady's ability to engage customer at POP, One would definitely feel that the big companies and their big projects of Customer Relationship Management are of no use when there are no people to implement it all the levels.

"According to a research by Reichheld and Sasser in the Harvard Business Review, 5% increase in customer retention can increase profitability by 35% in banking business, 50% in insurance and brokerage, and 125% in the consumer credit card market. Therefore, banks are now stressing on retaining customers and increasing market share".

The above situations like these are definitely creating an impression in the mind of customers that the corporate are denying legitimate right, needs and requirements.

Right from the days of customer centric market, this has been a regular activity that there are problems in customer care. In today's business environment there is no such industry, where customer care problems does not exist, even in the field of hospitality industry and service industry where in these industry's core business is custom care and the gap between the customers and their expectations and the service providers are increasing day by day. Today in the Heighten world lot many new innovative products and services are being invented, but at the same time does any company thought that the product/service they offer are really needed by the customers or it is just because the products are being produced and are dumped into the market.

As people are very much aware that there are whole variety of products and services available in the market. But how many of them do really buy them even though they are of top quality, with marvelous features and at affordable prices.

Managers at middle level and supervisory levels of Indian corporate are not ready to treat customers equally. Unless the attitude of the managers changes towards customers problems pertaining to service will always exist.

How companies are responding to the bad experiences of using the product or service, what are the measures taken to avoid such experiences by the customers. Companies must ensure that customers get a new experience in purchasing and using their products and the impact of such purchase must be for a long time and which can be encased into new opportunities in the long run. And differentiating from competitors, there by extending the change in purchasing experience.

One would definitely agree that, it is not always possible to give such a kind of experience and personal attention to each and every customer, but a company must make sure that customers should not leave the premises without satisfaction, and it is the right of the customer to expect highest degree of respect, let it be in the case of, hospitality, product availability, price, features or any other service (E.g.: Fiat is known for its best designed and engineered cars in the world, but in India it could not capture the market as expected because, after sales service levels were not up to the expectations of the customer, In order to boost sales in India, Tata Motors and Fiat came together and announced a strategic relationship in passenger car segment for sales and marketing of Fiat cars through Tata dealerships. Through these dealerships display a wide selection of Fiat cars along with service and spares will be provided across Tata dealerships in India. Dealers will display the Fiat models along with Tata cars).

And most importantly the consumer complaining behavior process is unique; it has to deal with at most importance. And it distinguishes between negative word-of-mouth that occurs prior to seeking redress (or in lieu of seeking redress) and negative word-of-mouth that occurs after seeking redress. There is an argument from the company's point of view i.e. how can any company spend time and manpower to attend a default and fraudulent customer and how treat them in the same manner as genuine and productive customer. Certainly they must be treated in a cordial way but one should not forget that they too deserve some importance in one way or the other.

There is every possibility that companies make mistakes but they must be such that they should be forgivable by the customer, meaning even though companies make mistakes and try to rectify at the earliest and inform customers that the mistake which has been committed is been rectified and at most precautions have been taken, not to repeat the mistake.

Eg: What Cadbury has done by giving advertisements in the media, that it has rectified its mistakes and promised the customer that it won't repeat the same mistake again.

If a person is a regular customer of friendly neighborhood grocery shop or any other shop or bank, one will definitely know the painless punch of corporate businesses. They might misguide, mislead with the bashing effect, display, intense publicity, promotion and enchasing on personal intimacy. One should be aware that in one way or the other the suppliers are the customers and consumers of their own produce. The individuals who supply the produce at certain rate cannot afford to purchase the same product just because it is been packed and placed in fully decorated place. In this kind of situation, are you (customer) the beneficiary, just ask yourself. Who do you think is the real beneficiary; if your answer is, neither the supplier nor the consumer, then one will get to know there is nothing, which is called as "Service".

Most Indians are habituated to have every thing fresh and never had tradition of packing food, let it be cooked or uncooked food, they prefer to have them in a natural way.

Eg: Fresh vegetables and fruits, do they really need packing, is there any need for branding products which are grown naturally or cultivated, does anyone feel it is absolutely necessary?

The ever changing customer expectations are forcing the corporate to provide excellent service which is not possible to each an every company, organizations which provides service beyond customer expectations will survive the future rest will be out of business. Organizations who wanted to survive are exploring, proliferating them selves by establishing new businesses in big way, there by depending on higher volumes. Some of them are collaboratively sharing their customer data there by offering vide variety of products to the same customer and leveraging customer base. These strategies adopted by the companies constantly put the pressure on the customer by offering vide range of product and there is fare chance that one might ignore such product offerings which are marketed by different departments, which are in a race generate revenue of their own. There is always a risk that customer may encounter different service levels of the different department of the same company.

For many years, Indian economy has been guarded from invasion of foreign companies in the form of Joint venture or fully owned or capitalistic form of economy. Only some state owned companies which were in key areas like Defense, Telecom, Oil and other essential commodities. A set of few private owned companies who were into consumer items, engineering and manufacturing prospered during that period. Right from the days of closely guarded economy and till the days of economic liberalization in late 1990, the private owned companies in the seller's market were very successful. But the whole scenario chanced after post liberalization.

Ever since the golden days (customer centric market) i.e. Since last thirty years to till date, marketers have been saying "Customer is the King" but, is the customer really a king? This is the main question which comes to everybody's mind and other questions such as how customers are treated? What quality of products do marketers offer? Are the products are user friendly? Etc., if these questions are answered completely with good outlook, a company can build up a brand which will be unique in any or combination of all the following attributes Price, Design, Quality, Usability, Service and shopping experience there by creating own and distinguished Brand. As an human being every individual expects to be treated with courtesy, similarly it is prime duty of marketers to treat customer with at most respect which he/she deserves. Here is a situation where CRM come in to picture, the essence of CRM should be understood as any activity which is completely customer centric and which enhances customer's expectations and satisfaction levels by giving him/her a wow effect with a human touch, at the same time maximize revenues from such services.

> *"CRM would help organizations to serve the customers on an individual basis, to enjoy a long-term relationship and to get rid of barriers and distortions created by non-value adding intermediaries. He also says that CRM would also help organizations to reduce marketing costs, target specific customers by focusing on their needs and to track the effectiveness of a given marketing action" by Dr. Thapan K. Panda, IIM Indore.*

"CRM has power to help bankers quickly and directly improve customer satisfaction. CRM is an added dimension to ensure that what the customer expects is consistent with what the bank is prepared to deliver. One expert in bank CRM initiatives recently said that CRM is an approach that is less focused on providing the right services to the customer than attracting customers who are the right fit for what the bank has to offer. Further, the primary value of CRM is its potential as a customer retention tool. People are starting to measure CRM in terms of increased customer satisfaction rather than ROI" by Rob Keene, Director, Banking Practice.

In the vide spectrum of business, in after adopting and practicing latest technologies like CRM, people soft and other similar technologies. How do people interpret and understand the meaning of Customer Relationship Management, many experts expressed their view in different forms but there are few seminaries which revolve round the "Customer's needs, expectations and satisfaction".

In the field of consumer service management, many unexpected problem do arise and they pose challenges to be solved, a doubt may arise in the minds of individuals that adopting all these CRM technologies are of waste of money and time. May be not, as per the latest studies, customer service problems are marginalized to some extent but could not overcome them completely. We cannot imagine big businesses without such customer service technologies. Company's internal environment (employees) and external environment (Customer traffic, Business expansion etc.,) do influence on implementation of such technologies, Employees must be trained continuously to implement it and also change their mind set to adapt to such changing environment (customer centric).

Unless people from top to bottom level in all departments focus and act on, what they actually wanted achieve in customer relationship management, interactive Customer Relationship Management software solutions will never deliver expected results.

It can be concluded that if any company intends to survive in today's competitive market it is essential that they must to treat customer as a king irrespective of using any technology. And giving at most importance to the direct or an indirect customer. Who knows a non productive customer of yours, may be a highly productive customer of your competitor.

International Trade Theory, Practice and Policy

International trade is exchange of capital, goods, and services across international borders or territories. It refers to exports of goods and services by a firm to a foreign-based buyer (importer) In most countries, it represents a significant share of gross domestic product (GDP). While international trade has been present throughout much of history, its economic, social, and political importance has been on the rise in recent centuries.

Industrialization, advanced transportation, globalization, multinational corporations, and outsourcing are all having a major impact on the international trade system. Increasing international trade is crucial to the continuance of globalization. International trade is a major source of economic revenue for any nation that is considered a world power. Without international trade, nations would be limited to the goods and services produced within their own borders.

International trade is in principle not different from domestic trade as the motivation and the behavior of parties involved in a trade do not change fundamentally regardless of whether trade is across a border or not. The main difference is that international trade is typically more costly than domestic trade. The reason is that a border typically imposes additional costs such as tariffs, time costs due to border delays and costs associated with country differences such as language, the legal system or culture. Another difference between domestic and international trade is that factors of production such as capital and labour are typically more mobile within a country than across countries.

Thus international trade is mostly restricted to trade in goods and services, and only to a lesser extent to trade in capital, labour or other factors of production.

Then trade in goods and services can serve as a substitute for trade in factors of production. Instead of importing a factor of production, a country can import goods that make intensive use of the factor of production and are thus embodying the respective factor. An example is the import of labour-intensive goods by the United States from China. Instead of importing Chinese labour the United States is importing goods from China that were produced with Chinese labour.

International trade is also a branch of economics, which, together with international finance, forms the larger branch of international economics.

Models

Several different models have been proposed to predict patterns of trade and to analyse the effects of trade policies such as tariffs.

Ricardian Model

The Ricardian model focuses on comparative advantage and is perhaps the most important concept in international trade theory. In a Ricardian model, countries specialize in producing what they produce best. Unlike other models, the Ricardian framework predicts that countries will fully specialize instead of producing a broad array of goods.

Also, the Ricardian model does not directly consider factor endowments, such as the relative amounts of labour and capital within a country. The main merit of Ricardin model is that it assumes technology differences between countries. Technology gap is easily included in the Ricardian and Ricardo-Sraffa model.

The Ricardian model makes the following assumptions:

1. Labour is the only primary input to production (labour is considered to be the ultimate source of value).

2. Constant Marginal Product of Labour (MPL) (Labour productivity is constant, constant returns to scale, and simple technology.)
3. Limited amount of labour in the economy
4. Labour is perfectly mobile among sectors but not internationally.
5. Perfect competition (price-takers).

The Ricardian model measures in the shortrun, therefore technology differs internationally. This supports the fact that countries follow their comparative advantage and allows for specialization.

Modern Development of the Ricardian Model

The Ricardian trade model was studied by Graham, Jones, McKenzie and others. All the theories excluded intermediate goods, or traded input goods such as materials and capital goods. McKenzie(1954), Jones(1961) and Samuelson (2001) emphasized that considerable gains from trade would be lost once intermediate goods were excluded from trade. In a famous comment McKenzie pointed that "A moment's consideration will convince one that Lancashire would be unlikely to produce cotton cloth if the cotton had to be grown in England."

Recently, the theory was extended to the case that includes traded intermediates. Thus the "labour only" assumption was removed from the theory. Thus the new Ricardian theory, or the Ricardo-Sraffa model, as it is sometimes named, theoretically includes capital goods such as machines and materials, which are traded across countries. In the time of global trade, this assumption is much more realistic than the Heckscher-Ohlin model, which assumes that capital is fixed inside the country and does not move internationally.

Heckscher-Ohlin Model

In the early 1900s an international trade theory called factor proportions theory emerged by two Swedish economists, Eli Heckscher and Bertil Ohlin. This theory is also called the Heckscher-Ohlin theory. The Heckscher-Ohlin theory stresses that countries should produce and export goods that require resources (factors) that are abundant and import goods that require resources in short supply. This theory differs from the theories of comparative advantage and absolute advantage since these theory focuses on the productivity of the production process for a particular good. On the contrary, the Heckscher-Ohlin theory states that a country should specialise production and export using the factors that are most abundant, and thus the cheapest. Not to produce, as earlier theories stated, the goods it produces most efficiently.

The Heckscher-Ohlin model was produced as an alternative to the Ricardian model of basic comparative advantage. Despite its greater complexity it did not prove much more accurate in its predictions. However from a theoretical point of view it did provide an elegant solution by incorporating the neoclassical price mechanism into international trade theory.

The theory argues that the pattern of international trade is determined by differences in factor endowments. It predicts that countries will export those goods that make intensive use of locally abundant factors and will import goods that make intensive use of factors that are locally scarce. Empirical problems with the H-O model, known as the Leontief paradox, were exposed in empirical tests by Wassily Leontief who found that the United States tended to export labour intensive goods despite having a capital abundance.

The H-O model makes the following core assumptions:

1. Labour and capital flow freely between sectors
2. The production of shoes is labour intensive and computers is capital intensive
3. The amount of labour and capital in two countries differ (difference in endowments)
4. free trade
5. technology is the same across countries (long-term)
6. Tastes are the same.

The problem with the H-O theory is that it excludes the trade of capital goods (including materials and fuels). In the H-O theory, labour and capital are fixed entities endowed to each country. In a modern economy, capital goods are traded internationally. Gains from trade of intermediate goods are considerable, as it was emphasized by Samuelson (2001).

Reality and Applicability of the Heckscher-Ohlin Model

The Heckscher-Ohlin theory is preferred to the Ricardo theory by many economists, because it makes fewer simplifying assumptions.

In 1953, Wassily Leontief published a study, where he tested the validity of the Heckscher-Ohlin theory. The study showed that the U.S was more abundant in capital compared to other countries, therefore the U.S would export capital-intensive goods and import labour-intensive goods. Leontief found out that the U.S's export was less capital intensive than import.

After the appearance of Leontief's paradox, many researchers tried to save the Heckscher-Ohlin theory, either by new methods of measurement, or either by new interpretations. Leamer emphasized that Leontief did not interpret HO theory properly and claimed that with a right interpretation paradox did not occur. Brecher and Choudri found that, if Leamer was right, the American workers consumption per head should be lower than the workers world average consumption.

Many other trials followed but most of them failed. Many of famous textbook writers, including Krugman and Obstfeld and Bowen, Hollander and Viane, are negative about the validity of H-O model. After examining the long history of empirical research, Bowen, Hollander and Viane concluded: "Recent tests of the factor abundance theory [H-O theory and its developed form into many-commodity and many-factor case] that directly examine the H-O-V equations also indicate the rejection of the theory."

Heckscher-Ohlin theory is not well adapted to, the analyse South-North trade problems. The assumptions of HO are less realistic with respect to N-S than N-N (or S-S) trade. Income differences between North and South is the one that third world cares most. The factor price equalization [a consequence of HO theory] has not shown much sign of realization. HO model assumes identical production functions between countries. This is highly unrealistic. Technological gap between developed and developing countries is the main concern of the poor countries.

Specific Factors Model

In this model, labour mobility between industries is possible while capital is immobile between industries in the shortrun. Thus, this model can be interpreted as a 'short run' version of the Heckscher-Ohlin model. The specific factors name refers to the given that in the shortrun, specific factors of production such as physical capital are not easily transferable between industries. The theory suggests that if there is an increase in the price of a good, the owners of the factor of production specific to that good will profit in real terms. Additionally, owners of opposing specific factors of production (i.e. labour and capital) are likely to have opposing agendas when lobbying for controls over immigration of labour. Conversely, both owners of capital and labour profit in real terms from an increase in the capital endowment. This model is ideal for particular industries. This model is ideal for understanding income distribution but awkward for discussing the pattern of trade.

New Trade Theory

New Trade theory tries to explain several facts about trade, which the two main models above have difficulty with. These include the fact that most trade is between countries with similar factor endowment and productivity levels, and the large amount of multinational production (i.e.foreign direct investment) which exists. In one example of this framework, the economy exhibits monopolistic competition and increasing returns to scale. There are three basic theories that global marketer has to comprehend: 1. Comparative Advantage Theory 2. Trade or product trade cycle theory 3. Business orientation theory

Gravity Model

The Gravity model of trade presents a more empirical analysis of trading patterns rather than the more theoretical models discussed above. The gravity model, in its basic form, predicts trade based on the distance between countries and the interaction of the countries' economic sizes. The model mimics the Newtonian law of gravity which also considers distance and physical size between two objects. The model has been proven to be empirically strong through econometric analysis. Other factors such as income level, diplomatic relationships between countries, and trade policies are also included in expanded versions of the model.

Regulation of International Trade

Traditionally trade was regulated through bilateral treaties between two nations. For centuries under the belief in mercantilism most nations had high tariffs and many restrictions on international trade. In the 19th century, especially in the United Kingdom, a belief in free trade became paramount. This belief became the dominant thinking among western nations since then. In the years since the Second World War, controversial multilateral treaties like the General Agreement on Tariffs and Trade (GATT) and World Trade Organization have attempted to promote free trade while creating a globally regulated trade structure. These trade agreements have often resulted in discontent and protest with claims of unfair trade that is not beneficial to developing countries.

Free trade is usually most strongly supported by the most economically powerful nations, though they often engage in selective protectionism for those industries which are strategically important such as the protective tariffs applied to agriculture by the United States and Europe. The Netherlands and the United Kingdom were both strong advocates of free trade when they were economically dominant, today the United States, the United Kingdom, Australia and Japan are its greatest proponents. However, many other countries (such as India, China and Russia) are increasingly becoming advocates of free trade as they become more economically powerful themselves. As tariff levels fall there is also an increasing willingness to negotiate non tariff measures, including foreign direct investment, procurement and trade facilitation. The latter looks at the transaction cost associated with meeting trade and customs procedures.

Traditionally agricultural interests are usually in favour of free trade while manufacturing sectors often support protectionism. This has changed somewhat in recent years, however. In fact, agricultural lobbies, particularly in the United States, Europe and Japan, are chiefly responsible for particular rules in the major international trade treaties which allow for more protectionist measures in agriculture than for most other goods and services.

During recessions there is often strong domestic pressure to increase tariffs to protect domestic industries. This occurred around the world during the Great Depression. Many economists have attempted to portray tariffs as the underlining reason behind the collapse in world trade that many believe seriously deepened the depression. The regulation of international trade is done through the World Trade Organization at the global level, and through several other regional arrangements such as MERCOSUR in South America, the North American Free Trade Agreement (NAFTA) between the United States, Canada and Mexico, and the European Union between 27 independent states. The 2005 Buenos Aires talks on the planned establishment of the Free Trade Area of the Americas (FTAA) failed largely because of opposition from the populations of Latin American nations. Similar agreements such as the Multilateral Agreement on Investment (MAI) have also failed in recent years.

Risk in International Trade

Companies doing business across international borders face many of the same risks as would normally be evident in strictly domestic transactions. For example,

- Buyer insolvency (purchaser cannot pay);
- Non-acceptance (buyer rejects goods as different from the agreed upon specifications);
- Credit risk (allowing the buyer to take possession of goods prior to payment);
- Regulatory risk (e.g., a change in rules that prevents the transaction);
- Intervention (governmental action to prevent a transaction being completed);
- Political risk (change in leadership interfering with transactions or prices); and
- War and other uncontrollable events.

In addition, international trade also faces the risk of unfavorable exchange rate movements (and, the potential benefit of favorable movements).

The Measurement of Efficiency and Productivity

Market orientation efficiency is conceptualized as the speed by which a company gathers information about customers and competitors, disseminates the information throughout the organization, arrives at a shared meaning, and implements a response. A reliable scale with demonstrated content and convergent validity is developed and the impact of market orientation efficiency on business performance is assessed based on multiple informant data drawn from two industries. From a managerial perspective, the scale can be used to evaluate a given firm's level of market orientation efficiency as a baseline measure and again as a measure of success once strategies designed to improve market orientation efficiency are set into motion.

Ultimate Goal of Operations Research

The term Operations Research (OR) describes the discipline that is focused on the application of information technology for informed decision-making. In other words, OR represents the study of optimal resource allocation. The goal of OR is to provide rational bases for decision making by seeking to understand and structure complex situations, and to utilize this understanding to predict system behavior and improve system performance. Much of the actual work is conducted by using analytical and numerical techniques to develop and manipulate mathematical models of organizational systems that are composed of people, machines, and procedures. This article introduces some of the methods and application that are affiliated with OR, and elaborates on some of the benefits that may be gained by incorporating OR into the actual business framework.

OR Activities

OR's role in both, the public and the private sectors is increasing rapidly. In general, OR addresses a wide variety of issues in transportation, inventory planning, production planning, communication operations, computer operations, financial assets, risk management, revenue management, and many other fields where improving business productivity is paramount. In the public sector, OR studies may focus on energy policy, defense, health care, water resource planning, design and operation of urban emergency systems, or criminal justice. To reiterate, OR reflects an analytical method of problem solving and decision-making that is useful in the management of organizations. In OR, problems are (1) decomposed into basic components and (2) solved via mathematical analysis. Some of the analytical methods used in OR include mathematical logic, simulation, network analysis, queuing theory, and game theory. The actual

OR process can in general be described via three steps. (1) A set of potential solutions to a problem is identified and developed (the set may be rather large). (2) The alternatives derived in the first step are analyzed, and reduced to a smaller set of solutions (the solution's have to be feasible and workable). (3) The alternatives derived in the second step are subjected to simulated implementation and, if feasible, exposed to an actual analysis in a real-world environment. It has to be pointed out that in the final step, psychology and management sciences often play a rather important role. Generally speaking, OR improves the effectiveness and the efficiency of an institution, hence some of the benefits offered by OR include:

- Decrease Cost or Investment
- Increase Revenue or Return on Investment
- Increase Market Share
- Manage and Reduce Risk
- Improve Quality
- Increase Throughput while Decreasing Delays
- Achieve Improved Utilization form Limited Resources
- Demonstrate Feasibility and Workability.

OR Functions and Methods

OR may assist decision-makers in almost any management function. To illustrate, OR supports the key decision making process, allows to solve urgent problems, can be utilized to design improved multistep operations (processes), setup policies, supports the planning and forecasting steps, and measures actual results. OR can be applied at the non-manager levels as well, as engineers or consumers alike can benefit from the improved and streamlined decision-making process.

When first encountered, the methods commonly utilized in OR may seem obscure. Technical labels such as multi-criteria decision analysis, linear and non-linear programming, discrete-event Dominique A. Heger, Fortuitous Technology, Austin, TX, 2006 simulation, queuing and stochastic process modeling, conjoint analysis, or neural networking further foster this general impression. Despite the wealth of labels available in the filed of OR, most projects apply one of three broad groups of methods, which may be described as:

- *Simulation methods*, where the goal is to develop simulators that provide the decision-maker with the ability to conduct sensitivity studies to (1) search for improvements, and (2) to test and benchmark the improvement ideas that are being made.
- *Optimization methods*, where the goal is to enable the decision maker to search among possible choices in an efficient and effective manner, in environments where thousands or millions of choices may actually be feasible, or where some of the comparing choices are rather complex. The ultimate goal is to identify and locate the very best choice based on certain criteria's.
- *Data-analysis methods*, where the goal is to aid the decision-maker in detecting actual patterns and interconnections in the data set. This method is rather useful in numerous applications including forecasting and data mining based business environments.

Within each of the three basic groups, many probabilistic methods provide the ability to assess risk and uncertainty factors.

OR in Manufacturing

As OR has made (over the years) significant contributions in virtually all industries, in almost all managerial and decision-making functions, and at most organizational levels, the list of OR applications is prodigious. Hence, this article focuses in the next few paragraphs on the manufacturing industry, and introduces some of the application where OR is being used.

The term operations in OR may suggests that the manufacturing application category represents the original home of OR. That is not quite accurate, as the name originated from military operations, not business operations. Nevertheless, it is a true statement that OR's successes in contemporary business pervade manufacturing and service operations, logistics, distribution, transportation, and telecommunication. The myriad applications include scheduling, routing, workflow improvements, elimination of bottlenecks, inventory control, business process reengineering, site selection, or facility and general operational planning. Revenue and supply chain management reflect two growing applications that are distinguished by their use of several OR methods to cover several functions. Revenue management entails first to accurately forecasting the demand, and secondly to adjust the price structure over time to more profitably allocate fixed capacity. Supply chain decisions describe the who, what, when, and where abstractions from purchasing and transporting raw materials and parts, through manufacturing actual

products and goods, and finally distributing and delivering the items to the customers. The prime management goal here may be to reduce overall cost while processing customer orders more efficiently than before. The power of utilizing OR methods allows examining this rather complex and convoluted chain in a comprehensive manner, and to search among a vast number of combinations for the resource optimization and allocation strategy that seem most effective, and hence beneficial to the operation.

Production Systems

Businesses and organizations frequently face challenging operational problems whose successful solution requires certain expertise in applied statistics, optimization, stochastic modeling, or a combination of these areas. To illustrate, a company may need to design a sampling plan in order to meet specific quality control objectives. In a manufacturing environment, operations that compete for the same resources must be scheduled in a way that deadlines are not violated. The manager of a supermarket must determine how many checkout lines to keep open at various times during the day and evening so that shoppers are not unnecessarily delayed. Or as a final example, the size of the areas reserved for storing work in process at a Dominique A. Heger, Fortuitous Technology, Austin, TX, 2006 number of bottleneck stations has to be determined so that a smooth flow of work results, even at the busiest (peak) production times.

The area of operations research that concentrates on real-world operational problems is called production systems. Production systems problems may arise in settings that include, but are not limited to, manufacturing, telecommunications, healthcare delivery, facility location and layout, and staffing. The area of production systems presents special challenges for operations researchers. Production problems are operations research problems, hence solving them requires a solid foundation in operations research fundamentals. Additionally, the solution of production systems problems frequently draws on expertise in more than one of the primary areas of operations research, implying that the successful production researcher can not be one-dimensional. Furthermore, production systems problems can not be solved without an in-depth understanding of the real problem, since invoking assumptions that simplify the mathematical structure of the problem may lead to an elegant solution for the wrong problem. Common sense and practical insight are common attributes of successful production planners. At the current time, the filed of OR is extremely dynamic and ever evolving. To name a few of the contemporary (primary) research projects, current work in OR seeks to develop software for material flow analysis and design of flexible manufacturing facilities using pattern recognition and graph theory algorithms. Further, approaches for the design of reconfigurable manufacturing systems and progressive automation of discrete manufacturing systems are under development. Additional OR projects focus on the industrial deployment of computer-based methods for assembly line balancing, business process reengineering, capacity planning, pull scheduling, and setup reduction, primarily through the integration of the philosophies of the Theory of Constraints and Lean Manufacturing.

Identifying Sources of Operational Risk

An operational risk is a risk arising from execution of a company's business functions. As such, it is a very broad concept including e.g. fraud risks, legal risks, physical or environmental risks, etc. The term operational risk is most commonly found in risk management programs of financial institutions that must organize their risk management program according to Basel II. In Basel II, risk management is divided into credit, market, liquidity and operational risk management. In many cases, credit and market risks are handled through a company's financial department, whereas operational risk management is perhaps coordinated centrally but most commonly implemented in different operational units (e.g. the IT department takes care of information risks, the HR department takes care of personnel risks, etc.)

More specifically, Basel II defines operational risk as the risk of loss resulting from inadequate or failed internal processes, people and systems, or from external events. Although the risks apply to any organization in business, this particular way of framing risk management is of particular relevance to the banking regime where regulators are responsible for establishing safeguards to protect against systemic failure of the banking system and the economy.

Background

Since the mid-1990s, the topics of market risk and credit risk have been the subject of much debate and research, with the result that financial institutions have made significant progress in the identification, measurement and management of both these forms of risk. However, it is worth mentioning that the near collapse of the U.S. financial system in September 2008 is a clear indication that our ability to measure market and credit risk is far from perfect.

Globalization and deregulation in financial markets, combined with increased sophistication in financial technology, have introduced more complexities into the activities of banks and therefore their risk profiles. These reasons underscore banks' and supervisors' growing focus upon the identification and measurement of operational risk.

Events such as the September 11 terrorist attacks, rogue trading losses at Societe Generale, Barings, AIB and National Australia Bank serve to highlight the fact that the scope of risk management extends beyond merely market and credit risk. The list of risks (and, more importantly, the scale of these risks) faced by banks today includes fraud, system failures, terrorism and employee compensation claims. These types of risk are generally classified under the term 'operational risk'. The identification and measurement of operational risk is a real and live issue for modern-day banks, particularly since the decision by the Basel Committee on Banking Supervision (BCBS) to introduce a capital charge for this risk as part of the new capital adequacy framework (Basel II).

Definition

The Basel Committee defines operational risk as: "The risk of loss resulting from inadequate or failed internal processes, people and systems or from external events." However, the Basel Committee recognizes that operational risk is a term that has a variety of meanings and therefore, for internal purposes, banks are permitted to adopt their own definitions of operational risk, provided the minimum elements in the Committee's definition are included.

Scope Exclusions

The Basel II definition of operational risk excludes, for example, strategic risk-the risk of a loss arising from a poor strategic business decision. Other risk terms are seen as potential consequences of operational risk events.

For example, reputational risk (damage to an organization through loss of its reputation or standing) can arise as a consequence (or impact) of operational failures-as well as from other events.

Basel II Event Type Categories

The following lists the official Basel II defined event types with some examples for each category:

1. Internal Fraud-misappropriation of assets, tax evasion, intentional mismarking of positions, bribery
2. External Fraud-theft of information, hacking damage, third-party theft and forgery
3. Employment Practices and Workplace Safety-discrimination, workers compensation, employee health and safety

4. Clients, Products, & Business Practice-market manipulation, antitrust, improper trade, product defects, fiduciary breaches, account churning
5. Damage to Physical Assets-natural disasters, terrorism, vandalism
6. Business Disruption & Systems Failures-utility disruptions, software failures, hardware failures
7. Execution, Delivery, & Process Management-data entry errors, accounting errors, failed mandatory reporting, negligent loss of client assets.

Difficulties

It is relatively straightforward for an organization to set and observe specific, measurable levels of market risk and credit risk. By contrast it is relatively difficult to identify or assess levels of operational risk and its many sources. Historically organizations have accepted operational risk as an unavoidable cost of doing business.

Methods of Operational Risk Management

Basel II and various Supervisory bodies of the countries have prescribed various soundness standards for Operational Risk Management for Banks and similar Financial Institutions. To complement these standards, Basel II has given guidance to 3 broad methods of Capital calculation for Operational Risk

- Basic Indicator Approach-based on annual revenue of the Financial Institution
- Standardized Approach-based on annual revenue of each of the broad business lines of the Financial Institution
- Advanced Measurement Approaches-based on the internally developed risk measurement framework of the bank adhering to the standards prescribed (methods include IMA, LDA, Scenario-based, Scorecard etc.)

The Operational Risk Management framework should include identification, measurement, monitoring, reporting, control and mitigation frameworks for Operational Risk. Operational disasters in financial institutions have grabbed any number of headlines in newspapers around the world in the last few years-as the case studies on our Wheel of Misfortune demonstrate.

For managers, these tales of incompetence, corruption and simple bad luck are both entertaining and disconcerting.

Disconcerting because, as the tally has risen, it's become clear that gross operational error and failure is much less isolated from the problem of day-to-day management than the financial industry had imagined.

Researchers now reckon that catastrophic events are the visible part of a wider spectrum of cover-ups, "near misses", and costly but undramatic events that plague most firms-and signal a failure in risk management practice and technology.

Operational risk has also turned out to be more costly in terms of capital than most institutions realised-recent estimates put it at 25% or more of risk capital. And that's rising, as operational risk emerges from beneath New Economy business models such as Internet banking, electronic trading and the outsourcing of core bank functions.

Meanwhile, as our scroll-over timeline explains, the regulators of international banking are about to ask major banks to set aside specific amounts of capital for operational risk. It's part of their long-term project to tie capital charges more directly to risk-taking.

Bank regulators are not alone in demanding a new approach. Corporate governance experts and stockmarket analysts have begun to address disingenuous questions to all sorts of financial institutions. Shouldn't top executives be able to name any "sudden death" risks that their firm is exposed to? Or at least have some idea of the scale of potential operational losses in their industry?

Top executives are themselves wondering whether decisions based on risk-adjusted return on capital (RAROC) might be flawed if operational risk is not taken into account. Might they simply exchange business lines with transparent market or credit risks for those with hidden risks?

All this explains why controlling operational risks at business-line level-simply "getting it right"-is no longer enough for many professionals. But, so far, financial institutions lack a framework of methodologies and tools to push operational risks through a coherent risk management cycle. Operational Risk Management Cycle;

1. Identify and assess
2. Analyse risk controls
3. Rank/score/measure/track
4. Cost
5. Contextualise and communicate
6. Monitor
7. Assume risk
8. Assume but reduce frequency
9. Assume but mitigate severity
10. Assume but risk finance
11. Avoid/Remove
12. Transfer .

In this piece of the Risk Jigsaw, we'll tell how the financial industry-led by bankers and their regulators-is constructing that framework.

Some of the new ideas have grown out of established risk management disciplines in financial institutions such as Audit and Market Risk, while others are drawn from activities as diverse as healthcare and the space industry.

As we go along, we'll explain the new concepts that are driving operational risk management, hear from some Expert Witnesses, and offer links to key information points on the web.

Saying what You Mean-The Definitional Problem

Defining operational risk sounds easy-it's the risk of something going unexpectedly wrong! Bankers add the caveat "outside of market and credit risk" because they already have specialist risk managers for these areas.

But general definitions are less useful when a manager or regulator tries to do something about enterprise-wide operational risk-such as improve operational risk controls across the board, or reserve capital against operational risk.

Counting something, or controlling it, means putting a line around it. Soon, regulators and RAROC analysts will need to decide whether to include, say, strategic business risks or reputational risk in their allocation of regulatory and enterprise-wide capital.

And managers will need to know whether their assessment of operational risk in a business line should include, say, the risk of a trader misunderstanding a sophisticated financial model. Some experts are sure model risk should be included, while others are sure it forms a more natural component of market risk-the button below maps out some other tricky boundary clashes. Luckily, busy practitioners can sidestep this industry debate by selecting a suitable definition from those below. For the moment, there's really no "right" general definition save one that's boldly drawn and fits the purpose.

Definitions developed by industry bodies and regulators have some practical advantages, so let's take a closer look at the components of operational risk as defined by the London-based British Bankers Association-a body that has been active in developing standard approaches to operational risk.

For the BBA, "Operational risk is the risk of direct or indirect loss resulting from inadequate or failed internal processes, people, and systems or from external events."

Patching up Processes

Historically, most financial institutions have built expert "ways of doing things" to achieve their objectives-whether that's administering a checking account in the retail business, or confirming the details of a million-dollar swap transaction in the money markets.

Processes of a more or less formal kind surround many of the risky activities of a bank. Some are routines performed by humans while others are part of the core infrastructure of the institution. The button below lists some key processes surrounding a capital markets trader.

Connecting a discrete set of actions into a procedure, and than a formal process, offers huge benefits to financial institutions-as it does to manufacturing industries-in terms of scaling, risk control and standardisation. Processes also help to defuse risk by institutionalising skills that would otherwise reside in a single individual. But processes can make a firm vulnerable in other ways.

Few employees understand a complex bank process as a whole, so the implications of sloppiness or breakdowns in the process chain are often unclear. And devious individuals find a process easier to exploit than a savvy manager because there's no immediate "sense check" of their actions.

Meanwhile, because turning a procedure into a process is usually associated with an increase in business line volumes and notional amounts at the expense of profit margins, processes tend to concentrate and leverage any existing operational risks. If something goes wrong, it goes wrong big time.

This cycle continues as processes speed up and are automated using the institution's computer systems-automation tends to improve consistency but it does not guarantee that the underlying process is structurally safe.

In financial institutions, most processes are designed with audited failsafes and checking procedures. These might be built into the process itself or take the form of independent monitoring by risk control groups such as Compliance.

But because processes interact with other risky variables-the external environment, business strategy, people-it's difficult to sound the all clear. For example, are the failsafes and "checks and balances" of the process appropriate now that the firm has opened offices in a new jurisdiction?

Given the new products a firm has introduced, could the firm suffer a massive loss if a step in the procedure is compromised? Does the process efficiently manage transactions that are exceptions to the norm, or are staff barely coping? Is risk information flowing from the process to decision-makers speedily enough to match market developments?

These questions help to show why the problem of risk managing processes has become more urgent over the over the last ten years as the rate of change in the financial industry has accelerated.

Institutions have automated processes, re-engineered them after mergers and acquisitions, and adapted them to improvements in industry-wide infrastructure and communications capabilities. Increasingly, banks have been rewarded with high margins for entering immature markets where, by definition, safe processes are not yet established.

They have also extended their activities overseas-beyond the easy reach of their established process infrastructure and monitoring capabilities.

And they have introduced new processes to monitor underlying processes-New Product Approval Process and formal Technology Audits being only two examples.

The Problem with People

It's said that the greatest asset of a services business goes up and down in the office lift every day. But like any other asset, people are a source of risk as well as reward.

Until recently, the risk associated with the staff of financial institutions was largely thought of in terms of simple fraud. The figures here remain eye-opening-FBI statistics for 1998 show that some 32% of convictions for crimes against US financial institutions involved bank employees. The internet age has also opened up a new frontier for fraudsters.

But people also cause damage to institutions through incompetence, error, bad decision-making and rule breaking.

And institutions can become dangerously dependent on key individuals, or on teams that are suffering a high staff turnover rate. As we explain below, some firms are starting to identify this kind of key dependency and to monitor business lines for the key people risk indicators.

Even in the case of fraud, greed in its simplest form is not always the most important factor. Traders who exceed their trading limits-rogue traders-often seem to incur the most damaging losses as they try to gamble themselves back into a break-even position.

The original rule-breaking might be motivated by an attempt to improve a bonus, but it's the fear of discovery and its consequences that encourages traders to go for double-or-quits.

That's why, as our next Expert Witness explains, there's increasing interest in the psychology of risk and decision taking.

Modern electronic trading and information systems can help by physically preventing certain actions as well as by automatically reporting infringements to risk managers and escalating key information through the management hierarchy. These increasingly intelligent process control tools help to turn reliance on people into reliance on properly designed systems.

But even where a business line or market has the electronic infrastructure to make this kind of monitoring practical-many derivatives markets, for example, continue to rely on phone and fax trading-people risk is reduced, not removed. Systems that are used by people are always vulnerable to compromise by them. And a real-time risk report delivered by a state-of-the-art system is of little use if managers do not react to it appropriately.

It's also difficult to enforce control through automatic systems when businesses are immature or when volumes have grown suddenly. Other kinds of financial business-such as advisory services or those dependent on third-party agency sales-are structurally reliant on people for expertise or distribution in a way that is difficult to engineer away.

That's why financial institutions have started to look at individual and group behaviour as a way of understanding risk. Researchers believe the reason why individuals break rules-more crucially, why their colleagues let them get away with it-is sometimes rooted in the corporate culture of an institution.

Does the institution reward success without looking closely at how it is achieved? Do senior managers favour dominant personalities and connive with the bullying of subordinates?

Making sure that reporting systems are independent of business lines, risk sensitive, automatic, consistent and secure is an important aspect of the control of operational risk. But in many cases on our Wheel of Misfortune, losses spiralled out of control because a compromised executive was high enough in the hierarchy to disguise the losses.

Often, the problem is a fatal reliance upon an individual by senior managers and committees, compounded by the reluctance of staff further down the reporting line to break rank and voice concern.

Increasingly, corporate governance rules around the globe are encouraging firms to establish formal mechanisms for individuals to step outside the normal reporting line-to blow the whistle on wrong doing that has either a social cost or a cost to shareholders.

And as our last Expert Witness mentioned, the way that groups of professionals take critical decisions is also coming under scrutiny. Many disastrous losses-often misleadingly recorded as credit and market risk losses-happen because a group of managers or an oversight committee take a decision in a way that, with hindsight, seems to ignore extreme risks in favour of attaining preagreed goals. One palliative is to make sure the person or committee with the power to take action on the risk information understands what they are being told, and its implications. This is, in part, a problem of risk communication. The development of methodologies such as value-at-risk in recent years is, in part, an attempt to get to grips with this problem.

But confused or wrong-headed decisions are also rooted in poor corporate governance and tie in with the problem of enterprise-wide risk management.

All Systems Down

The reliance of most financial institutions on computer systems and technology infrastructure is absolute, as the avalanche of reports produced in advance of the millennium date-change made clear.

From individual business lines to the core support functions of an institution, systems are the principal means for storing and managing vast amounts of transactional, financial and corporate data. They are used to analyse that information, to automate all or part of many critical bank processes, and to communicate with customers.

It's a mistake to think of these systems as an interconnected whole. Instead, most institutions rely on a series of partially interconnected systems of various shape, size and age.

Often, management information systems or data warehouses are used to extract information from underlying systems and present it to managers to help them in making strategic and risky decisions.

Some of the most intractable system risks reside in the relationship between the system and an institution's business plans. Technicians cannot plan for flexibility in capacity, levels of redundancy or absolute levels of security without clear directions from business managers.

As business plans or volumes change, it's important that these decisions are revisited and that the firm as a whole monitors its system dependencies. If a system is left unaltered, a risk decision has been taken-albeit unconsciously.

Systems audits can help to make these tacit decisions more transparent, but they do not necessarily help managers in weighing up the risks and rewards of new system investments. Some researchers believe that the new science of real options-the application of financial options concepts to the valuation of decisions about physical assets-will help managers in the future.

But at a more practical level, as our Expert Witness explains, the most pressing problem for senior managers is to identify, monitor and manage critical risks in the huge range of systems supporting their institution-including those supporting emerging e-commerce and multi-channel banking initiatives.

Enemy at the Gate-external Risks

External risks take many forms, but they have one defining feature-it's difficult for firms to influence whether the risk event takes place. So the risk management of an external event focuses on mitigating its effect.

The most dramatic external risks are natural and man-made physical catastrophes such as the bombing of Canary Wharf, London's financial district, by terrorists in 1992.

The direct physical impact of these risks is insurable. But payouts cannot compensate for an interrupted relationship with a customer, or for the effect on future business plans or staff.

The problem of ensuring that a business can continue despite a physical catastrophe-business continuity-has evolved into a small industry. Major banks now spend millions of dollars each year to ensure that, if disaster strikes, they can relocate within hours to a functional version of their main or trading offices-complete with IT systems that are constantly primed with backup data from the bank.

But this cannot remove the vulnerability of institutions to public or financial market infrastructure. A recent and dramatic example of this was the systems failure at the London Stock Exchange in the summer of 2000 which prevented the exchange from opening.

Fundamental social and technological trends can also threaten institutions-from a rise in general fraud to sustained attacks on corporate web sites by external hackers and fraudsters.

In the summer of 2000, the UK's financial services regulator Howard Davies echoed the concerns of regulators around the world when he claimed that banks systems were being "probed for weaknesses hundreds of times a day"-and that there was sometimes insufficient segregation between the internal systems of banks.

But regulators are themselves a source of external risk. An unforeseen shift in the regulatory or political environment can ruin the profitability of an institution, or leave it vulnerable to catastrophic litigation.

The Big Picture

Many of the operational risks described above are already managed by specific risk functions within institutions-line managers, operations managers, market risk, credit risk, technology risk, internal audit, security, legal, compliance, insurance and so on.

But most of these functions have responsibility for specific risks, services or business lines. They cannot give a firm a wide-angle view of its operational risks.

The reasons why institutions and experts think this wider view is important tend to vary according to individual priorities. But the most pressing are the efficient monitoring of critical risks across an organisation, the interaction of risks, risk measurement and the efficient use of capital, and corporate support for risk-reducing investments at business-line level. Some leading financial institutions have established specific operational risk managers at a senior level to give them this wider view-the purist approach, in that the operational risk function can then itself be checked over by the institution's internal audit group.

Other firms have extended the remit of internal audit to include operational risk management, arguing that their audit group has to hand the skills, infrastructure and manpower to take action on operational risk.

Some firms report that giving internal audit a wider remit makes the function more efficient. Rather than simply ensuring that the proper reporting and control procedures are in place in each unit, audit can take a more active view of risk/reward and reduce duplicated checks and controls. Whatever the framework, taking the wider view means bringing together information about risk in a consistent fashion so that corporate management and the specific owners of the risk can take action.

The button opposite offers easy access to some of the new information management tools that are being marketed to help managers do this more efficiently.

One interesting aspect of these tools is that by making approaches to operational risk control and measurement more consistent within and across firms, they also make it easier for firms to benchmark their risk standards and publish this information to external audiences of regulators, investors-and key customers.

Seeing the Wood for the Trees-Critical Dependencies and what-if Scenarios

One approach to identifying operational risk is to look for critical dependencies in people, processes, systems and external structures. Once identified, the dependencies can be managed or engineered away by adding failsafes and system redundancies.

This approach is commonsensical, and has the great advantage that the risk of an event happening does not have to be measured in any quantitative way. It simply has to be identified as critical to the safety of the firm or process.

Many of the formal ideas that have come into the financial industry for system and process analysis have their roots in engineering-appropriately enough, given the increasing dependence of financial institutions on technology.

For example, some consulting firms now specialise in identifying the critical dependencies in power, communication and security systems-such as the failure of a critical power line, cable or firewall. Click the dependency diagram opposite to read how our next Expert Witness tracks back to a specific critical risk.

Dependencies often arise out of the interplay between business plans, process design and system architecture-which means that senior managers and business line managers must be involved in risk identification as well as risk management solutions.

And because a disaster would affect the whole firm, senior managers need to understand enough about the risks and their relationships to take the right decision.

It's not just a question of identifying physical dependencies. Many firms have begun to bring together groups of experts to discuss all the various risks in their part of a financial business line or process.

These structured discussions are different from most traditional forms of risk audit in financial institutions because they concentrate not on checking control procedures, or on the filling in of periodic reports, but on risk identification, the promotion of risk awareness in business line personnel, and detailed risk scenario building.

Risk scenarios are important because they help managers to work through what might happen if a particular mishap occurred. These "what if" scenarios are often simply descriptive and hypothetical. But some institutions are experimenting with more formal, quantitative techniques that model firms as systems.

The approaches include applying the latest scientific ideas on network topologies and complexity theory.

At the moment, though, it's difficult to apply this kind of sophisticated analysis to whole firms-so it's mainly being used to track down dependencies in specific business lines and processes.

The Data Game-more Questions than Answers

When a risk threatens a whole firm, and can be removed simply and cheaply, decision-making is easy. But some decisions demand hard numbers.

It costs money to install redundant systems-how much should be spent? If the chosen means of managing the risk is to reserve capital, how much capital is required? If a company decides to insure itself, how does it assess whether a high premium is worth paying?

It's difficult for firms to answer these questions-and move through the risk management decision cycle we identified earlier-without first answering three questions that depend upon data.

- How frequent are the events that generate each specific risk?
- How costly will any loss event be if it occurs?
- How likely is it that risk control efforts will reduce either of these numbers?

These questions are similar to those asked by market and credit risk specialists. But operational risk is a more difficult nut to crack because of the paucity of data, the many different frequencies and severities of loss, the multiple categories of risk that have to be considered, and the difficulty of linking a loss event to a single cause.

As our next Expert Witness explains, some key concepts here are expected, unexpected and catastrophic types of event. These concepts can help managers compare the character of risk profile associated with different business lines, and they also help explain part of the data problem.

Take the case of a failure to process a transaction of some kind. In institutions that process large volumes of transactions, these failures are relatively frequent. Firms are likely to be able to gather significant data on the more common low-impact costs associated with these breaks-fines, penalties, reimbursement to customers or counterparties, cost of mending the transaction, and so on.

Other kinds of medium-impact risk, such as significant bank

fraud, are more difficult for banks to analyse because they do not have enough data on loss and frequency within the institution to support a valid statistical analysis. This is not always because data do not exist-sometimes it's a question of availability and quality.

For example, in the US bank fraud and money laundering data is already gathered systematically by the regulatory authorities. But it was only in October 2000, after pressure from industry associations, that the US Treasury's Financial Crimes Enforcement Network indicated it might publish the data periodically in association with the American Banking Association.

It is not yet clear whether the data will be released with enough contextual detail to make it useful for quantifying the risk of different kinds of fraud in different kinds of institutions.

For many kinds of medium-frequency, medium-impact risk, however, there are simply no readily available databases of loss. So one of the most exciting developments in operational risk is the emergence of banking industry initiatives to solve this problem.

In the summer of 2000, the British Bankers Association announced that over 20 financial firms were joining together to collect data on operational risk events. By autumn 2000, some of the firms were actually supplying their internally collected data to the BBA, using the association's standard categorisation of loss and risk types.

The BBA pools the data and removes any identifying tags before republishing the complete dataset to contributing banks.

A similar venture, MORE, has been set up by Connecticut-based risk consultancy NetRisk, with the support of industry associations and various Canadian and US banks.

The most important feature of both these efforts is the attempt to produce a rich but standard set of data that will help banks quantify risk and link it to root causes, while at the same time preserving bank confidentiality.

These initiatives should help the banking industry to put numbers against the operational risks that are frequent and also those that are unexpected. But they will not solve the problem of the most extreme and infrequent events.

Extremely high impact, but low frequency, risks pose a different kind of problem. This kind of loss is difficult to conceal from shareholders, and is often reported in the press, so some data is publicly available. Bringing this data together in a consistent form is a significant task, but a number of consultancies-listed in our Operational Risks Tools button above-offer such public loss databases as packages.

But the real problem is that, even at an industry level, there are not enough extreme events of a particular type to allow the statistical modelling of their frequency or severity. Most firms respond to these extreme risks through attempting to prevent them or by insuring against them, rather than by reserving specific amounts of capital against them.

But they can't be ignored in the numbers game, or institutions will be building a blind spot for the most deadly risks of all. The regulators are also keen that these risks are accounted for in the total levels of capital available to the financial industry.

One of the cutting-edges of operational risk research is therefore the application of a body of theory known as Extreme Value Theory to the scarce data that is available on catastrophic risks. Although highly technical, EVT offers some hope that it will become possible to put meaningful figures against the risk of massive operational failure.

But EVT cannot help solve a more fundamental data problem. Data takes time to collect and it often has to be aggregated across institutions to make the sample large enough for statistical analysis.

Some experts point out that aggregate historical data cannot help banks identify the risks specific to their institution, or the risks that are lie in wait over the horizon of the data sample.

Risk Indicators and Scorecards

Collecting historical loss data at an industry or institutional level is one way to put a number against operational risk-but it's not the only way.

Institutions can also try to identify sets of quantitative "risk indicators" that seem likely to be related to the level of operational risk in a business line. As our next Expert Witness explains, quantitative risk indicators could bring a valuable element of objectivity to traditional operational risk assessment techniques. For example, in a business line that depends upon the safe handling of transactions, some key quantitative risk indicators might include the ratio of reported transaction "breaks" or failures compared to transaction volumes, the ratio of transaction volume to trained staff, and the ratio of system downtime to uptime.

After all, a back-office operation with high volumes, skeleton staff and poor systems would seem more likely to make operational errors than a similar low-volume operation with longer-serving employees and a robust systems infrastructure.

Quantitative risk indicators can be transformed into weighted components of a more general risk scorecard for a business line or whole firm with the help of expert judgement. But this introduces a subjective element into the measurement.

So some leading banks are starting to apply statistical techniques, such as discriminant analysis and principal components analysis, to explore the relationship between a risk indicator and loss levels, and to weight the indicator's relative importance within a larger set of indicators.

In an ideal world, all operational risk indicators would be quantitative, and their weighting within the overall risk score of a business line would be decided statistically, and backtested. Operational risk modelling would end up looking something like advanced credit modelling-a series of weighted risk ratios backtested against the available data.

In the real world, some bankers say it's difficult to avoid assessing operational risk using qualitative factors. That's why the new science of quantitative operational risk management sometimes begins to sound like the rather older art of risk auditing-armed with new information management tools and risk/reward concepts.

Indeed, some practitioners argue that risk managers who try to track operational risk at group level should simply incorporate audit scores for each business line into their enterprise-wide risk assessments.

The tension between quantitative and qualitative assessments of risk is likely to be a continuing theme in operational risk management. The problem is at its greatest in business lines and support functions such as fund management or legal risk that that rely heavily on individual expertise and integrity.

But even techniques for awarding qualitative scores can be improved. For example, qualitative scoring can be linked more closely related to risk levels, rather than control levels. That is, the weighting given to each element of the control environment can be modified to reflect the severity of any loss given a failure of control, and the scoring can be made independent, and benchmarked for consistency.

Moving from Measurement to Capital Allocation

Quantitative measures and improved scorecards can be used to compare the risk levels in different business lines, track risk trends, improve controls and prioritise risk management efforts. But some firms are also starting to use them to allocate portions of economic risk capital to particular business lines.

There are various ways to approach this problem. One is to work out the total capital the bank ought to set aside to cover operational risk by looking at the amounts of capital other banks set aside (the benchmarking methodology) or by a statistical analysis of industry-level operational losses in the relevant business lines.

Internal scorecards can then be used to adjust the portion of the capital charge allocated to each particular business line.

This mixed methodology is not the only approach to calculating or allocating capital for operational risk. In the past, firms that allocated capital to operational risk tended to use non-interest expense as a rule of thumb or, alternatively, examined the revenue/ expense volatility associated with a business.

Into the future, many firms hope they will be able to a purely statistical/actuarial approach that links the analysis of data collected at business-line level to firm-and industry-wide loss and risk data.

But for the moment, scorecards have some practical advantages from the point of view of forward-looking line managers and enterprise-wide risk managers.

For a start, the cause of a high score is transparent because it can easily be traced back to the scores on the card. By contrast, if a business line is deemed "risky" because of historical or industry-wide data, it is often unclear what the manager can do to reduce the risk score.

So scorecards help motivate managers to reduce the amount of economic capital allocated to their business line by ironing out problem areas. Likewise, group managers can quickly establish stronger incentives for line managers to improve controls.

From Risk Insurance to Alternative Risk Transfer

Some operational risks are impossible to engineer away or to risk manage adequately. Others are so difficult to identify and scale that an institution can never be sure that its internal risk management has been effective.

Where the potential losses seem likely to be of medium severity, a financial institution can reserve capital or use self-insurance techniques to mitigate their impact. But in the case of a catastrophic risk, institutions either have to accept the risk as part of doing business, or transfer the risk to external providers of risk capital.

Over the last few years, new kinds of insurance and alternative risk transfer mechanisms have held out hope that this kind of risk transfer will become more practical and cheaper.

Insurance has developed in two ways. Firstly insurance policies have developed to cover types of operational risk that are ill-served in traditional bank cover. Our next Expert Witness believes an improved set of insurance products will offer a stiff challenge to some novel ideas that have recently been mooted within the banking industry-such as mutual insurance techniques.

Secondly, insurers have begun to offer coverall policies for extreme levels of risk, arguing that the massive amounts of capital available to insurers gives them a special role in managing catastrophic risk.

But critics of the insurance strategies for operational risk claim that the insurance market is an opaque and inefficient way of pricing risk. They say the delay and uncertainty associated with insurance payouts might destroy a wounded institution.

In the case of alternative risk transfer mechanisms, on the other hand, capital would already in the hands of the wounded bank. ART tools-so far only a concept in the financial institutions sector-would take the form of structured instruments sold to the capital markets by the bank itself.

For example, some time in the near future a financial institution might sell a special bond to investors that offered an above-market interest rate, with the stipulation that the bank would cease paying any interest on the billion-dollar principal in the event of an operational disaster.

The premium the bank had to pay to the market to accept this embedded option would be, in effect, the market price of its operational risk-and the world would have seen the first operational risk derivative for a financial institution.

Some investment bankers say this kind of traded market in operational risk would price major bank risks more efficiently than the traditional insurance market. But the banking industry's own internal insurance specialists are more cautious.

They say they are still trying to work out how well their existing insurance polices complement the risks the bank is running. They don't think they'll be in a position to understand the cost reduction and risk management benefits of newfangled instruments for some time to come.

But it would be a pleasant irony if the derivatives technology that lay behind some of the most famous operational losses in the 1990s eventually helped to tame the most unpredictable piece of the risk jigsaw.

3

Strategic Market Management

Travel policies aren't designed just to keep costs down. You also need to consider your team's needs, the system's ease of use, and convenient locations and schedules.

If you've been to the supermarket or the drug store lately, you've likely learned the basic rule of purchasing: Frequent customers get the best prices and the best service. American Airlines first invented a frequent shopper's program when it launched Advantage to encourage travellers to bring all their business to one supplier.

Thirty years later, even small firms and their clients can save money and make taking to the road a little easier for their travellers by applying this basic rule of purchasing. This edition of Transit Authority will outline the nine components of a corporate travel program that small and midsize firms can institute for their own employees and partners or recommend to their clients. Our goal: finding the delicate balance that keeps travel costs down and road warriors happy.

At companies with larger travel spends (where the annual travel tabs run over $100 million), managing the travel program is a serious business handled by a dedicated staff. When travelling for the firm, their employees are urged — or even ordered — to book their trips through a designated travel agency or Internet travel site, using airlines and hotels with which the firm has negotiated discounts. Travellers charge their tickets to a single charge card, drive cars from the firm's designated car-rental company, bring their meetings to preferred hotels, file their expense reports online. The best practices of their corporate travel programs can be adapted on a smaller scale by companies and firms of every size.

Optimizing travel comes down to making decisions about nine things: the corporate travel policy; the manager of the program; the type of travel agency that will serve as your intermediary to suppliers; the airlines, hotels, car-rental, charge-card and online travel-booking companies with whom you will partner; and the system you will use for tracking and reporting spending data. We'll look at and offer best practices for each piece of the puzzle, with a focus on small and midsize companies and their business customers.

Start the Journey with a Map

Whether your employees are travelling on firm business or billing every charge back to a client, they are only human. Everyone likes to fly first class — and will, unless someone sets clear limits. Every firm and company should have a travel policy outlining the basic rules, signed off on by top management and distributed to every employee who travels. Keep in mind, however, that buying travel is not like buying paper clips; flying far from home is a stressful and emotional business, and the time of executives is a valuable commodity not to be wasted. A bus may be the cheapest option for getting from Chicago to New York, but odds are good that Southwest Airlines will be the better value in terms of time and effort saved.

While travel policy should come from the top, be sure to include a broad contingency in the discussion, including at least one of the most frequent travellers and the assistants who will make the actual reservations. Many firms also consider a two-tier policy, one for road warriors, senior partners, and executives, and a second for those who travel only to an occasional conference. Keep the policy concise and clear, covering the basic goals and guidelines for each of the nine major components.

Building a Framework

Companies have two options for selecting the framework for the travel management function: whether to handle it internally or to outsource it to a travel agency. Unless your annual travel budget is over $1 million and your office is open 24/7, the best practice usually is to contract with a professional travel agency. Keep in mind, though, that while you can outsource the tasks involved in making reservations, providing customer service, collecting spending data and negotiating contracts with suppliers, you cannot outsource management functions. It's imperative, therefore, to designate an employee of your own to oversee the program, manage the relationship with the travel agency, insure best practices in pricing and execution, and negotiate some deals of your own.

Consolidating all travel through a single travel agency is the best way to collect data, provide 24-hour service to travellers on the road, and rarely cause for objection by travellers themselves. In the not-so-distant past many firms had travel agents physically sit in their buildings, but rising personnel costs make that unfeasible today, and technology makes it unnecessary; travel agency call centres provide excellent service to small firms and companies at a fair price.

Even less costly is the option of booking travel online, through dedicated small-business programs offered by the major online travel agencies: Expedia, Travelocity, Travelport, and Orbitz. All four systems produce monthly spending reports for your firm or company and can be configured so that when travellers say they need a hotel in Phoenix, for example, the Hyatt with which you have a negotiated discount will be highlighted. Shifting traveller behaviour so that they book their own trips online instead of calling Mary at the agency down the block may take some doing, however. A clear policy from top management is imperative; even then, expect about 50% compliance unless your top executives are prepared to not reimburse travellers unless they comply.

Beyond the fees you can save, letting travellers self-serve by making their own reservations invariably results in lower costs. Perhaps the biggest surprise travel managers have realized from online booking is that when travellers are offered a wide range of options on their computer screen, a surprisingly high number do the right thing and change their plans slightly to take advantage of lower-priced options. In fact, if we had to offer a single piece of advice for cutting travel costs, it would be this: Get as many travellers as you can to book their travel online as fast as you can.

Note that many small companies report that they are being inundated by offers from Southwest Airlines' SWABiz program. The savings there are real, as travellers are entering their own information directly into Southwest's computer system and saving the agency transaction fees. But, travellers will see only flights and fares for one carrier, and lose the ability to comparative shop.

The travel industry is built on discounts and market share bonuses. No matter what agency or online system you are using, opt to pay them flat fees for services rendered and have any discounts you earn flow back to your firm. The point is to underline to both the agency and the suppliers that your firm is the customer here, not the travel agency.

Trains, Planes, and Automobiles

While larger companies are often best served by pushing all their travellers to use one airline and then negotiating discounted rates, small companies generally fare better allowing travellers to just pick the airline or hotel with the lowest fare on each trip. Remember that every dollar not spent falls right to your bottom line; saving a few thousand dollars in expenses may be as valuable as ten times as much in additional sales.No matter how hard you try, though the need for some high-end travel will not go away. These are where the airlines derive their biggest profit margins. Track them and try to negotiate a discount for all first-and business-class tickets with a single major airline that offers frequent flights from your home city. Virtually every airline, hotel and car-rental company offers discounts to business customers; make it someone's formal responsibility to negotiate on your behalf and then to nudge travellers to use these vendors. Airline programs typically offer small-business programs that yield free tickets with the purchase of a given number; take advantage of them. Beware the prepaid miles programs, however, which generally cost about 53 cents per mile; firms that let travellers choose their own lowcost flights online report that they average about 22 cents a mile. When employees are travelling on client business and billing their expenses back, there is a fiduciary responsibility to travel at the same level as the client would. Many firms follow client travel policies in such cases, and sometimes use the client's travel agency as well. Be careful about how you handle negotiated discounts in such cases; KPMG and Price water house Coopers in 2004 paid $17 million and $54.5 million, respectively, to settle a class-action lawsuit that charged them with billing clients for full fares and then keeping corporate discounts they got back from travel suppliers.

Checking in with a Hotel Program

While it's possible to push your travellers to use one or two major airlines without inconveniencing them much, hotels are a different story. Location really does make a difference. Staying in a particular hotel often offers tangible and intangible benefits: saving cab fares and wear and tear, keeping you close to the action at a conference or meeting, and allowing for mingling with important contacts or potential new customers. Rather than insist that everyone always stays at a Marriott or a Holiday Inn, a best practice is to focus on the five or six cities to which your firm travels most frequently, and negotiate discounts with a hotel or two in each. If your travellers or their assistants are using a corporate Internet site, set the system up so that these properties appear first and are highlighted as your preferred properties.

Maximize your business at these properties by requiring employees to register any meetings they will be holding with the travel manager, who in turn can encourage them to use the same properties as much as possible. Managing meetings is politically sensitive, as many meeting planners receive gifts and rewards from the hotels to which they bring business. Like every purchasing decision, though, it's important to base the choice of a meeting location on what's best for the firm, not the individual doing the buying. Centralizing and managing your meeting spend is likely the biggest single remaining opportunity for travel management for smaller companies.

Other Pieces of the Puzzle

Of all the pieces of the travel framework, moving travellers to a single car-rental supplier is the easiest. The issue here, again, is cost vs. Convenience; in general, on-airport companies cost more, off-airport companies cost less. But any preferred car-rental program brings one important advantage: free insurance. With car-rental companies typically charging $9-14 a day, and the average rental lasting 2.5 days, the savings from directing your travellers to just one are compelling.

The most important piece of the travel program, though, is a single corporate charge card to which all travel expenses must be billed. This is a relatively easy step to enforce; mandate that charges not booked on the credit card will not be reimbursed. Charge cards (like the American Express or Diner's Club corporate cards, which are not "credit cards" as they must be paid off every money)-capture the data that shows what your travellers actually bought, and are the key to rebates, discounts, and enhanced services. When dealing with the data, don't allow the sheer magnitude to overwhelm you. Pick out the key items or objectives that matter most and track those. Some companies have developed a dashboard or scorecard of key travel program measurements they track quarterly: percent of compliance to travel policy for air, car, hotel; average airline cost per mile through the agency and through online booking sites; rate of online booking adoption; average hotel room rate in key cities. Those are your fundamentals. Establish the parameters for success for each key measure and work toward achieving those. When you get there, develop new measures.

Passenger Space Travel and the Wright Brothers' Vision

It is a great pleasure and a great privilege to be invited to contribute to the Centenary celebration of one of the truly world-changing inventions of the 20th century – Orville and Wilbur Wright's development of controlled, powered flight. It is also a particular pleasure to speak at the session on space tourism, of which I am confident the theme will be recognised in coming years as the most significant at this Symposium. The topic I was invited to discuss is the market demand and transportation infrastructure for space tourism, but it seems only appropriate to begin by giving some thought to the relation of this subject, passenger space travel, to the Wright brothers' achievement and vision. If the word genius has any value, then we can certainly say that Orville and Wilbur Wright were engineering geniuses, not in the popular sense of being able to solve incomprehensible mathematical problems, but in having the rare combination of different abilities that enabled them to do something important that no-one else at that time was able to do. It seems reasonable to guess that if the Wright brothers were alive today, they would be working to realise passenger space travel and the future developments to which it will lead. So we might ask: "If the Wright brothers were alive today, what would they think of progress in space travel so far?" Well, if we look at their own experience in developing air travel, and at the present situation in space travel, I think we have to conclude that they would be *shocked and appalled*.

To see the truth of this we need to remember the treatment the Wright brothers received from the U.S. Government. At the same time as they were pursuing flight as a hobby, Professor Samuel Langley, secretary of the Smithsonian Institution, was funded by the U.S. Army to develop what he called an "aerodrome". Though Langley was a fine researcher, he did *not* make the conceptual breakthroughs necessary to achieve flight. However, the Smithsonian supported Langley, even years after his death, and refused to recognise the Wrights' achievement. It even collaborated in 1914 with Glenn Curtiss in flying a modified variant of one of Langley's failed attempts at an aeroplane — whereupon they claimed that this proved that Langley was the co-inventor of flight with the Wright brothers.

Orville and Wilbur could not accept such dishonesty — and so the Smithsonian refused to recognise their invention. It was not until *44 years* after the Wright brothers' first flight, 1947, that the government-funded Smithsonian finally acknowledged what everyone else in the world already knew — that the Wright Brothers alone invented flight.

This may have been the most shameful episode in the Smithsonian's history. So it would be comforting to believe that its shockingly dishonest mistreatment of the Wright brothers — who contributed perhaps more to U.S. technological prowess and prestige than anyone else in the 20th century — was a unique aberration. However, we have to face the fact that such self-serving behaviour is not anomalous; it is typical of governments everywhere, including particularly "democratic" ones, as they act to protect the interests of economically powerful groups within the economy against others, notably newcomers and the general public. It is indeed quite similar to the British government's decades-long refusal to award the "Longitude Prize" to John Harrison, the genius inventor of the chronometer. The defining feature of governments is that they employ force to achieve their purposes, and controlling this force to work for the public good, instead of for the benefit of the people comprising the government, is the central problem that humans face in trying to create and maintain free and fair societies.

In this context it is relevant to refer to the work of another American genius, Professor James Buchanan, who received the Novel Prize in 1986 for his work on the economic analysis of governments' behaviour and how to control it. The basic assumption of the field of economics concerns human psychology — it that humans are intelligent animals who use their brains to improve their situation. Adam Smith, the father of economics, analysed the implications of assuming that people act in their own self-interest in the case of business people and their customers; however, although he also noted that government officials "...have generally an interest to deceive and even oppress the public", he did not analyse the implications of this in detail. Buchanan and the colleagues with whom he pioneered the field of Public Choice economics analysed its implications for the behaviour of politicians and bureaucrats, and for the formal constraints needed on government. Niskanen extended this work, showing that in order to constrain government organisations, or "bureaus", to act in the public interest, their activities need to be the subject of close scrutiny not by politicians but by large numbers of the general public.

It is widely recognised that the USA has an exemplary Constitution, designed both to ensure the provision of the services that only government can provide, and also to protect the people from government's inexorable tendency to become tyrannical. However, governments become more tyrannical the larger they grow, and the U.S. government is surely no exception to this, despite the Constitution. In order to appreciate this we do not need to consider anything controversial such as foreign policy; we need only consider the case of Prohibition when the U.S. government imposed a disastrous law invasive of private liberty and against the wishes of an enormous number of its own population — or the fact that the U.S. government today keeps a larger proportion of the national population imprisoned than any other government in the world. So the shockingly dishonest mistreatment of two of the nation's greatest geniuses, whom we are celebrating at this symposium, by a government organisation should not be thought of as an aberration, but as typical. Every government system is different in innumerable details, and the 44 years that it took the U.S. government to finally admit what everyone else in the world already knew can perhaps be seen as the "cycle time" of the U.S. Federal government system in correcting an error.

This digression brings us directly back to our main topic — since it is now 42 years since Alan Shepard performed the first space flight by a U.S. Citizen. Of course Shepard was a government employee — it's as if the U.S. Army-funded Langley had succeeded in developing controlled, powered flight. It is therefore *extremely striking* that no private US citizen has yet been permitted to travel to space, but only a tiny number of government employees and related invites selected by the U.S. Government's 45-year old monopoly space agency, Nasa. In addition, despite having spent an astonishing $1 trillion of taxpayers' money on nominally civilian space activities (that is, nearly $1,000/second for 40 years, measured in 2003$), the U.S. Government *has not reduced the cost of travelling to space at all.*

So if we were to ask the Wright brothers what they thought of space flight today, perhaps in such terms as: "Don't you think our space agencies are doing a wonderful job?" they would not be impressed — they would surely laugh bitterly: "Are you joking? What did you expect? You left it to the U.S. Government. *Look how they treated us!*

The U.S. Government's 45-year old monopoly space agency, Nasa currently has a travelling exhibition called "Starship 2040" which includes a mock-up of a small module which it suggests might be feasible for tourism by 2040 — which would be *79 years* after Alan Shepard. Based on this we can perhaps guess what would have happened if Langley had indeed invented flight: at the rate of development of space travel proposed by the U.S. Government, passenger air travel would have started in 1982. In fact, by that date private passenger air travel, as initiated by the Wright brothers, already exceeded 1/2 billion people/year, or 1.5 million passengers/day! Fortunately, 44 years seems to be a better estimate than Nasa's estimate of 79 years. For it is surely not unrealistic to hope to see private suborbital space flights – that is, short trips of just a few minutes like that made by Alan Shepard himself – starting by 2005. If they do start then, it seems likely to be with little or no help from government space agencies, which continue to spend $20 billion/year of taxpayers' money on non-science space activities of little economic value, as discussed in Aviation pioneered by the Wright brothers contrasts sharply with space flight pioneered by governments, most notably in providing transportation services to the general public whereas space agencies provide no such services to the public, for whom their activities are largely incomprehensible.

In terms of cost-performance the results are predictably disastrous: despite Nasa's use of $1 trillion of taxpayers' money, the first private U.S. Citizen to pay for a space flight, Dennis Tito, had to fly on the 1,657th Soyuz rocket– essentially the same vehicle that carried Yuri Gagarin 40 years earlier in 1961! Tito also faced public abuse from the then Nasa administrator. If that $1 trillion had been used as productively as the cumulative investment in the civil aviation industry launched by the Wright brothers, we would have a nearly $1 trillion/year space travel industry today. This failure of "space" to follow in the economically successful footsteps of "aero" represents a massive hiatus in "aerospace" development in the U.S.A. Due largely to the influence of the cold war.

As a consequence, the U.S. Government decided to compete with the Soviet Union on its own terms in space, and established a monopoly agency which quickly developed self-serving habits, such as holding invitation-only press events (paid for by taxpayers), which are extremely effective in minimising critical media scrutiny. If the Wright brothers were developing passenger space travel today – well, obviously they would develop services that the public want to buy. Government space agencies periodically pay for surveys of public support for their budgets; but what they have never done – except finally, grudgingly, in just the last two years, with a tiny budget, and with minimal publicity – is ask the public what they want, and specifically whether they would like to travel to space.

Passenger Demand

In a paper presented at the 1986 IAF Congress, a colleague and I wrote: "Great interest must therefore attach to any detailed market surveys that are performed to determine the likely level of demand for space tourism services of various kinds". At that time the idea of space tourism was not considered a serious topic within the space industry, and the proposal was met with silence – which is the first point to be made about passenger demand for space travel.

Lack of Data

Surely the most striking feature of the data on the demand for passenger space travel is *how very little data there is*. In view of the fact that Nasa is required by U.S. Federal law "to encourage to the maximum extent possible the fullest commercial use of space", and other government agencies such as Esa, Nasda and the BNSC have similar responsibilities, it is clearly wrong for them to ignore a potentially major new market for space transportation. Such a decision might be acceptable if the agencies were achieving great success in their preferred activities, but the economic performance of the non-science activities in which they have collectively invested $1 trillion is disastrous: the resulting commercial turnover is about 1/50 of what ordinary companies would have achieved with the same investment.

However, this behaviour is in close agreement with Niskanen's analysis of the economic behaviour of bureaucratic organisations, in which, as he explains succinctly, individual officials "have no incentive to know or seek to know the public good, nor to work for the public good". It is particularly striking that space agencies continue to rigidly ignore the passenger market even in the early years of the 21st century while the space industry is shrinking drastically for lack of demand: U.S. aerospace employment has fallen to its lowest level for 5 years, and both the European monopoly launch supplier, Arianespace, and the remaining European monopoly manufacturer of large satellites, EADS, are cutting staff by a further 30%.

Prior to the first market research data published in 1994, "guesstimates" had been published by Ehricke, Citron and the author. As part of a Nasa study of future launch markets, some more detailed "guesstimates" were also published in 1994. In view of the growing evidence that tourism is the only activity capable of growing large enough to develop space economically, it seems clear that having relied on government monopoly organisations for access to space has greatly delayed its realisation. Indeed, in view of the growing interest in suborbital space travel services, which could easily have started during the 1970s, this delay caused by space agencies has reached decades already.

Worldwide Demand

The second very striking feature of the data on the demand for passenger space travel is that it is hugely positive, across all categories— age, sex, income-level and country — everywhere and every time that people have been surveyed. In 1993 I was finally able to use a small budget to perform the first ever market research on the subject, as a Science & Technology Agency Fellow in Japan; with a number of colleagues I distributed a pamphlet and questionnaire to 3030 people selected quasi-randomly from all age-groups, and roughly nationwide. A substantial majority of the general population, both men and women, said they wished to travel to space: the youngest were the most keen, but even many older people also said they would like to buy such a service.

The response to the same questionnaire delivered by telephone in the U.S.A. The main difference is that U.S. women are somewhat less enthusiastic than men, which is presumably due to the military connection and more "macho/techno" image of space flight in the U.S.A. than in Japan.

In response to the question "How many months' salary would you pay for a space flight?", some 70% of those wishing to travel to space in Japan, North America and Germany said they would pay several months' salary, and in each country a few percent said they would pay even 1 year's salary or more. Bekey usefully surveyed various different studies as of 1998, as Crouch did in 2001. More recently Kelly Space & Technology Inc and Futron Inc, in studying potential markets for reusable launch vehicles for Nasa, surveyed the potential demand for space tourism – using Nasa funds for this purpose for the first time. Both studies concluded that passenger travel offers the most promising market for space transportation.

The great popularity of passenger space travel makes the lack of data even less excusable. It is indicative of space agencies' failure to follow aviation's successful lead, as well as their failure to do work that has economic value. There are many striking examples of space agencies refusing to act appropriately, even after having paid for and published research stating these facts. For example, in the U.S.A. the Nasa administrator refused for more than three years to make its report "General Public Space Travel and Tourism" available through its website, and even today it is not directly findable – only indirectly through a link to another site. In Japan, the director of planning at the government's National Aerospace Laboratory (NAL), even after having paid $4,000 for a survey in the U.S.A., and having coauthored four papers including statements such as "the demand apparently has the potential to grow to many times the most optimistic projections for existing commercial space activities", stopped all work on the subject, while continuing to spend hundreds of millions of dollars/ year on activities with little economic value, for six years — until it was decided to merge the NAL with other research organisations.

These examples are sadly typical of space industry officials who feel no pressure to contribute to economic growth. At a time when commercial demand for space transportation (i.e. satellite launch) has been shrinking progressively, and the U.S. and Japanese economies are in their worst crises for 50 years *due precisely to the lack of investment in commercially promising new businesses*, this deeply irresponsible attitude has been disastrous for taxpayers.

In summary, it is now recognised worldwide that there is a potentially very large market for passenger space travel services. There remains a great need for more market research, as discussed in. This should be performed in collaboration with aviation and other travel-related organisations, of which the thinking is based on supplying passenger services.

This matches the facts that the most vigorous advocate of passenger space travel within the U.S. Government is the FAA's Associate Director for Commercial Space Transportation (AST), and the main organisation working for it in Japan is the Japanese Aeronautical Association (JAA). However, it is important that the need for more market research on space tourism should not be used as an excuse for further delaying work towards its realisation; it should rather be widened to include research on a range of related matters. These include the planning of many aspects of passenger space flight services as seen from the point of view of passengers, including vehicle specifications, passenger cabin interior design, orbital accommodation facilities and thence to the entire range of infrastructure needed.

Transportation Infrastructure

In trying to envisage the details of the future development of passenger space travel services, and what vehicles and other infrastructure will be needed, the historical development of passenger air travel offers a useful precedent. In combination with elements of the hotel industry and the cruise-liner industry, civil aviation seems to offer a fairly complete model for passenger space travel services. For the regulatory aspects, in addition to aviation and other safety regulations there will be a need for traffic rules, police services, specialised pilot services (as on difficult-to-navigate waterways), and possibly an equivalent of coastguard services. However, what we may expect to see a few decades in the future depends both on what is technically possible, and on how much is invested in coming years to realise passenger space travel.

Technical Possibilities

Very similar to the situation concerning demand, there is strikingly little information on the technical possibilities for passenger space travel, but all the information that does exist is positive. The lack of data is due to government space agencies — never having commisioned a feasibility study of a dedicated passenger launch vehicle in more than 40 years. In order to understand the potential it is perhaps useful first to dispel the remains of a very widespread myth — that in order to provide space travel services a vehicle like the U.S. Government's "space shuttle" is needed. From this it is commonly concluded that, since that vehicle costs about $100 million/passenger/flight, space tourism is therefore a fantasy, or at least conceivable only in the far future after several more decades of government-funded space technology. The most important point to note is that the "space shuttle" was designed to military specifications; its hypothetical cost/passenger is therefore of no more relevance to space tourism than the cost of carrying passengers in a bomber aeroplane would have to commercial air travel. Hence the only relevant data are those relating specifically to dedicated passenger vehicle design studies. Over the past decade or more, a number of such studies have been published based on varying degrees of effort. However, they show considerable consensus about the cost of developing a fully reusable passenger-carrying launch vehicle capable of repeated flights to and from low Earth orbit, with most estimates clustered around $10 billion.

Designs of single-stage, vertical takeoff and landing (VTOL) rockets include Pacific American Launch Systems' " Phoenix", a passenger-carrying variant of the German " Beta", and the " Kankoh-maru" designed as part of the Japanese Rocket Society's (JRS) space tourism research program started in 1993. Designs of two-stage horizontal takeoff and landing (HTOL) vehicles include the "Spacecab", "Spacebus" and precursor vehicles proposed by Bristol Spaceplanes Ltd., several designs studied by Penn and Lindley at the Aerospace Corporation, and a recent study done at Boeing. Development and operating costs for several configurations are usefully tabulated by Bekey in. The estimated development costs in these studies range from a few billion dollars to about $16 billion.

What is perhaps most striking about these figures is that even the largest is less than one year of G7 space agencies' current spending on non-science activities — which have little economic value in terms of generating commercial space revenues. Thus such an investment could be funded by using about 5% of space agencies' annual budgets over a decade, which would clearly not be a significant burden to taxpayers. Indeed, if planned government space projects' funding were reduced by 5%, and their timetables extended a little, the vast majority of the general public would not even be aware of the change – but at the end of the period, space activities would enter a new era with the start of lowcost, reliable access to orbit.

If the actual cost of developing the transportation infrastructure required for passenger space travel was even ten times higher, this would be only of the same order of magnitude as the international space station (ISS), which has little measurable economic value (particularly since its future depends on an unreliable transportation system).

Consequently developing a passenger vehicle would be greatly preferable. How best to achieve the desired result organisationally is a different issue discussed further below. The estimated timetable to reach initial passenger service is about 10 years, if the resources were provided without interruptions. In that case the transportation infrastructure in 2030 might look. First published in 1999, this scenario has lost 4 years at time of writing, but it could probably still be achieved if sufficient investment was started in the near future. Its value would be some $1 trillion greater than continuing government space activities as they are today, as discussed further in.

The range of on-orbit infrastructure would be determined primarily by the requirements of daily life of members of the general public living in a zero-gravity environment. This would have great economic value through the flowering of new business opportunities in every sector of economic activity, in contrast to the minimal effect of traditional space agency activities.

As a step on the way towards the $1 trillion/year scale of activity which might be expected from the scale of public investment made to date. In the present depressed state of the world economy, including particularly the aerospace industry, such activity is economically very desirable. Furthermore, it is the *only way* of achieving commensurate economic benefit for taxpayers from the public investment in developing space capabilities to date.

Actual Progress

How much progress we will actually make towards the future illustrate, depends of course on how much is invested in achieving passenger space travel, how soon it is invested, and how effectively it is invested. This particularly includes achieving efficient, complementary roles for both government organisations and private companies. Unfortunately it is currently unclear how much space agencies are capable of contributing to this very desirable outcome, due to their inappropriate organisational structures..

This problem can be seen from the orders of magnitude difference in cost between G7 space agencies' procedures, and what can be taken as a proxy for commercial "best practice" today. This was put into sharp focus recently when it was stated that the Russian company NPO-Energia builds Soyuz crew vehicles for $12 million, Progress cargo craft for a little more than $6 million, and Soyuz launch vehicles for about $16 million. By contrast, Nasa estimates the cost of developing a 4-to-6-person "orbital space plane" (OSP) to be launched on an existing expendable rocket by 2010 at $13 billion or more.

Even after allowing for the fact that the OSP is intended to be reusable, and ignoring the higher cost of U.S. expendable rockets, it is clear that its cost/flight would not approach that of Soyuz in even 1,000 flights. When the difference in reliability between the two systems Soyuz having made nearly 2,000 flights, including hundreds of successful manned flights are taken into account, it is clear that Nasa's technical capabilities are of little economic value. Indeed, at the time of writing, the latest news is that Nasas proposed Orbital Space Plane may actually be a non-reusable capsule, which closes the circle: Nasa is now proposing to use $13 billion of taxpayers money to redevelop an Apollo capsule 40 years after the original.

Some people might conclude, puzzled, that the US space industry cannot compete with 50 year old Russian technology! But this is not so. Even despite the Soyuz's advantages of having low labour costs and development costs written off long ago, if given a free hand US companies can get at least close to the same costs, as can be seen from a single example. HMX Inc proposed its reusable XV cargo carrier in 2000 for Nasas Alternate Access to

Space program (AAS). Total program costs for four XV launches carrying 300 lb payloads were estimated at $145 million.

If produced, the first flight would have been in 2003; this would have been invaluable after the loss of the space shuttle Columbia, and would save US taxpayers billions of dollars. However, the AAS program was imposed on Nasa by the Office of Management and Budget (OMB) and the Congress in an attempt to get value for money for U.S. taxpayers; consequently, out of $62.7 million that Congress provided for the AAS program in 2003, Nasa brazenly redirected $40 million to its favoured OSP program, and announced that AAS will not continue in 2004 !

Why is AAS resisted by Nasa in favour of OSP? The answer is plainly because it is not in the short-term economic interest of Nasa and its client companies to permit such a simple lowcost solution to their requirements. Unfortunately, as Niskanen also explains, nor would it be in the short-term interest of the politicians who nominally "oversee" Nasa and its budget. One might paraphrase Winston Churchills famous description of Russia as a riddle wrapped in a mystery inside an enigma by saying that G7 space agency cost estimates are a scandal wrapped in a sham inside a farce.

In truth, Nasa's own cost estimates in this case are economically meaningless. Quite apart from being undependable and prone to balloon, they refer to the development of a service for which there is no demand except from Nasa itself, devised in a "sui generis" manner and hence under no pressure to be an economically competitive or "best-practice" result, and following no agreed standard so that the resulting service cannot be judged. An aviation expert involved in the JRS space tourism study programme accurately described the difference between civil aviation and space industry practice in vehicle development by saying that the latter are like children making model aeroplanes: they make up rules as they go along, deciding what is acceptable (to themselves) on an "ad hoc" basis rather than following agreed rules derived from accumulated experience, and designed to achieve a target level of performance.

That is, after more than 40 years, governments' role in space activities is still at the same stage as the early days of aviation when government aircraft development projects suffered repeated disasters from which the fundamental lesson was learned that the three roles of customer, manufacturer and safety regulator must be performed by independent organisations. If they are not, the conflicts of interest that arise between political and commercial objectives ensure failure. This is well illustrated in the book " Slide Rule", which describes the simultaneous development of the successful, company-developed R100 and the disastrous, government-developed R101 airship projects. As a result of experience, governments (reluctantly) corrected their role in aviation from (disastrously) developing aircraft directly, to (successfully) supporting the development of commercial aviation. U.S. government actions such as the 1925 Airmail Act privatising the air mail, and the 1926 Air Commerce Act giving the Department of Commerce responsibility to promote aviation, were in much the same vein.

In order to make progress in this situation, the single most important step for the space industry is to collaborate with the civil aviation industry, as discussed in. As Antunano has described, the "aviation approach", its fundamental way of thinking, is the opposite of space agencies: the objective of aviation authorities is to enable as many people as possible to enjoy the services they wish. Consequently instead of government defining rules for selecting candidates for space flight, passengers select themselves, and it is necessary only to advise them of possible risks.

However, space agencies currently have no plans to even study the feasibility of passenger travel services, let alone initiate the fundamental rethinking needed to generate economic value for taxpayers in this way from their massive investment in space technology development. The huge cost to taxpayers' of permitting the present economically wasteful situation to continue, that is the cost of governments' continuing failure to amend their mistaken approach to space development contrary to what they did successfully in aviation is discussed next.

Economic Cost of Delay

As described in Section 3.1 above, the development of passenger space travel services is economically very desirable. As a corollary, delaying this development represents a very large economic cost to taxpayers, which can be considered as comprising four components, namely the direct cost of $1 trillion to date plus $20 billion/year spent on non-science space activities with little economic value, and the economic, social and macroeconomic costs of the lost potential value of new economic activities, as discussed further in. In the following we consider the economic cost of not benefiting from the commercial space activities that could have been generated.

In addition to space agencies' investment of $1 trillion over recent decades, G7 governments have spent some $2 trillion on nuclear power and ten times this on economically unproductive military activities. Using these funds for political purposes instead of for taxpayers' economic benefit hinders the innovation which is vital for the continuation of economic growth. These three fields also employ a very significant fraction of all engineers; employing these highly skilled people in economically unprofitable work greatly reduces the economic value of technological progress — to the point that it becomes a threat to the stability of the economic system.

Each individual decision to use taxpayers' money for purposes other than to create wealth by developing services for which there is potential demand, is made in the belief that there will always be another year's budget from the "golden goose" of government. Collectively, however, these economically damaging decisions have nearly killed the golden goose, by gradually choking off the possibilities for growth. These cumulative wasteful actions have contributed greatly to the present situation of spiralling government debts, collapsing corporate profits, and ever-rising unemployment — in the USA as well as in Japan, and elsewhere. Indeed, this cost has now reached such a scale that it is causing serious dislocation of not only the US economy but the world economy as a whole, which is in serious distress due to excess capacity in many older industries and lack of new industries, leading to the highest level of unemployment for decades in almost every country today. G7 space agencies have contributed their share to this problem, by adding to taxpayers' debt burden by $20 billion/year while refusing, year after year after year, even to study the possibility of developing a new service that the public are known to want to buy. The potential being wasted in this way is illustrated in the following fictional analogy:

> *"After the invention of the camera, government established the National Camera Science & Applications Administration (NACSAA) which grew rapidly to employ many thousands of researchers developing camera technology. Highly trained "cameranauts" used the resulting government cameras, which cost many millions each, to take photographs of specially chosen subjects "for the benefit of the people". NACSAA prepared voluminous educational materials describing NACSAA's history and activities, and urged members of the general public to take more interest in camera technology. The possibility of developing cheaper cameras as consumer products was said by the leaders of NACSAA and the "camera industry" to require decades more government-funded technology development. Surveys showing a widespread wish among ordinary people to use cameras and own photographs themselves were publicly criticised as "unpatriotic", and said to show lack of respect for NACSAA history and for NACSAA's "cameranaut heroes". However, in response, NACSAA started a Photographic Commercialisation Initiative (PCI) which provided a range of new services to the public, including discount sales of government photographs, rental of government cameras to selected members of the public who underwent training at NACSAA in "non-cameranautic photography", and a travelling exhibition to widen access to NACSAA photographs and NACSAA history....."*

It is clear that, in such a hypothetical situation, the existence of NACSAA and its political and economic interest group would have created enormous resistance to the development of a genuinely commercial, consumer-oriented camera and photographic industry. This would have imposed a very large economic cost on the public due to not having the benefits of the innovations that have in reality arisen in the absence of NACSAA's repressive influence.

In order to appreciate the scale of this "invisible cost", we need only consider the century-long, true "gale of creative destruction" that has in fact been brought about successively by the invention, development and commercialisation of cinematography, colour photography, instant photography, photocopiers, fax systems, television, video, highspeed photography, Schlieren photography, X-ray photography, holography, IMAX, cineplexes, laser discs, laser printing, disposable cameras, video-conferences, digital cameras, digital film standards, Internet graphic protocols, computer graphics, data compression algorithms, DVDs, colour faxes, mobile-phone cameras, video email, and many other actual developments in imaging technology, many of which have already gone through several generations of technology.

All of this astounding creativity, which has had enormous economic value and created millions of well-paid jobs, is driven by *demand from the general public,* from the "mere consumers" whom NACSAA – and government space agencies – spurn. The growth of passenger space travel, which is finally being grudgingly recognised as the only activity which can energise the stagnating space industry, through the power of consumer demand, can surely be expected to generate at least as great a profusion of innovative and profitable new activities as photography. Barely scratches the surface of what will be done by private citizens once they have access to space.

It is important to recognise also that the cost of not benefiting from innovation would have been invisible to those living in the world of NACSAA, and the existence of such a cost would have been vociferously denied by the leaders and political supporters of NACSAA, who would have been eloquent in their praise of its wealth of accumulated experience, the excellence of its staff, the importance of its historic achievement, and so on. Like the hypothetical NACSAA, G7 space agencies' use of US$1 trillion over 45 years – *without having improved on the access to space provided by the Soyuz launch vehicle* – represents an extreme miscalculation of taxpayers' money.

The fact that, during the first four decades of their history, the agencies never even investigated whether the taxpayers for whom they supposedly work would like to visit space, further illustrates how far space agencies are from being "servants of the people": *They do not even want to know what the public wants*— precisely as Niskanen describes.

In the Wright brothers' centenary year it is time to face the fact that, as presently constituted, government space agencies are not only not capable of developing space economically, they are actively preventing it from happening.

They do this by spending hugely on activities that have minimal economic value, while confusing the public about what is worth doing in space, and obscuring the truth about the enormous economic potential of developing passenger space travel.

Unlike government expenditure on nuclear power and military activities, the development of space technology has created capabilities which have the potential to contribute greatly to economic growth by supplying a wealth of popular new consumer services. It is therefore economically very desirable to redirect government space activities so as to achieve greater economic benefit from the technological capabilities developed to date by supplying passenger space travel services.

Conclusions-Where Next?

Once the need to change the present situation is acknowledged, we must face the question how to realise the productive and profitable institutional and political reform that is required, which is discussed elsewhere, including in. Fundamentally it is necessary to follow the Wright brothers' lead, and provide services which the public want to buy.

In order to do this economic policy-makers must be made aware of the enormous cost of the present disfunctionality of government space funding; the value of the goal of passenger space travel must be recognised officially; the public must be educated about its feasibility (undoing space agencies' cumulative influence in spreading the false idea that only statistically unusual people can survive the "rigours of space flight"); and detailed collaboration must be established with aviation organisations, of which the spontaneous inclination is to develop popular passenger services.

This collaboration must be carried out in such a way as to aid the private sector, as airmail contracts did in the early days of flight. The development of suborbital passenger vehicles and related services should also be encouraged. However, these changes will not be easy to achieve, due to the continuing influence of those with vested interests in preserving the status quo.

Unfortunately, as Public Choice economics explains, governments are very slow to change, and frequently do so only in the face of crisis. We must hope that the government of a country with the required capabilities will take the initiative before the condition of the world economy deteriorates much further; the benefits of doing so are potentially very large. At a time when overproduction in older industries and lack of new ones is reaching crisis level, it is alarming that there is a faction within government arguing that this situation is unavoidable; that war is a means of "economic stimulus" (as well as social control); and that rich countries should take control of the world's "dwindling resources" to maintain their living standards far above the average. Such narrow-minded blindness is tragically mistaken; in truth the future is a cornucopia — there is almost no limit to the potential availability to humans of any known resource. The false belief in a "closed world" rests ultimately on meaningless cost estimates made by G7 space agencies. We can be sure that the Wright brothers would not have been taken in for a moment.

Among other components of the present unusually severe recession, civil aviation is suffering down-sizing, bankruptcies and overall shrinkage within the richer countries. The failure of space to contribute to the economy in any way commensurately to the massive public investment which it has received is because it has systematically put short-term political and corporate interests ahead of the wishes of the general public. The result is sadly predictable: unlike aviation, the space industry supplies almost no services that the public want to buy.

In order to achieve the limitless possibilities for peaceful, plentiful growth that can only be realised through passenger space travel opening space to economic development, the public must learn the hard lesson of the Wright brothers' own harsh experience at the hands of government— and design institutions and rules that ensure that governments' investment in space benefits the general public. Above all, this requires that the goal of space investment is changed to follow aviation's lead and ensure successful development of commercial passenger travel services. The contrast between the histories of aviation and space is key: space must learn from aviation that the only road to real growth is to supply services that the public want to buy. This must be recognised as the most valuable goal of space development. It is so simple and obvious that the only possible resistance is from those with vested interests in preserving existing arrangements. Space agencies' continuing silence on the matter testifies to their recognition that they cannot justify their long-standing negative stance in open debate; they're "hunkered down", hoping the golden goose will continue to lay. In recent years the most economically important new products have been personal computers and mobile telephones (together with the internet protocols which link them all together), of which sales revenues have reached hundreds of $ billions/year.

Both the worldwide boom in sales and the still-continuing rapid technological improvements seen in these two industries were unpredicted, indeed seemed almost unthinkable, even just a few years before they began. Both arose and continue because *they provide products and services that most of the general public wish to buy*. There can be little doubt that the development of passenger space travel has the potential to create an economic boom that will grow far larger than either of these two, and continue far longer. This is because these new services are not only known to be extremely popular among the general population — giving the potential to emulate the "Lindbergh Boom" in aviation — but they also involve opening access to new territory, which has itself been the stimulus for major booms in history. This probability is a further reason why governments mired in a global recession should urgently study the possibility in depth.

It was the Wright brothers' vision and achievement to give the human race access to the sky, thereby fulfilling millenia of dreams. The true continuation of their vision is unquestionably to give humans access beyond the sky, which is collectively our ultimate dream. It is now clear that this requires reorganising governments' role in space development to follow the hugely successful model of civil aviation that the Wright brothers pioneered, rather than continuing the economically unsuccessful model of government monopoly space agencies.

As described in Section 1, for reasons clearly explained in the field of Public Choice economics, government space agencies are not capable of putting the economic interest of the general public ahead of their own contrary interests. The centenary of the Wright brothers' world-changing first flight, which is also the 42nd anniversary of the first space flight (but only the second anniversary of the first private passenger space flight), is high time for governments to face this, and take urgent steps to ensure the further flowering of the Wright brothers' vision, to the immense benefit of us all.

4

Hospitality and Maintenance Operations

Tourism product development is mainly undertaken to facilitate product diversification, development or improvement of tourism products with the help of knowledgeable and qualified staff. It aims at enhancing visitor experience by building consensus and strategic alliances with business stakeholders in order to bring about socio-economic growth. Tourism product development seeks to support in the maintenance, development and enhancement of the tourism product.

A large number of companies offer training programs and advice on tourism product development. The services include sustainable tourism product planning and development, presentations, seminars, campaigns and strategies for destination marketing organizations, individual operators and agencies. These companies make use of a community and stakeholder-based approach to assist businesses and destinations to plan for successful tourism in the long-term from cost-effective, environmental and communally sustainable perspectives. These companies provide an extensive range of specialized services designed to help individual tourism operators, associations and product clubs, educational institutions and government agencies effectively attain their short and long-term goals. Some of these companies are designed to assist government and quasi-government agencies in the development of the tourism industry, principally by coordinating and aiding timely action between public and private sector interests. Tourism product development aims at long-term sustainable development by the execution of a number of strategies. These strategies bring into focus a generic idea to increase competitiveness, build an inclusive industry by promoting closer integration of people and develop and maintain the environment. Tourism product development is designed to increase the income in the sector. Tourism product development involves implementation of a comprehensive plan of action that will guide towards dealing with estimated increase in business over the short, medium and long-terms.

Tourism product development helps in improving product quality by complying with the standards set by international benchmarks. It helps in product improvement by tourism training. It helps in product diversification by acting as a channel, facilitator and controller for development through sports and community based development with stress on culture, heritage and eco-tourism.

New Product Development

New product development is one of the most important components of product policy and product management. Product lines and products are appraise and are positioned effectively. Brand decisions are taken wisely. For a higher level of growth, a firm has to look beyond its existing products. A progressive firm has to consider new product development as a cardinal element of its product policy. Innovation is the essence of all growth. This is especially true in marketing. In an age of technological advancements, change is a natural outcome – change in food habits, change in expectations and requirements. Any business has to be vigilant to these changes taking place in its environment. People always seek better products, greater convenience, newer fashion and more value for money.

A business firm has to respond to these dynamic requirements of its clientele and these responses take the shape of new products and new services. Through such a response, the firm reaps a good deal of benefits. New products become necessary from the profit angle too. Products that are already established often have their limitations in enhancing the profit level of the firm. Profits from products decline as they reach the maturity stage of their life cycle. Thus, it is necessary for business firms to bring in new products to replace old, declining and losing products. New products become part and parcel of the growth requirements of the firm and in many cases, new profits come to the firm only through new products. New products can be broadly classified into two groups: new products arising out of technological innovations and new products arising out of marketing oriented modifications. The first group involves innovations leading to intrinsically new products with a new functional utility behind them. The second group involves mere marketing oriented innovations in existing products; it gives rise to new versions of the existing products.

New Product Development

In business and engineering, new product development (NPD) is the term used to describe the complete process of bringing a new product or service to market. There are two parallel paths involved in the NPD process: one involves the idea generation, product design, and detail engineering; the other involves market research and marketing analysis. Companies typically see new product development as the first stage in generating and commercializing new products within the overall strategic process of product life cycle management used to maintain or grow their market share.

Types of New Products

There are several general categories of new products. Some are new to the market, some are new to the company, some are completely novel and create totally new markets. When viewed against a different criteria, some new product concepts are merely minor modifications of existing products while some are completely innovative to the company.

* Changes to Augmented Product
* Core product revision
* Line extensions
* New product lines
* Repositionings
* Completely new

These different characterizations are displayed in the following diagram.

Product Newness based on Company and Market

The process

There are several stages in the new product development process...not always followed in order:

1. Idea Generation (The "fuzzy front end" of the NPD process, see below)
2. Ideas for new products can be obtained from customers (employing user innovation), the company's R&D department, competitors, focus groups, employees, salespeople, corporate spies, trade shows, or through a policy of Open Innovation. Ethnographic discovery methods (searching for user patterns and habits) may also be used to get an insight into new product lines or product features.
3. Formal idea generation techniques can be used, such as attribute listing, forced relationships, brainstorming, morphological analysis and problem analysis
4. Idea Screening
5. The object is to eliminate unsound concepts prior to devoting resources to them.
6. The screeners must ask at least three questions:
7. Will the customer in the target market benefit from the product?
8. Is it technically feasible to manufacture the product?
9. Will the product be profitable when manufactured and delivered to the customer at the target price?
10. Concept Development and Testing
11. Develop the marketing and engineering details
12. Who is the target market and who is the decision maker in the purchasing process?
13. What product features must the product incorporate?
14. What benefits will the product provide?
15. How will consumers react to the product?

16. How will the product be produced most cost effectively?
17. Prove feasibility through virtual computer aided rendering, and rapid prototyping
18. What will it cost to produce it?
19. Test the concept by asking a sample of prospective customers what they think of the idea
20. Business Analysis
21. Estimate likely selling price based upon competition and customer feedback
22. Estimate sales volume based upon size of market
23. Estimate profitability and breakeven point
24. Beta Testing and Market Testing
25. Produce a physical prototype or mock-up
26. Test the product (and its packaging) in typical usage situations
27. Conduct focus group customer interviews or introduce at trade show
28. Make adjustments where necessary
29. Produce an initial run of the product and sell it in a test market area to determine customer acceptance
30. Technical Implementation
31. New program initiation
32. Resource estimation
33. Requirement publication
34. Engineering operations planning
35. Department scheduling
36. Supplier collaboration
37. Logistics plan
38. Resource plan publication
39. Program review and monitoring
40. Contingencies-what-if planning
41. Commercialization (often considered post-NPD)

42. Launch the product
43. Produce and place advertisements and other promotions
44. Fill the distribution pipeline with product
45. Critical path analysis is most useful at this stage

These steps may be iterated as needed. Some steps may be eliminated. To reduce the time that the NPD process takes, many companies are completing several steps at the same time. Most industry leaders see new product development as a *proactive* process where resources are allocated to identify market changes and seize upon new product opportunities before they occur (in contrast to a *reactive strategy* in which nothing is done until problems occur or the competitor introduces an innovation). Many industry leaders see new product development as an ongoing process (referred to as *continuous development*) in which the entire organization is always looking for opportunities. For the more innovative products indicated on the diagram above, great amounts of uncertainty and change may exist, which makes it difficult or impossible to plan the complete project before starting it. In this case, a more flexible approach may be advisable.

Because the NPD process typically requires both engineering and marketing expertise, cross-functional teams are a common way of organizing projects. The team is responsible for all aspects of the project, from initial idea generation to final commercialization, and they usually report to senior management. In those industries where products are technically complex, development research is typically expensive, and product life cycles are relatively short, strategic alliances among several organizations helps to spread the costs, provide access to a wider skill set, and speeds the overall process. Also, notice that because engineering and marketing expertise are usually both critical to the process, choosing an appropriate blend of the two is important. Observe that this article is slanted more toward the marketing side. For more of an engineering slant, see the Ulrich and Eppinger reference below. People respond to new products in different ways. The adoption of a new technology can be analyzed using a variety of diffusion theories such as the Diffusion of innovations theory.it include economical support of social serctor

Protecting New Products

When developing a new product many legal questions arise, including: How do I protect the innovation from imitators?; Can the innovation be legally protected?; For how long?; How much will this cost?. The answers are complicated by the fact that several legal concepts may apply to any given innovation, product, process, or creative work.

These include patents, trademarks, service marks, tradenames, copyrights, and trade secrets. It is necessary to know which are applicable and when each is appropriate. This varies somewhat from jurisdiction to jurisdiction. The advice of a lawyer that specializes in these matters and is knowledgeable with your corporate philosophy regarding IP protection is essential. Generally, copyrights are fairly easy to obtain but are applicable only in certain instances. Patents on the other hand, tend to involve complex claims and approval processes, tend to be expensive to obtain, and even more expensive to defend and preserve.

Fuzzy Front End

The Fuzzy Front End is the messy "getting started" period of new product development processes. It is in the front end where the organization formulates a concept of the product to be developed and decides whether or not to invest resources in the further development of an idea. It is the phase between first consideration of an opportunity and when it is judged ready to enter the structured development process. It includes all activities from the search for new opportunities through the formation of a germ of an idea to the development of a precise concept. The Fuzzy Front End ends when an organization approves and begins formal development of the concept.

Although the Fuzzy Front End may not be an expensive part of product development, it can consume 50% of development time, and it is where major commitments are typically made involving time, money, and the product's nature, thus setting the course for the entire project and final end product. Consequently, this phase should be considered as an essential part of development rather than something that happens "before development," and its cycle time should be included in the total development cycle time. Koen et al. (2001) distinguish five different front-end elements (not necessarily in a particular order):

1. Opportunity Identification
2. Opportunity Analysis
3. Idea Genesis
4. Idea Selection
5. Concept and Technology Development

The first element is the opportunity identification. In this element, large or incremental business and technological chances are identified in a more or less structured way. Using the guidelines established here, resources will eventually be allocated to new projects.... which then lead to a structured NPPD strategy. The second element is the opportunity analysis. It is done to translate the identified opportunities into implications for the business and technology specific context of the company. Here extensive efforts may be made to align ideas to target customer groups and do market studies and/or technical trials and research. The third element is the idea genesis, which is described as evolutionary and iterative process progressing from birth to maturation of the opportunity into a tangible idea. The process of the idea genesis can be made internally or come from outside inputs, e.g. a supplier offering a new material/technology, or from a customer with an unusual request. The fourth element is the idea selection. Its purpose is to choose whether to pursue an idea by analyzing its potential business value. The fifth element is the concept and technology development. During this part of the front-end, the business case is developed based on estimates of the total available market, customer needs, investment requirements, competition analysis and project uncertainty. Some organizations consider this to be the first stage of the NPPD process.

The Fuzzy Front End is also described in literature as "Front End of Innovation", "Phase 0", "Stage 0" or "Pre-Project-Activities".

Enterprise Risk Management

Enterprise risk management (ERM) is the process of planning, organizing, and controlling the activities of an organization in order to minimize the effects of risk. Enterprise risk management includes not just risks associated with accidental losses, but also financial, strategic, operational and other related types of risks.

In recent years, many external risk factors have lead to a heightened interest in ERM packages. Industry and government regulatory bodies, as well as investors, have begun to scrutinize companies' risk-management policies and procedures. In an increasing number of industries, boards of directors are required to review and report on the adequacy of risk-management processes in the organizations they administer. In a service driven economy, businesses cannot afford to let risks remain unidentified. Currency fluctuations, wide distribution channels and an unprecedented dependence on technology are just a few of the new risks businesses must assess. Many organizations are choosing to implement an Enterprise Risk Management process to ensure that a uniform approach is adopted towards risk identification, analysis and treatment. The Sarbanes-Oxley Act of 2002 became the driving force behind Enterprise Risk Management. Financial institutions are good examples of companies that have benefited from effective ERM.

There are a few basic strategies that can be adopted in the process of Enterprise Risk Management. Experts in ERM recommend a five-year financial plan whereby a business can identify, prioritize and map all aspects of the most critical risks. Businesses must subject themselves to regular financial audits in accordance with government accounting standards. ERM calls for stricter corporate governance that provides greater transparency to stakeholders. More empowerment and responsibilities are given to Internal Audit Departments. A greater emphasis is laid on the code of ethics. ERM improves the way a company handles the more predictable risks that businesses face. It allows a company to avoid bad investments, and conversely, make investments that might intuitively seem too risky. Companies that have adopted risk management methodologies report fewer failed ventures and less damage from unforeseen events.

An Alternative Method for Developing New Tourism Products

The principal motivation behind such a paper came to us

when we started searching for Indian tourism related marketing literature. We found, after going through national as well as international journals that there is hardly any report of the multivariate method conjoint analysis being used developing new products in Indian tourism sector. In terms of a methodology conjoint analysis provides excellent forecasts and its use has ever been increasing right from its inception in the early 70's. It has also received widespread acceptance and use in various industries and sectors with the usage rate increasing tenfold in the 1980s. But Indian tourism sector, it seems, still uses managerial expectations and apprehensions to develop new products. Our argument in this respect is simple and straightforward.

A new product must satisfy the needs and wants of the consumer and not the needs and expectations of the management team. In India, it also presents a verysorry state of affairs concerning the incompatibility between the developments in the academia and the industry. Apart from wide use of conjoint analysis in multifarious fields it has also undergone much refinements so as to make it more powerful in solving complex marketing decision situations over these years. In the current paper we attempt to demonstrate the power of conjoint analysis and identify areas in the Indian tourism sector where it can be effectively administered for better predictable efficacy. We also discuss the simplicity and flexibility of this method along with certain special uses to show the reader that this method goes beyond just identifying new products and attempt to simplify managerial decisions relating to other marketing concepts and objects.

Tourism undoubtedly emerges as one of the most remarkable economic and social phenomena of the last century. Apparently it seems that it is all set keep this position for the next century as well. Every year a bigger portion of the world population takes part in tourism activity and for the majority of countries tourism has developed as one of the most dynamic and fastest growing sectors of economy. On a global scale the number of tourists is constantly increasing. Especially in the past 50 years the growth of tourism has been phenomenal in terms of its expansion. Between 1950 and 1999 the number of international arrivals has shown an evolution from a mere 25 million international arrivals to the current 664 million, corresponding to an average annual growth rate of about 7 per cent. In addition to its strong overall expansion, the development of modern day tourism is also characterized by its ongoing geographical spread. Numerous countries have been successful, not only in attracting significant numbers of tourists, but also in turning tourism into a source of wealth. A notable diversification in tourism destinations has taken place, with those of Asia, North Africa and Latin America and the Caribbean being the emerging destinations joining in.

With these developments taking place around lets understand India's interests as well as the needs of the hour. India has the potential to release foreign exchange earnings from current $3 billion to over $10 billion and attract 10 million tourists by 2008. This is possible even with the existing infrastructure, may be a marginal investment in certain specific segments, rational management of hospitality industry and adjusts in the mindset of various players in the field. But India's share in world tourist arrivals and receipts is dismally insignificant.

In the post liberalized scenario Indian private sector is assumed to play a greater role in the development of tourism sector compared to government efforts. Therefore, it is a concerted effort by all players in the private sector that can properly position India as a better tourism destination option by uniquely designing products and promotions that distinctly focuses on specific market segments with definite needs. Traditionally India's tourism is promoted on account of its diversity and vast variety offering in terms of its flora, fauna, cultural heritage etc.

Now the problem lies in properly designing products that suit to different needs of international tourists. Reports indicate that though recreation and leisure holidays remain as the principal segment of tourism purpose but other small areas are registering a better growth such as visiting friends and relatives, religious purposes/pilgrimages, health treatment etc. In the last ten years, especially the share of this category has been rising. This pattern reflects the trend towards market diversification and the division of holidays, with people travelling for shorter periods of time and for different reasons. This growth has basically detracted from the share of total trips made for leisure, recreation and holiday purposes, the share ascribed to travel for business and professional purposes having remained relatively stable.

Against this backdrop, we strongly feel, there is a need to understand the changing preferences of the international tourist and identify suitable products/packages that yields better choice and in turn can increase revenues. Therefore the importance of appropriate marketing research further gets emphasized as compared to the past practices of going bymanagement intuitions. Need has come to promote specific products/packages rather than promoting the whole of India as a tourism destination. Hence, we propose a flexible but enormously powerful multivariate method *Conjoint Analysis* and show how this can identify ideal new tourism products that can better address the future needs.

What is Conjoint Analysis?

As a research method, conjoint analysis portrays consumers' decisions more realistically as tradeoffs among multi-attribute products or services. The authors, in this paper, revisit this technique in developing new tourism products and show the flexibility and prowess of this methodology that helps evaluate any set of objects or concepts related to tourism marketing. The authors also point out the importance of conjoint models that help in predicting optimum combinations of new tourism products, estimating customer judgments to predict market shares among objects with differing sets of features, isolate groups of potential customers and identify opportunities for feature combinations not currently available among tourism product offers. With the increase in use of information technology and personal computer based programs, the authors finally conclude the ease in estimating the entire process, i.e., from generating combinations of predictor variables to creating choice simulators.

Conjoint Analysis is a "what-if" experiment in which buyers are presented with different possibilities and asked what they would buy. Despite its name, conjoint analysis is not like other multivariate methods such as factor analysis, cluster analysis etc. Rather it is a type of thinking experiment that is designed to show how various elements of products or services (elements such as price, brand name and features) predict consumer preferences for certain hypothetical products or services. Conjoint analysis is a multivariate technique used specifically to understand how respondents develop preferences for products or services. It is based on the simple premise that consumers evaluate the value or utility of a product or service (real or hypothetical) by combining the separate amounts of utility provided by each attribute.

The Conjoint Model

Essentially in conjoint analysis the analyst tries to understand the "preference structure" of a respondent. It is actually a family of techniques and methods, all theoretically based on the models of information integration and functional measurement. In terms of the basic dependence model conjoint analysis can be expressed as $Y1 = X1 + X2 + X3 + \ldots + XN$ *(nonmetric, metric) (metric)* From the above it is clearly evident that the flexibility of conjoint analysis primarily arises from its ability to accommodate either a metric or a nonmetric dependent variable and use of categorical predictor variables. Moreover, it makes quite general assumptions about the relationship between dependent and independent variables. We have presented the operationalization of this in the later part of our paper. But this clearly shows the suitability of conjoint model in the field of tourism, as very often an analyst is likely to come across categorical variables while identifying ideal new product designs.

The basic method of conjoint analysis asks consumers to imagine products or services that vary along some dimensions of interest and to score these products or services in some way. The scoring is usually done by ranking or rating as per the preference of consumers. These scores are then used to decompose for the purpose of estimating the values of each attribute level in the experiment. The interesting difference here from other methods is that the respondent need not tell the researcher about the attraction or evaluation of specific attributes of a given product or service. Because the researcher constructs the hypothetical products or services in a specific manner, the importance of each attribute and each value of each attribute can be computed from the respondents' overall rating.

Therefore to be successful in a conjoint experiment the analyst must be able to properly and in clear terms describe the product or service in terms of both its attribute and all relevant values of each attribute. The respondents may be asked to rate the hypothetical products (may be using a 10-point scale) or rank all of them that are presented to them by the analyst. Conjoint method is also sometimes referred as a "trade-off analysis" because in making a judgment on a hypothetical product, respondents must consider both positive and negative characteristics of the product to form a preference. Thus the respondents must weigh all the attributes simultaneously in making their judgments.

By drawing a contrast between specific treatments (combinations or stimuli or hypothetical products/services) the analyst attempts to understand the overall preference for each treatment. This overall preference that represents the "total worth" of a treatment is thought of as based on the "part-worths" for each level of each attribute. Here the general form of the conjoint model presented as Total worth for product*ij*...*n* = Part-worth of level*i* for factor*1* + Part-worth of levels for factor2 + ... + Part-worth of leveln for factorm Where the product/service has *m* attributes (referred as factors), each having two or more levels (a mandatory requirement). Thus the hypothetical product consists of leveli of factor1, levels of factor2, ... upto level n for factorm. In general most of the dependence methods assume a linear relationship. However, conjoint analysis is not limited to types of relationships between the dependent and independent variables. It can make separate predictions for the effects of each level of the independent variables and does not assume they are related at all. Thus conjoint method can easily handle non-linear and even curvilinear relationships.

Extensions and Special Topics in Conjoint Analysis

One of the most common uses of conjoint analysis is to group respondents with similar part- worths to identify specific marketing segments. Often it may become necessary for the researcher to identify these groups and understand their relative magnitude to ascertain the attractiveness in the tourism sector. Through conjoint analysis an analyst can also do a marginal profitability analysis of the hypothetical products and services. If the cost if each feature is known, the cost of each proposed product can be combined with the expected market share and sales volume to predict its viability.

Conjoint analysis can also give birth to choice simulators. First the conjoint models for each respondent (or group) is estimated and validated. Second selection is made of a set of stimuli (treatments) that may resemble the competitive scenarios. Then simulation is done for the choices of all respondents (or groups) for the specified sets of stimuli and predictions are obtained for each stimulus by aggregating their choices. Conjoint analysis with large number of attributes seems to be very difficult to handle. But one variant of the main analysis method known as Adaptive Conjoint Analysis (ACA) developed by Sawtooth Software handle these with great ease. One more extension is developed utilizing the conjoint principle known as Choice Based Conjoint model. Traditional conjoint analysis assumes that the judgment task based on ranking or rating captures the respondent choices. But some researchers have argued that this may be less realistic way of reflecting the actual market setting. Past research has shown that choice is often a two-stage process. Therefore it would be more prudent to ask the respondent to identify a choice set from among the options laid down rather than rating them. This helps the analyst to observe the threshold above which the respondent makes his/her choice.

Assumptions and Cautionary Issues in Conjoint Analysis

Even though we presented the conjoint model in an attractive manner but it involves certain care to be observed by the researcher. One of the key issues to be addressed in the conjoint experiment is of realism though most of it deals with hypothetical concepts. Respondents must be able to visualize in real terms what kind of hypothetical tourism products are being presented by the researcher. In designing the experiment the analyst must specify differing attributes as the respondents to arrive at a choice ultimately trade these off. These attributes should also be relevant to ones own marketing program. Using appropriate levels is another key issue that should be realistic and believable. The success of the conjoint experiment also depends on the selection of proper study design, selection of respondents, specifying the main effects model, specifying the data collection method and above all professional execution of the experiment. Conclusion We did not attempt to explain the procedure of conjoint analysis;

rather the scope of this paper is to show the power of this model in addressing the new product development issues in the Indian tourism sector. Due to cost considerations, conjoint analysis usually should be reserved for studies of product improvements or new product developments.

The ability of conjoint analysis to model market response is especially valuable in its application to Indian tourism sector. Therefore the reader should note that the conjoint method should not be used for the primary purposes of measuring the importance of product attributes or market segmentation as cheaper methods provide adequate data for these purposes.

Conjoint analysis places more emphasis on the ability of the researcher/manager to theorize about the behaviour of choice than it does on analytical technique. Though this technique has strong theoretical foundations, its applications have increased dramatically without corresponding theoretical development. Today it is simple to use conjoint analysis especially after the easy availability of many personal computer based software programs. Some of the popular computer programs for conjoint analysis are MONANOVA (Monotonic Analysis of Variance), LIMAP and SPSS etc.

What is Tourism Product Development?

Tourism product development involves co-ordinating effort behind viable, sustainable projects that will help to develop North East England as a successful tourism destination.

It includes:

1. Developing tourism related products focusing on quality, sustainability and industry involvement to gain maximum economic benefit
2. Ensuring a product matches and exceeds customer expectations
3. Enhancing public product through provision of signage and interpretation
4. Promoting local distinctiveness
5. Creating new niche areas to entice and target new visitors to the region

6. Looking at existing products in the region and improving their current offer to ensure visitors have a wonderful experience and make repeat visits
7. Improving the quality of the existing tourism accommodation product– to ensure visitors have a wide choice of quality accommodation in the region to choose from
8. The way in which marketing, investment (including capital) and business development are aligned around product priorities to have a greater impact
9. A coordinated response to evidence from research

What Exactly is a 'Tourism Product'?

The term "product" is something of a misnomer since leisure and tourism are service industries and the bulk of leisure and tourism activity is concerned with the customer's experience.

Examples of tourism products are:

* Short breaks
* Leisure centres
* Nature reserves
* Museums
* Attractions
* Holidays
* Art galleries
* Events
* A 30 min horse riding session
* Local food/craft product

Some products are tangible: you can see and touch them. However many tourism products cannot be seen and are therefore intangible. You can't see a short break, but you can experience it. It is this aspect of intangibility that makes tourism products so difficult to describe. It could be argued that hotels, leisure centres, tourist attractions etc. are simply facilities in which the intangible products are experienced, e.g. a short break could well involve staying at a hotel.

In essence a tourism product can be defined as a visitor service, activity, attraction or an experience (in itself, a collection of services, activities and attractions). A product is 'something' you decide to take to market to satisfy a want or need. Therefore a product is identified through prioritisation and decision making, guided by a process.

Niche Tourism Product Development

A "niche" is a specific segment usually with a well-defined tourism product that can be tailored to meet the particular interests of a set of visitors that share similar interests/aspirations/lifestyles etc.

Examples of some of the existing regional niche tourism product development areas in North East England are:

* Cruise Tourism
* Gardens
* Luxury Group Travel
* Mountain Biking.

Developing Tourism Products and Services

Tourism is a vital and increasingly important part of the regional and local economy. Successfully developing the tourism products available to visitors and locals increases the diversity and appeal of North East England as a destination, attracting more visitors and higher spending customers.

Tourism product development involves looking systematically at our region, areas, offering, markets and niches to determine which are the right tourism businesses, markets and products to develop: those with the potential not only to thrive economically, but to improve the overall offer and experience of the region.

It also aims to help identify the 'wrong' sort of developments: those that are likely to fail, impact negatively on the local environment, or degrade or devalue the overall area and regional offering.

This guide explains the North East England product development process and is intended for tourism development staff and businesses working on larger scale projects. However the principles can be applied to any project of any size. In all cases, Business Link can provide tailored help and advice for specific projects or businesses.

Commercial Implications of Market Research on Space Tourism

In the post-Cold War era, the justification for the space industry to continue to receive the large government budgets on which it has depended to date is being questioned. In particular, the value of government investment in the development of new launch vehicles when there is over-supply in relation to the worldwide launch rate of just a few tens of launches per year is questioned. Yet in the absence of a new generation of fully reusable launch vehicles with much lower launch costs than today, the space industry has little possibility to grow into a commercially profitable and self-sustaining industry. Justifying such investment will require the development of new launch markets which have the potential to grow to traffic rates many times greater than the present limited demand for satellite launches.

One possible source of demand for future launch services, and so of future revenues and profits to finance the development of erasable launch vehicles, is tourism-the making of short visits to low Earth orbit by fare-paying customers. In the modern world tourism represents one of the largest, most international industries, and it is growing fast, particularly in the more economically advanced countries. Furthermore, space travel has a high level of popularity among the general public. The desire of many people, particularly the young, to explore the unknown world of space and face new challenges seems likely to create growing demand for popular space travel. Thus it seems possible that the commercial demand for space tourism could be very high, and that the widespread desire of humankind to have the experience of going to space for themselves could become a driving force for the space industry in the future.

However, the attractiveness of "space tourism", or "orbital tourism" (at least in the early stages), as a potential target market for commercial companies will depend critically on the actual scale of future demand for space tourism services at different prices. To date very little data has been collected on this subject in any country. During the summer of 1993 a market research questionnaire on the potential demand for orbital tourism was completed by more than 3000 people from all age groups in Japan. The questionnaire was distributed face-to-face mainly in large companies, universities, schools, obtaining a response rate of well over 90%. Details of this survey, and initial results have been published in, but the idea of space tourism was very popular. Nearly 80% of those under 50 said that they would like to travel to space, and 45% of those over 60, with no significant difference between the 1465 men's and 1565 women's answers. Some 70% of those who wished to travel to space said that they would pay three months' salary or more, and the great majority said that they would like to stay in orbit for a few days. In the following we discuss some further details of the results.

In considering whether a new service such as passenger flights to Earth orbit could become a profitable business, companies must estimate both the costs that they would incur in providing the new service, and the revenues that they could earn. The costs depend on how low engineers can reduce the manufacturing and operating costs of reusable launch vehicles, and the revenues depend on the size of the potential market for the service, that is on how popular the service could become. Consequently in order to assess the feasibility of this business we need to do both engineering and market research. Currently the Japanese Rocket Society is studying the engineering and other aspects of space tourism in its Space Tourism Study Program. The authors of this paper have been carrying out preliminary market research.

Limitations of Market Research

In principle, if firm data were available concerning the future demand for space tourism at different price levels, it would be possible to plan a business to provide such a service, provided that the vehicle costs could be reduced sufficiently. In practice, however, any conclusions that can be drawn from market research data on this subject can be only tentative, for a number of reasons. First, the reliability of all market research concerning future products and services is inherently limited. There have been many cases of new products' sales being very different from the results of market research, both greater or less. This is due fundamentally to the impossibility of predicting the future, and more particularly to peoples' inability to foresee their own future behaviour accurately.

Second, this uncertainty is particularly strong in the case of a new and futuristic service such as space tourism about which peoples' expectations are particularly likely to be mistaken. Thus the reliability of market research results must be more uncertain than usual. This is not to say that the results must be inaccurate, but rather that it is not possible to know how accurate they are.

Third, it is uncertain how representative the market research data that have been collected are of the Japanese population as a whole. The authors tried to ensure a wide distribution to people outside the space industry. As discussed in, by distributing the questionnaire on a face-to-face basis, the response rate was nearly 100%, which avoids the common bias of receiving answers only from those who are interested in the subject.

There are nevertheless some biases in the results. For example, 64% of Japanese households are salaried, and their income is some 5% above the average, while 36% are self-employed and their income is some 10% below the average, but only 2% of the participants in our survey were from the self-employed population. However the proportion of self-employed participants who said that they would like to go to space was not very different from the self-employed, 77% versus 81%. Consequently, while recognising this limitation in the survey, it was not felt necessary to correct the data as a result.

Fourth, it is uncertain how representative our data are of the populations of the advanced industrial countries as a whole. Although similar market research has not been carried out in these countries, the market for space tourism seems sure to be international. Consequently, in order to understand the true potential market we need to consider at least North America, Western Europe and Australasia as well as Japan, the total population of which countries is some 6 times that of Japan.

There may be significant differences in demand between these countries due to the cultural differences between them, which are significant. But there are also important common strands in modern popular culture. Science fiction and particularly space fiction, international organisations such as the Young Astronauts Club, and the worldwide popularity of big-budget space-related films such as "2001" or "Star Wars" suggest that people in many countries enjoy these ideas. Thus, although it is possible that Japanese people are more interested in space travel than other countries, it seems likely that such an interest is also widespread in America and Europe.

However, there are also significant differences between Japanese consumer behaviour and that of Americans and Europeans. One difference is the much higher savings ratio in Japan (which is related to the low interest rates, the high rate of investment, and the low level of unemployment in Japan). Because of their high savings, typically amounting to one year's income held in financial assets, Japanese are able to spend relatively large amounts on things that have particular value for them, such as education, weddings, foreign travel. Another difference is the relatively equal income distribution in Japan compared to America or Europe. From this we might guess that demand for space tourism services may be higher in the latter countries while the price is so high that only the rich can afford it, but may be relatively greater in Japan if the price is low enough to become affordable by a large proportion of the population.

Fifth, since the number of people who said that they would pay one year's income or more to go to space was considerably fewer than those who said that they would pay less, the figures must be considered statistically less reliable. That is, a small number of unrepresentative answers could bias the results significantly. Likewise, the 3-4 % of non-student participants in each age-group over the age of 20 who said that they would pay 3 years' or 5 years' salary for a trip to orbit may be unrepresentative, so that the proportion of people with similar opinions may be significantly less than this. Even so, and even if these people are wrong in the sense that in the event of such a service becoming available many of them would not actually pay such a high price, we must still recognise that for a significant number of people the idea of going to space is clearly a powerful dream. However, although there may well be significant demand for space tourism even at very high prices of more than 10 million, this will probably be mainly from uncommonly rich people, rather than from people with average incomes paying a multiple of their annual salary. Consequently, in analysing the results we have included these multi-year answers with those who said that they would pay one year's salary. Despite these limitations of our market research data, it is nevertheless interesting to use the results as a basis for estimating the future demand for space tourism services. Indeed we have no choice but to do this if we are to develop a successful commercial service. We must also remember a fundamental difference between scientific research and business. Businesses do not require proof before they invest in a project, but reasonable probability. Investment entails risk because the future is uncertain. Businesses that wait for proof risk being beaten by bolder competitors.

Demand Curve

Initial results of our survey are described in. For the present analysis, in order to derive a demand curve for space tourism, we excluded teenagers, as lacking experience about financial matters, and those over 70 years old, as being unlikely to travel to space. By making the assumption that the participants in the survey are representative of the Japanese population as a whole, we can estimate the proportion in each age group who say they would pay each price, in terms of months of salary. National income statistics allow us to estimate the monetary value of the monthly salaries for different age groups. By using national population data broken down by age we can then estimate the total number of people in Japan who would go to space at different prices.

In order to estimate the number of people who would travel to space each year, we need to develop a traffic growth model, and we plan to do this in the next phase of our analysis. For the present, in order to obtain a single figure representative of a future space tourism business, we simply divide the total demand by 25, that is we assume that 4% of those who wish to would go to space each year. The results of this simpler case with an exponential curve fitted. At first sight the demand, seems very high. For example, at prices of \5 million and \2.5 million the demand figures of 100,000 and 500,000 passengers per year are some 10-20 times higher than the estimate published by Citron in 1985 of 5,000-10,000 passengers per year at a price of $50,000, and 20,000-50,000 passengers per year at $25,000. However, in order to compare these figures accurately we need to make some adjustments. First we should adjust the earlier figure for inflation from 1985 to 1993, which reduces the difference to some 5-12 times for the lower price. If we further adjust the figures to use a "purchasing power parity" exchange-rate between the yen and dollar, which is arguably more appropriate for comparing consumer prices between Japan and the USA, the difference falls to perhaps 3-7 times.

The earlier estimates were for world demand, whereas the market research data was from Japan alone. The earlier data relate to just a trip in a launch vehicle, whereas a large proportion of the market research data represents people who wish to stay a few days in orbit. Finally the earlier estimates included projections of growth over the next 30 years, whereas the market research data has no explicit time-scale.

The annual revenue that would be earned at each price level, with quartic (solid) and quadratic (dotted) curves fitted. Annual revenues reach a peak of some \1.35 trillion ($13.5 B), though there is some uncertainty about the price at which the maximum revenue would be earned. In the smoothed curves it lies between \1.2 million and \2.4 million.

Since these figures seem very high, it is interesting to consider possible reasons for discounting them. It might be argued that for the various reasons discussed in the previous section these figures should be discounted by a factor of 5 or 10. To discount them even further, to perhaps 1/20 of the market research data, seems excessive: In a country where many people pay three months' salary for a foreign holiday, it does not seem unrealistic to expect that many would pay the same or more for a trip to space, which is clearly a particularly popular dream.

Alternatively it might be argued that once it became a commercially available service, space flight would lose its glamour, and so people would find the reality less attractive than the dream today. While this argument probably has some value, on this qualitative level it is possible also to argue the opposite: that in the coming years, a visit to orbit to see the Earth from space and to experience living in weightlessness could become the defining experience of the new post-cold-war era, in which advanced technology will be used for peaceful more than for military purposes, as foreign air travel might be said to have become in the late 20th century. In addition, the marketing industry, which grows ever more influential with the spread of the mass media, would surely be pleased to be offered the challenge of keeping the idea of space travel exciting. In view of its existing popularity, and of the almost limitless range of interesting future entertainments that can be developed in orbital facilities and beyond, it does not seem a serious danger that space tourism might fail through being considered boring.

Another possible response is to say that the survey is unrealistic because low-cost, airline-type launch operations are not feasible. Although this has been the opinion of many in the space industry over the past quarter-century, the tide of opinion is now changing. Hudson's work on SSTO VTOVL vehicles, which had been largely ignored through the 1980s, has been endorsed, and even senior figures now openly support the concept. To design a vehicle to achieve the cost targets necessary to start a commercial space tourism service is one of the objectives of the current Space Tourism Study Program of the Japanese Rocket Society (JRS). After considering these arguments for considering the results to be unrealistically high, we should also note a number of arguments for correcting the figures upwards.

These are first, the figures used for average salaries are those for Japanese manufacturing industry in 1990, which are significantly lower than national average incomes in 1993 at the time of the survey. Second, we have not included bonuses, which typically represent some 25-40% of annual income in Japan. Third, since we are considering the demand for a service to be available some years in the future, we should allow for economic growth in estimating salaries. If incomes grow at 3.5% per year, this would represent growth of 50% over 12 years, and 100% over 20 years. Fourth, it is a well-recognised feature of consumer expenditure in advanced countries, that once a certain income level is reached, spending on leisure activities increases proportionately faster than on other expenses, taking a larger share of income. Future spending on space travel would fall into this category. If we were to make allowance for all these factors, it is therefore arguable that we should increase the price at each demand level by as much as 100%.

As discussed above, it seems reasonable to assume that world demand for space tourism services might be 6 times greater than demand in Japan alone, although to be sure about this will require further surveys. Consequently, if we took the demand,as provisional estimates of world demand for space tourism, we would be effectively discounting our questionnaire results by some 90%. Thus it seems a reasonably conservative interpretation of our data to assume that world demand for orbital tourism services could reach a level of more than \1.2 trillion ($12 billion) per year at a service price of between \2.4 million ($24,000) and \1.2 million ($12,000).

It therefore seems reasonable to conclude that the commercial revenue earned by space tourism services would be several times larger than the entire launch industry today, and has the potential to grow to many times its size. Consequently, in considering the design of a reusable launch vehicle from a commercial point of view, developing a vehicle for the tourist market seems to be an attractive target.

Pattern of Development

The JRS Space Tourism Study Program assumes that the first phase of space tourism will comprise short trips to orbit lasting a few hours. However, it seems likely that once space tourism begins, like other commercial activities the variety of space tourism services will grow progressively and, in particular, orbital accommodation will become available. At first no more than a simple "hostel" comprising a few accommodation units, these orbital vehicles will later become large and sophisticated "hotels", offering a range of entertainments that exploit the unique features of the orbital environment, as discussed in. It is therefore interesting to consider the possible pattern of development of such services.

Any distinction between demand for different services, in our questionnaire participants were asked to state a preference between a day-trip to orbit, a trip lasting 2-3 days, a week-long stay in orbit, and a stay of 2 weeks or longer, without reference to price. The replies showed a strong preference for stays of a few days or longer, as described in. From a commercial point of view the important questions are: "How much more would guests pay for a longer stay in orbit?"; "How much higher will the cost of providing such services be?"; and "How much greater would demand be for these services?" Participants in the survey were not asked how much they would pay for different lengths of stay in orbit, but were asked to state their preference for a single visit length, independent of price. Consequently our data does not allow us to determine confidently the relative demand for trips of different lengths. Nevertheless, in the absence of more precise data, it seems reasonable to use the increasing popularity of different trip lengths at the same price as a proxy for the growth of demand that would occur as better services were offered.

As orbital accommodation services grew, the share of space tourism revenue accruing to launch vehicle operators would fall, as a larger proportion is paid for accommodation. Thus a significant proportion of the revenues would accrue to operators of orbital accommodation rather than to launch companies. It is notable that the demand for stays of 2-3 days and 1 week show the same pattern of dependence on price, with a revenue peak at a price below \2 million. This is different from the demand for day-trips, which shows a different pattern, with demand being relatively inelastic and growing only relatively slowly as the price falls. However, this is of course affected by the increasing attractiveness of the alternative offerings at the same price. It is an important gap in the present data that, because the demand for longer stays in orbit is, not surprisingly, greater than the demand for day-trips at the same price, we can deduce little from our data about what the demand for day-trips would be at a time when this was the only service available-other than it would be greater than the figures in our results, which represent only those who would prefer a day-trip to a longer stay at the same price.

Thus, as space tourism services develop, as in other forms of tourism the overall price that passengers pay will comprise two separate components, that for flight to orbit and that for accommodation in orbit, and the price of each will fall progressively as demand increases. Stays in orbit will become available at a given price only once flight to orbit has fallen sufficiently below that price. Longer stays will become available later, when the price of shorter stays will be less than that of the longer stays.

If we make a simple assumption that the unit cost of launch services will fall according to a learning-curve of 90%, the cost of a flight to orbit will fall by about 30% as demand grows approximately 10 times from the day-trip phase to 2-3 days in orbit, and by about 37% as demand more than doubles again by the 1-week stay phase. Thus if the price of the service remained constant, as assumed in the questionnaire, the cost of accommodation would be successively 43% and 60% of the cost of flight to orbit. This is comparable to the rough estimate published in that the cost of a few days' stay in orbital accommodation will be approximately 50% of the cost of a flight to orbit. In the future we will analyse this in more detail, breaking down the data collected in our survey according to age and other factors. It will be interesting to compare the results with "bottom-up" economic analysis of orbital accommodation using inputs from the hotel and real estate industries.

It is noteworthy that the growth in demand for orbital accommodation, measured by number of guest-days will be faster than the growth in launch demand, due to the growing length of stays. Consequently the service of providing accommodation in orbit has the potential to achieve greater reductions in cost (measured per guest-day) due to learning-curve benefits than have launch services. At a time when 1 million people visit orbit each year, orbital accommodation for 10,000 people or more will be required.

Commercially Justifiable Investment in Passenger Launch Vehicle Development

From the point of view of those considering investing in the development of a passenger launch vehicle, a question of central importance is "How high an investment cost can we expect to recover from profits from sales of vehicles?" In order to answer this we should make bottom-up estimates of vehicle operation and maintenance costs, propellant costs, staff costs and indirect costs. By comparing these with estimates of traffic rates at different prices, it would be possible to estimate justifiable vehicle price against passenger fare. By making further assumptions about vehicle production and sales, it would be possible to derive a figure for the maximum development cost that would be commercially recoverable. This is one of the intended outputs of the JRS passenger launch vehicle design study.

For the present paper we take a simpler approach. We assume a certain profit margin on the price that passengers pay. By doing this we can estimate the profit per year obtainable according to the vehicle utilisation. From the overall traffic we can estimate the number of vehicles needed, from which the maximum supportable investment can be calculated by making conventional financial assumptions.

However, we must also take into account the fact that the flight price will fall progressively below the overall service price, which we do by assuming a 90% learning curve, as above. The initial assumptions of the JRS passenger launch vehicle study, that each vehicle carries 50 passengers, and flies to orbit 300 times per year. In addition we assume a 2% profit margin on the price of the passenger flight (which is less than the overall service price).

On this analysis, the most profitable flight price is about \1,200,000, corresponding to a service price of some \1,700,000. Development of a vehicle designed to fly passengers at such a price could be financed commercially at a development cost of up to some \150 billion ($1.5B), 25% more than a vehicle with passenger flight costs of twice this level. To provide the service would require 50 such vehicles, compared to only half this number of a vehicle with twice the passenger cost. The results of such a simple, preliminary analysis can only be considered tentative. However, the underlying concept is fundamental to the future of the launch business.

If further research on both the demand for space tourism and on the cost of supplying the services that people want supports our results, it is clear that carrying passengers to orbit and back has the potential to become a mainstay of the space launch business. No other payload which has so far been proposed in the space industry literature offers such a potential. The only other candidate for which launch demand could be of a similar or greater magnitude is the project to deliver solar-generated microwave power from space to Earth. This will become feasible only after a number of technologies have been developed beyond their present stage, in addition to the development of low-cost launch vehicles. By contrast, space tourism can start as soon as an appropriate vehicle is developed.

Further Results

Another interesting and potentially valuable subject not mentioned in the above discussion, which can also be analysed using the survey data, is market segmentation. As in terrestrial tourism, there seems to be a relatively inelastic demand for a high-priced service, and a separate, more price-elastic demand for low-price, mass-market "pack tours". From our results the possibility of a number of other more detailed categories of customer are apparent-graduation travel, young family holidays, "full moon" travel. These suggest directions for developing a range of distinctive space tourism offerings, which we will investigate further.

5

Strategic Planning to Promote Tourism

Introduction

The tourism is one of the main economic activities in the world. It generates an important investment and it can contribute to the economic growth and the social progress of the developing countries not only for its economic spill but also when favoring and encouraging the performance of activities that assist the demand of the tourists like lodging, feeding, transport, amusement, the knowledge of traditions, attractions and of the culture, among other, with the consequent generation of direct and indirect job positions; In addition it attracts national and foreign investment and it impels the regional infrastructure by means of the urbanization and construction of new and improved communication means (terrestrial, sea, air).

A great amount of foreign currencies enters the countries because of this activity, derived from the international exchanges, but also, the internal tourism that the national population practices inside its own territory, contributes to balance the national economy by means of the redistribution of the income. At the same time, for the amount of services that it requires, the tourism is a factor of employment creation of in different activities. For instance in Mexico the Tourism contributes with more than 7.7% of the national Internal Raw Product (PIB) and contributes with more than 9% in direct and indirect job positions, reason why it is one of the strategic sectors in the national economic development.

Evolution of the Tourism's Conceptual System

The study of the tourist phenomenon at the present time requires a revaluation of the models that have been used for this aim, with the purpose of generating a holistic vision in its analysis. Science contemplates a series of specific knowledge that explain the concrete phenomena of real life, through it, scientists understand their study object, as long as the method allows to carry out valuations with certainty of the wisdom and agree to the theoretical structure to prepare.

Science in its historical evolution has suffered transformations, passing from the traditional reductionism to the totalizing approaches, with the firm conviction of achieving transcendence in the acquired knowledge.

The study of the social science, different from the so called hard sciences, has softening elements appreciated in the systems of human activity, reason why it cannot be approached from exact sciences' characteristic scientific perspectives.

The scientifically acceptable tourism has recaptured defined theoretical structures starting from their main manifestations (economic, social, and psychological) that are shown as weak to remark their theoretical synopsis when valuing the phenomenon from the whole that embraces. The scientific thought of Tourism, should be understood from totalizing methodologies view, able to overcome the antagonism of the singular vision of a science in particular. The prime scientific outcome, from which the tourist study can start, is constituted by its constant evolution, basic elements of the living systems that show the alignment of phenomena to the conditions of the environment, as well as its structural components.

In order to approach the epistemological problematic of the tourism, one can use the Systemic Emergent Paradigm as a methodology that provides a dialectical synthesis in the study of the composition of relating qualitative and quantitative combined elements to their different manifestations by means of constituting the aspects that compose it from a holistic optics, able to refer the phenomenon in all its possible manifestations. Therefore it is convenient to try to approach the study of the tourist phenomenon from the perspective of the Systemic, with the intention of being able to propose a model of tourist system that shows the involved elements and their possible interactions. This way, it is sought to analyze the theoretical currents about the Science of Systems and the Tourism with the purpose of generating a reference mark to lead us toward a model of categorization of the tourism from the systemic considerations.

Science and Systems Sciences

The rational knowledge is derived of mankind's necessity to give answer to the events that surround them, and so it is that the philosophical method arises, along with the metaphysics and the Greek scholastic, giving a controllable order to the thought that separates the ideology from the application.

The systemic thought emerges of the Aristotelian teleology of "the whole it is more than the sum on its parts", agreed in the Hegelian and Marxist dialectics that constitute the advance of the holistic vision.

Evolution of the Tourism's Conceptual System

Overcome by the emergence of the Descartes reductionism whose proposal breaks into fragments the whole problem in as many simple and separate elements as it is possible, generating the resolute method of Galileo where the complex phenomena are reduced to parts and elementary processes.

Bertalanffy (1995), introduced the idea of the organisms like systems, showing by fact that the laws of the systems behave as analogies, that is to say that formally identical laws are applied to completely different phenomena.

The General Systems Theory or Theory of the Organized Complexity, treats phenomena that cannot be simplified, that to say that cannot be reduced, it embraces the living and not alive systems through isomorphic principles, leaving intact the internal interactions, studying the system like a whole and embracing its complexity. In general, inside the system conceptualization, the authors that have defined it agree that it is a group of coordinated parts and in interaction to reach a group of objectives. The systems approach is used to solve complex problems of the organisations from a global perspective, it carries out an analysis of the entirety of the components as well as its interrelations, and it tends toward the application of a holistic perspective, it tries to reach the dialectical synthesis between the quantitative and qualitative methods, considering them as complementary and it is not only limited to the knowledge of the system but rather it promulgates its improvement.

Darwin's theory of evolution, postulates the living beings as a result of a slow evolution where the diverse species have derived from each other by natural selection. The evolution leadsto the spontaneous appearance of systems of a grater and grater complexity where not alone the complexity increases in the system but also its effectiveness.

Epistemoligical Problems of Tourism

The advance of the scientific research of Tourism shows leisure (playful activity, vacation or free time), as main element of its theoretical consideration. Leisure according to Bullon (1990), leads to free time or work break that according to Mune (1986), represents the social wealth that constitutes the time in which the productive forces recover their vitality, through a playful self-regenerating of all that is human. The use of leisure time is a psychological activity since it depends on what each individual intends. The recreation on the other hand is any kind of use that the mankind makes of its free time, whenever this use is carried out in a pleasant attitude. This way the tourism is a peculiar form of recreation, but not its only presentation. Reason why trying to study the tourism through the use of the recreation and the free time, requires subordinating the recreation, human innate element to a specific use of the free time, which turns into an exhausting task that would not lead to its theoretical conformation.

Evolution of the Tourism's Conceptual System

The concept of Tourism has been approached from the practical definition deduced from the shortened interpretations emitted by the OMT (1991) that refers to the displacement of people outside of their residence place for different reasons, fact that scorns the tourist dynamics including it in the tourist's emblem as the only element of their conformation.

The tourism has been glimpsed from the tourist's vision whose elements that validate the tourist concept, are contemplated by 1) the activities to develop 2) the existence of a displacement 3) the permanency in the visit place for at least 24 hours where a night stay should exist to be considered as the use a tourist service 3) the interaction of the tourists with the hosting community. The debate on what is or not a tourist, derives from the previous elements, since only people that complete such condition are considered as tourists, therefore one should not considered 'a tourist' as the person that moves inside their habitual environment, consume tourist products, develop tourist activities and interact with the hosting community, however they are considered inside a tourist segment, they carry out tourist expense and act as tourists, but according to the previous considerations they should be classified as non tourist, due to the absence of one of the elements that gives them that categorization which is the displacement outside of his residence place.

The economic and social slopes have marked the rule to be able to locate the tourist issue as part of their theoretical happening, the first one with the economic science, in the offer-demand model where the tourism is an activity that generates revenues, job positions and expense with a multiplier and transformer effect on the regional development.

The social approach promulgates the social psychology that tries to refer it from the intercultural contacts, the sociological theory that shows tourism like a social phenomenon,, and the tourist anthropology that includes tourism inside its ethnic-cultural dynamism. These approaches present tourism like a playful activity that has as main function, the one of fomenting the human understanding among people of different cultures.

The epistemological problem of the tourist knowledge resides, more than in the same object, in the paradigm that studies it. The tourism has shown obstacles and continuous epistemological errors within the evolution of its theoretical knowledge, exposed in the theoretical lack pointed out by Bullon (1985), and revealed by the lack of general principles to harmonize its theoretical structure.

The tourist researcher should depart from its own knowledge, linking their experiences with the phenomenon, their rational understanding, and to be able to combine it with the knowledge of the scientific theory, to be able to propose a dialectical that leads to new and transcendent knowledge. This implies not to copy ordinary arguments, but making a dialectical rupture with the traditional foundations.

Systems Theory and Tourism

The best way to approach tourism is through the General Theory of Systems, in accordance with Leiper, who proposes the recommendation of a systems approach as a means for the research that deal with relative general matters related to the interdisciplinary issue.

The design of the tourist dynamics began to be develop from a particular systemic approach, cybernetics, based on it, the classic approaches are shown like the Molina tourist system, that is explained as an open system, established by the integration of a group of parts or subsystems that are related to reach a common objective, related in turn with their environment. For Boullon (1985), the tourist system is composed of three perspectives: to) an offer demand model that centres its interest in the operation of the commercial tourism b) a social anthropological approach that is in charge of the leisure and free time manifestations and c) inside the industrial tourism model that is interested in the massive production the commercialization and the profit. This tourist division denotes the disintegration of what should be a single system, what makes allusion to this model's inability to be able to integrate the elements and the relationships of the tourist system.

However, so much the system of Molina as well as Boullon's respond to the mechanical and organic models that locate tourism inside the relationships of exchange of information with the environment where the change is primarily endogenous even ending up changing the structure of the system. Alfonso Jiménez (2004), takes Leiper's model as a reference to dismember his contribution framing the tourist subsystems, inside an entropic process, feedback by the haemostasis established by the exterior environment, qualitative data (motivational of trip) and quantitative (statistical) and the environment of the impacts in the local populations based on the analysis of the origin region and the destination region,which stuck the development of the systemic advance of tourism when carrying out new interpretations of already established models.

The tourist system of Osorio (2005), is a soft complex system, composed by a net of numerous relationships that have a self-organisation and evolution capacity, subject to determining external changes of its transformation, among which there is the dynamic element that determines the form of making tourism, the static element referred to the destination, the consequential element that refers the impacts of the two previous elements, these elements form the subsystems that provide evidence of the relationships that happen in the tourist system.

However, in the model, soft complex systems are not defined nor complex systems taken as a reference that are defined based on the mathematical structuring of their variables and take fractal geometry as a reference; specifically the behaviour of the mathematical variables and their stationary capacity, in a bifurcation point known as saturation of the system.

The above-mentioned constitutes the contributions carried out inside the research on tourism with systemic linking, although it is certain that they represent relevant advances to the study of the tourist issue, the study of the tourism in Mexico has not been developed due to the epistemological incongruity applied of the knowledge of the Systems Science and the use of the new systemic methodologies that would allow to establish a more direct approach to try to define it.

Tourist System Evolution

The tourist system presents a constant evolution expressed in the factors of the international tourism development such as: a) the increase of the personal income, b) larger leisure times c) the revolution transportation d) technological changes e) and the freedom of travelling. The previous factors allow contemplating tourism like an economic political group that surpasses, the continental, national and regional issue being constituted in the tourism of masses that has shown an evolutionary, interesting tendency, generated from the transformations of the demand, derived from the new tourist demands. The traditional way of making tourism has evolved reaching all tourist areas, generating new specific segments of the market where the tourist is no longer willing to carry out an unjustified expense. It takes more and more seriously the role of preserving the environment, and grants bigger attributions to the experiences generated of the interactions with other people.

The changes experienced in the tourist phenomenon have radically transformed what could be glimpsed as the traditional tourist system, under the new perspectives, composed by the demands, the knowledge, and forms of making tourism in the contemporary world. The evolution that is presented in the tourist system emanates of its central element, the tourist that when acquiring new experiences, in different environments, creates entropy that when being absorbed by the remaining elements of the system, is used to propitiate haemostasis contributing to its evolution and transcendence.

The tourist system as such has been transformed in different action fronts that show the evolution of the commercialization relationships expressed in the use of the web (internet) that allows the direct interaction between the tourists and the providers of services, the approach of the tourists to know the places, regions, communities and tourist spaces to visit, allowing to compare prices, qualities, and even to try to make a judge on the degree of experiences that will have.

The evolution of the tourist system, toward the conformation of the alternative tourism (process that promotes a fair way of travelling among the members of different communities), it pursues the mutual understanding, the solidarity and the equality among the participants.

The tourist comes off of his elitist character and congregates a renovating environment and social activity, promoted by the consumers themselves, as a result of their evolutionary process where the tourists request, without any imposition, to be given the opportunity to participate in the conservation, development and improvement of the social and environmental atmospheres that surround the tourist activity. In its new placement the tourism creates job positions, protects the natural and cultural resources, at the same time that promotes human understanding. In accord ance with Barreto (1996), the tourists should not carry out lucrative functions, what leaves the concept of business tourism in a difficult position since although tourists services are being used, and they can behave as tourists in their free time they cannot be considered as such, because they don't fulfill the requirement of being travelling for pleasure, they are not owners of their time and they present burden attitudes due to the pressures of the work.

The tourist concept should not come from their motivations, behaviour and attitudes since these are centered in the subjective area, which would not help to dismember its concept because we would already have so many definitions as approaches for its analysis.

The concept of tourist should come from a holistic perspective that will allow us to use a rational valuation for its conception. The tourist is the main element of the tourist system that generates negative entropy that comes from their diversification, necessities, expectations and attitudes, reason why its conceptual treatment should be approached not by the causes of its displacements but for the effects that generates inside the tourist system.

The tourist like the main entropy element of the system may be specified based on their participation inside the tourist system, considering that people have the ability to belong or to stop belonging to the systems, what takes us to the following view. The tourist is that person that belongs to the tourist system and alters its operation, by means of the entropy, independently of the activities, attitudes, or perceptions that they present, tourists generate changes inside the other elements that try to understand to be coupled to its considerations, and in turn it is influenced by the other elements, for the determination of decisions in the tourist system.

Evolution of the Tourism's Conceptual System

Design Of The Model

The general postulates of the Systems Method and its methodologies, as well as the Domain of Science Model by John' Warfield were considered for the design of the model. In a summarized form, the steps and development of the methodology are shown next:

1. Object of study or problem: To outline the elements of the tourist system.
2. To visualize the concepts like a mental representation of the reality inside the psychological Cosmo vision: We can understand this stage like the part of the interaction and mental construction on the study concepts, enlarging our understanding of reality. This happens when we interact and think of such concepts and we relate them with our cosmo vision.
3. Importance or value for humanity. For this work the importance resides in establishing the elements of the tourist system.
4. Systemic Cosmo vision: The reconstruction of the concepts is given in this stage until reaching an approach to a theory with a holistic vision. A way to reconstruct the concepts is changing some original attributes. Changing some original attributes of the existent tourist systems, their order and disorder elements are established.

Evolution of the Tourism's Conceptual System

Considerations of the model

According to the elements and their interrelations the following principles are proposed: The tourist system has entropic elements defined by the vulnerability of the phenomenon to the social, political and economic events. The personal and social security constitutes the bases on which the tourist makes a purchase election. The tourist system, finds its balance in the destinations that try to clean up their image as safe destinations.

In tourism free time is valued in terms of knowledge, experiences, and satisfactions, what determines in turn how they will decide to spend the new free time. The Tourist is the main entropic element of the tourist system whose participation favours changes in the other elements at the same time that it is influenced by them. The elements of negentropy of the tourist system produce information, and structuring of the system, that are useful to propitiate firstly its survival and invoke its development. The handling of electronic information systems (Tic´s), creates negentropy at the time that the options, of making and consuming the tourism are considerably increased.

Evolution of the Tourism's Conceptual System

The identification of the tourist segments and the determination of activities according to their necessities, cooperate to balance the tourist system. The knowledge of the socio cultural environment to visit, favours positive information to the system. The stationary demand, generates fluctuations in the prices, therefore the stability of the system depends on the capacity and sustentation of the linking elements (tourist companies). The elements of tourist linkage (tourist companies) are able to create like every organisation, elements of entropy and negentropy by their own, therefore they are considered as direct modifiers of the tourist satisfaction, haemostasis creator.

The linking elements need to improve their goods and services with the purpose of directing their product to create positive entropy reflected in the increase of their revenues and quality of services. The elements of tourist interactions include the crisscross environments that are considered, to the moment of the tourist experience, and that in general determine the behaviour and evolution of the system. The regulators conform the supra system, able to implement the changes according to the evolutionary aspects of the tourist system in legal, productive, social, cultural matters and in the generation of new knowledge. Each element of the tourist system is subordinate to a regulator.

The evolutionary element of tourism is the one of greater transcendence to consider its future states and conditions. The main element of the tourist evolution this constituted by the tourists that when returning to their origin place, evolves and influences in the evolution of the remaining elements, presenting bigger impact in the linking elements (tourist companies) and in the regulating elements, (unions, organisations, governments and institutions) tourist.

Next, in a synthetic way, some of the discoveries that have been found in the course of research are described, as well as some preliminary conclusions: The tourism is an open system, customizable, and dynamic integrated by entropic, negentropic and homeostatic elements that determine its condition in an evolutionary phase.

The tourist system is conformed by all the elements that are presented in its manifestation, they create alteration situations in its interior, and aim to establish a balance, while the consideration of tourism like a series of isolated knowledge, a group of dismembered policies, or a group of diffuse procedures, they belong to a social, economic or managerial part different from the one constituted by the tourist system.

The tourism seems to evolve toward the social, environmental, and economic reconciliation, manifested in its sustainable considerations and reflected in the demands of the tourists to respect those environments. Therefore it is a suitable tool to propitiate the social, and economic development, the care for the environment and the cultural invigoration. The linking elements (tourist companies) have the internal capacity of being self regulated, and of balancing the tourist system, at least in terms of what the satisfaction of goods and services concerns, the levels of worldwide competition cause the necessity to respond favourably to the tourist evolution captured in the reference frame.

The tourist companies should consider the role that the human element plays in the process of tourist conomic transformation, reason why they should be focused in the creation of real scenarios, to satisfy their demand, since the human factor is considered to be the essential element of the tourist system. The objective of the tourist system is to provide visitors with the suitable conditions to take a trip, in consequence the reconciliation in the actions of the regulating elements, meaning the participation of the governments, the unions, the institutions and tourist organisations, should result in combined efforts to develop the tourist system, and not in disperse actions that hinder its development. The main mission of the tourist regulators responds to propitiate favourable homeostatic changes, developers of the system, in legal, productive, environmental, social, cultural and educational matters whose commercial, economic bureaucratic barriers or of different nature hinder its function to the degree that their lack of actions have a negative impact in the tourist system. The governments, unions, organisations, and institutions of quick answer, generate favourable conditions for their internal tourist environments, due to their quick action to identify the elements of improvement and to carry out their developing function of the tourist system.

The tourist evolution allows glimpsing the integration of the economic, political environmental and social environments of the tourist issue through its manifestations, generated trough the history of its conformation.

The documented applications of the Science of Systems in tourism that have been found have been incongruous with the advances that this science has had. Prove of it is the categorization of tourism using primarily the cybernetic model of first level of the 50's or incomplete or mistaken approaches to propose tourist systems. This obeys the lack of a modernized and deep knowledge of this Science. The Systemic Science provides a new research method, and useful tools for the theoretical and praxiologic study of tourism.

Rules for Successful Tourism Marketing

Tourism is an important economic activity because it brings in dollars from outside the community. It continues to be a fast growing sector and is typically included among the top three industries in the country. In addition, tourism provides a "front-door" to non-tourism economic development efforts such as business recruitment. Roger Brooks, a nationally recognized expert in tourism development spoke about rules for success at the 2004 Wisconsin Governor's Conference on Tourism in Green Bay. Many of his rules apply to the tourism marketing efforts of small city downtowns and business districts. Presented below is a summary of his keynote address titled *15 Immutable Rules of Successful Tourism.*

Success Begins With a Good Plan

Creating a Tourism Development & Marketing Plan is the first rule for successful tourism. The plan should include several details like product development, upgrades and improvements, repositioning and/or branding, attractions and events, visitor amenities and services, marketing and public relations, public/

private partnerships, recruitment, funding and budgets, and organizational responsibilities. The plan should integrate existing comprehensive plans and economic development and Main Street efforts.

Importance of Front-line Sales

Your front-line employees can be your most valuable sales team. This is because they establish the first contact with the customer. The front-line employees should be knowledgeable about your community and should promote other stores, attractions and amenities to visitors to keep them in the area longer.

Critical Mass: In order to attract and keep visitors in your community, there must be several retail and dining establishments within walking distance. Shopping and dining in a pedestrian setting is one of the top activities for visitors. An average rule of thumb for rural communities is to have nine retail stores and four dining/treats establishments within two or three blocks.

Turn Negatives Into Positives: Almost every community and attraction has its challenges. Think creatively on how to convert these negatives into positives. You can then attract people to your area using clever promotional tactics. For example, when an article in the Washington Post labeled Battle Mountain, Nevada the "Armpit of America", the town took a positive spin on that title by having an annual event sponsored by Old Spice drawing thousands of visitors.

Be Unique: In order to be successful, you must be worth the trip. A visitor must be able to differentiate you from the competition and you must strive to be creative and set yourself apart from others. Being unique will make a visitor travel the extra distance.

Telling Stories: Museums and interpretive centres should always tell stories, not just display artifacts. Stories can keep visitors in the area longer, which means additional spending. Visitors also remember stories, and captivating stories are told and passed on to others. More people pick destinations by word of mouth than any other method.

Four-Times Rule: People are willing to travel a distance if you offer something that appeals to them. There should be enough for visitors to see and do in your area. In general, you should be able to keep visitors busy four times longer than it took them to get there.

Marketing vs. Product Development

Before you market your community, make sure it is appealing to customers. If your product is not of great quality, then your marketing efforts are wasted. Product development should always be a top priority, and it never ends. Having a good mix of product development and marketing is also important.

Selling the Experience

Always sell the experience associated with an activity and not the place. If you are using pictures in your marketing campaign, avoid using scenic images. Scenery lasts in the mind for only a few moments. Instead, use images of people laughing and having fun. Viewers are more likely to remember images that include people's emotions.

Branding: Even at the community level, branding is critical for success in tourism. Branding is much more than just a logo; it is what sets you apart from your competition, it is your image and your value. Do not try to be "all things to all people."

WOW Photography: Nothing sells tourism like great photography. Photographs used for tourism purposes should have a "wow" appeal in the viewer and should make the viewer want to go to the place depicted. As mentioned earlier, you are trying to sell an experience and your photos should evoke emotion in the viewer. Photography should be the key element in brochures, public relation efforts, and especially on the web.

Close the Sale: Most communities and attractions spend a significant amount of money on advertising. The primary "call to action" in advertising is to get the potential customer to call and get a brochure, or for them to visit your web site. If this is the case, the brochure and web site should be good enough to close the sale. Otherwise, your advertising effort is largely wasted. Pay attention to certain small details while advertising. For example, for brochures, the best colors to use are red and yellow as these colors get the viewers attention. In addition, most brochures end up in racks along with scores of other brochures and the top three inches is all that is visible to the potential customer. Keep this in mind when designing brochures.

Public Relations

Even though you need both, publicity is much more important than advertising. Implementing a professional public relations campaign can have several benefits: it will build brand, improve your image, increase credibility and will provide a greater return on investment than advertising alone. Public relation is how you build your brand and advertising is how you maintain your position. Studies show that for every $1 invested into a public relations campaign, you get a $3 return.

Effective Web Sites

According to a Nielsen/Netratings study, nearly 75% of the U.S. population has access to the Internet from home. In addition, 94% of Internet users make travel arrangements using the Web. The Internet is by far the number one resource for planning travel and vacations.

If you have a tourism related web site, can your potential customers find you easily on the Web? How does your web site compare with the competition? Make the online experience interactive for the customer and remember to promote attractions, not just the place or your organization. Several thousands of dollars spent on web site development and maintenance is not a waste of money. You can even make sure your web site is displayed at the top of a Web search by paying a fee.

Frequency in Advertising

Frequency is more important than variety in placing advertising. People viewing your advertisement should develop Top of Mind Awareness (TOMA). For example, when the words "fast food" are mentioned, most people think of McDonalds because they make a good use of frequency in advertising.

Successful Budgeting for your Medical Tourism Marketing Campaigns

If marketing can be called the vehicle that brings dreams to reality, a marketing budget can certainly be referred to as the fuel that drives the vehicle. A marketing budget has long since outlived the traditional moniker of being a financial tool that helps an organization assign enough resources to achieve its marketing objectives.

Today, a marketing budget is a proud badge of recognition that demonstrates that an organization has purpose in its marketing. It says that an organization knows EXACTLY what marketing it intends to perform and how that marketing is going to help its bottom line.

In order to design a marketing budget, on organization first needs two things; an executive in charge of marketing and a manager in charge of executing the marketing plan. The former petitions the keeper of the funds for enough budget dollars to successfully help the organization, while the latter determines exactly how much resources the former should ask for.

The most successful budget style that I have encountered is the Cost Center Budget approach. With this approach, Medical Tourism is assigned what we call a cost centre. This puts it on par with all the organization's important strategic and operational departments such as Finance, Accounting, and Sales. More importantly, it means that your organization can now capture ALL the medical tourism costs in one place.

This is a very important management tool that will enable senior management to assess the performance of the organization's medical tourism operations. Within this Cost Centre, Medical Tourism Marketing is assigned a Cost Centre Group. This means that all the marketing activities associated with medical tourism can be tracked from a financial perspective. Also, it isolates the marketing expenses from the other medical tourism efforts, such as Customer Service, Information Technology (IT), Sales, Public Relations (PR), Education and Training, and Business Processing.

What are your marketing budget elements? In other words, what goes into your marketing budget? There's the obvious; Salary and Fringe Benefits, IT Expense, Advertising, Event Marketing, and Promotional Merchandise. In addition however, your organization should budget for Professional Services, New Business Promotion, Purchased Services and Travel.

Professional Services will include any expenses that the organization incurs to solicit the services of professionals. Included in this line item are creative design, graphic design and website design.

Website design, in my opinion, should always merit its own line item due to its importance and the need to isolate and, therefore, manage its expenses. Website marketing is rapidly becoming the most effective (and cost effective) way to attract customers. However, the costs associated with its design and maintenance can become very complex and easily lost with the other design costs that an organization may incur.

New Business Promotion costs are those costs incurred for new products, new markets or new customers. It's very important for an organization to capture these costs separately from ongoing promotion. Most marketing professionals operate under a timeless adage that it costs seven times as much to capture a new customer as it costs to retain an already existing customer.

In my opinion, anything that's costing my organization seven times the cost of anything warrants its own specific attention. Plus, proper capture of these costs enables proper management of them and can provide guidance to actually reducing them, thereby becoming more efficient. ALL costs associated with new products, new markets or new customers should be captured in this bucket.

Purchased Services are those services that an organization elects to "buy" versus "build". These costs can include printing, service measurement (customer surveys), project expenses, mail management, and special promotions not associated with any current product or service, nor with any new product or service, such as an organization's community activities. The key to identifying which costs belong in this bucket is that they are for services (usually professional services) other than those included in the Professional Services bucket.

Travel costs might appear to be obvious and one might wonder why they warrant special attention. In one of my previous organizations, I have direct experience that suggests that excluding travel costs that are incurred because of marketing, from a marketing budget can skew the results of a marketing campaign.

Imagine a campaign that involves travel to a particular conference where your organization is a sponsor and has a booth or other display space. The costs for travel, lodging, meals and other related expenses can be appreciable and should be included in the budget in order to determine how successful that event was for your organization. ALL expenses that are incurred to get people somewhere for a special reason, should be included in the marketing travel costs bucket. While this article attempts to simplify the budgeting process somewhat, it should be clear that capturing all your marketing efforts is important for your organization. For a particular campaign like marketing to a specific U.S. state, or a particular U.S. ethnic sector, or for a specific purpose in the U.S., the campaign should be set up to capture all the aforementioned costs.

You can never have too many campaigns; each unique in its cost collection efforts so that the success of each can be uniquely and separately assessed. In order to accomplish this goal successfully, the marketing manager and marketing department should know EXACTLY what each campaign involves. This can be achieved by creating a communications plan for your campaign.

The Marketing Manager should be responsible to ensure that all the costs are properly captured and reported up to the executive responsible for marketing. Also, the marketing manager should be responsible for determining what results are expected. How many new customers? How many referrals? How much sales? What incremental sales are expected? By balancing the expected results against the cost, an organization can establish an expected Return on Investment (ROI). And, by balancing the actual results against the cost, an organization can establish an actual ROI. Does your actual medical tourism marketing campaign ROI meet or exceed your expected ROI?

When I was in charge of marketing at a previous employer, I created a campaign for every promotion. We tracked every campaign. We were able to identify and continue successful campaigns and actually improve them. We were also able to discontinue unsuccessful campaigns so they didn't drain much needed resources. That particular product achieved $40 million in revenues in the first year and a retention ratio of almost 80%

in the second year. Both achievements are considered excellent for the competitive market of the product. We are so committed to the concept of using marketing budgets, that we have created a presentation that demonstrates how to create a medical tourism marketing budget.

Make sure your organization has a budget method that enables it to capture all medical tourism marketing costs. Make sure that you establish expected results, against which actual results can be compared. Using a marketing budget for each campaign will help you achieve this. It will help you demonstrate the success of your Medical Tourism Marketing Program.

6

Strategic Framework for Tourism Industry

Management

Juneau needs a vision and framework for carrying out tourism. The vision defines what Juneau wants to achieve from the tourism sector and the framework specifies how, when and where the various professional and community discussions and actions about tourism take place. The framework also needs to define roles among the various public and private sector entities involved in tourism. It needs to lay out where tourism is going so that both businesses and residents can make plans with a common understanding of direction and scale. And it needs to prescribe the actions that move Juneau toward its tourism goals. When building a new strategic framework, which is happening through the adoption and implementation of this plan, transitions must be incorporated into the planning process. Roles need to be handed off at appropriate times, dictated either by funding cycles or tourism seasons.

Vision and Objectives

Juneau intends to succeed at both cruise tourism and destination travel – with success being defined on Juneau's terms. That success entails maximizing the benefits of tourism in Juneau, while minimizing the costs and impacts. Juneau looks to tourism, expecting social, economic, and environmental benefits. Juneau seeks a more positive image among its neighbors in Alaska, and with its visitors and travel industry partners. Juneau intends tourism to help create a more diverse economic base. To that end, Juneau will work to create a positive atmosphere for business investment and operations, especially those businesses that are locally owned and operated.

Juneau wants, through tourism, to bolster its commitment to its heritage and cultural values. Juneau intends to be a high quality destination, providing rich and positive experiences for its visitors. It intends to make those visitors feel warmly welcomed.

Overall Guiding Principles for the Tourism Plan

This tourism plan is based on the development and management of a partnership between the people of Juneau, local tourism businesses, and the international cruise tourism industry. In the sections that follow, relationships of that partnership are described, responsibilities outlined, and venues for working out issues among the partners are laid out in considerable detail.

In a partnership approach, all partners invest to achieve results that cannot be achieved outside that partnership. In this case, investment ranges from financial, to time, to energy, to the sharing of Juneau with outsiders. A true partnership plan recognizes and values all these levels of investment.

This plan is based on the principles of sustainable tourism development. That means that social, economic, and environmental resources must be utilized in such a way that they keep their integrity, and at such a pace that they can withstand the impacts of use. Our guideline in building this plan is to assume that at the start of each season social, economic, and environmental resources should be in as good or better shape than at the start of the previous season.

Strategic Directions – Tourism Positioning

The market and product analysis conducted as part of this tourism management planning process revealed that Juneau has a superb opportunity to strengthen its destination tourism sector. The combination of an outstanding natural resource base, diverse history and culture, and coastal community location make it attractive to the growing nature, adventure, heritage, and Eco-tourism travellers. This potential notwithstanding, it is clear that Juneau will have to establish leadership in realizing this potential. Industry cannot make Juneau a successful destination by itself – it needs a partnership with government, particularly in marketing and training areas.

Juneau's competitive position in the Alaska cruise market is already strong. The cruise industry indicates its continued desire to bring its customers to Juneau.

There is general agreement that the volume of visitors (about 700,000 in 2001) represents a near-capacity situation for Juneau harbor. Industry advises that they will be allocating an additional ten percent capacity for 2002, although there is no guarantee they will be able to fill that capacity with customers given the September terrorism events.

Beyond that, they expect growth to settle down to about four percent per year. The most appropriate course of action for Juneau to assume in the cruise sector involves maintenance of its current competitive position, but to prepare for the possibility of continued vigorous growth.

Juneau has not realized success in the development of a meetings and convention market in southeast Alaska, in spite of its stature as a state capital. However, with general improvements in tourism product quality and greater attention to both destination and waterfront development, we believe that this situation can be reversed. Based on the technical product and market analysis prepared for this tourism management plan, the recommended strategic directions for Juneau tourism are as follows:

1. Premier destination, combining nature, adventure, heritage, and cultural experiences Attracting high value customers Focusing on guided experiences
2. Maintain and strengthen Juneau's competitive position in the Alaska cruise tourism market Build on current strong tour product mix Significantly enhance visitor experience in downtown Juneau
3. Position Juneau as a small meetings and convention host in Alaska, the Pacific Northwest, and matched niche markets.

Rationalize and Modernize Juneau's Approach to Tourism

Unlike most communities throughout North America, Juneau experiences annual tourism visitation well in excess of its population. In 2001, Juneau hosted over 800,000 visitors, of which about 700,000 were cruise arrivals. The cruise industry is a major contributor to Juneau's economy, generating estimated economic benefits in 1999 of about $90 million and 750 jobs. Clearly, Juneau is in the tourism business and must organize itself to respond to the opportunities, challenges and issues it faces in ensuring that tourism sector activities enhances, rather than comprises, the community's quality of life.

Current Management Approach

Juneau's approach to tourism management has largely been delegated to semi- independent boards and agencies as shown below.

* Agency
* Role and Responsibility
* Docks and Harbors Board
* All matters related to Juneau's port including primary interaction with the cruise ship industry
* Juneau Convention and Visitor Bureau
* Primarily focusing on destination marketing and responsible for attracting meetings and conventions to Juneau
* In 2000, Juneau created a Tourism Planning Manager position within the City staff organization, reporting to the Deputy City Manager. The primary purpose for this position was to respond to tourism issues raised by the community. Juneau also decided to proceed to prepare a tourism management plan to provide a blueprint for appropriate tourism sector management.

Alternative Models for Tourism Management

There is a range of potential models the CBJ could implement for its tourism management function. Tourism management can take a lassies faire approach at one extreme, or it can extend to a full partnership approach with the tourism industry, guided by a tourism management plan. In some regions of the world, government assumes a more controlling role, directing the path and nature of tourism development and tightly holding access to operation, development, and marketing rights. In light of the scope and scale of Juneau's tourism sector, the opportunity for growth in the destination market segment, and the need to better manage community impacts, we recommend a much more proactive approach to tourism sector management and Juneau's current position. This is illustrated in the chart below. McDowell Group, October 2000, The Economic Impacts of the Cruise Industry in Southeast Alaska.

The recommended position for Juneau in establishing itself as a full partner with the tourism sector is premised on two initiatives:

- This Tourism Management Plan, approved by the Assembly and establishing the framework for CBJ policy and program support for tourism.
- The creation of an appropriate agency or tourism entity – responsible for implementation of the Tourism Management Plan on behalf of the CBJ and all stakeholders.

Update the Comprehensive Plan

The CBJ adopted a position on tourism in its Comprehensive Plan to guide its actions related to the tourism sector. With the adoption of this Tourism Management Plan that position should be updated to achieve consistency.

The adopted tourism policy in the Comprehensive Plan CBJ is aimed at encouraging tourism in a collaborative manner:

Policy 2.12. It is the policy of the CBJ to encourage tourism, convention and other visitor-related activities through the development of appropriate facilities and services, while protecting Juneau's natural and cultural attractions for local citizens and visitors alike, and to participate in the accommodation of the future growth of tourism in a manner that addresses both community and industry concerns.

Included in the plan are a number of implementing actions to carry out the intent of this policy. Both the policy and the implementing actions are now superseded by the formal development of a tourism management plan by the CBJ. Given the proposed adoption of this plan by the CBJ, the Comprehensive Plan will need to be updated accordingly. The recommended amendments to the Comprehensive Plan are structured to recognize the Tourism Management Plan as the mechanism by which the CBJ will promote and manage tourism. In this way the Comprehensive Plan recognizes by reference the (adopted) Tourism Management Plan as the "Implementing Actions" of the CBJ position on tourism.

The Comprehensive Plan amendments are recommended as follows: Delete Policy 2.12 and the "Implementing Actions" pursuant to this policy and substitute the following amendments

1. Policy 2.12. The promotion and management of tourism by the CBJ shall be governed by the following vision for tourism:
2. Policy 2.12.1 The CBJ shall encourage tourism in accordance with the Tourism Management Plan, adopted on [insert date] by the Assembly.
3. Policy 2.12.2 The CBJ shall re-confirm the Tourism Management Plan including any amendments consistent with the vision and objectives for tourism, annually, based on the recommendations of the Juneau Tourism Partnership and the CBJ staff.

Motivation of Nature Tourism

In the following essay through a behavioural perspective, which means not considering external factors, we try to understand why nature tourism is one of the fastest growing segments of world tourism. To understand why this is happening is to comprehend the intrinsic motivation "nature tourists" have to pursue this type of tourism. To recognize this motivation we must search for clues in the theories of travel motivation proposed throughout the travel research literature, and try to see if these diverse theories can actually help us identify the motivation of nature tourists and hence the growth of this tourism segment. The following essay is able to draw from several authors and their theories important conclusion on whether the models or frameworks presented can be useful to understand nature tourism and if so conclude why they are valuable. We firstly define what nature tourism is and from there we review several travel motivation theories that are applicable to this type of tourism.

To know what nature tourism is we must understand a broader classification of tourism that includes nature tourism, and that is alternative tourism. "Alternative tourism can be broadly defined as forms of tourism that set out to be consistent with natural, social and community values and which allow both hosts and guests to enjoy positive and worthwhile interaction and shared experiences".

Newsome, Moore & Dowling, 2002). Under alternative tourism we can see the presence of natural, cultural, event and other types of tourism. Nature tourism, called by Newsome & et al. (2002) "natural area tourism", is in short "tourism in natural settings".

The proposed classification of Newsome, Moore and Dowling (2002) and theirconception of nature tourism is confirmed by Ceballos-Lascuráin (1996) when he defines it as "all tourism directly dependent on the use of natural resources in a relatively undeveloped state, including scenery, topography, water features, vegetation and wildlife."

Newsome, Moore & Dowling (2002) include under nature tourism: adventure, nature- based, wildlife and Eco-tourism. McKerchner (1998) expands the scope of nature tourism including: adventure tourism, Eco-tourism, alternative tourism, educational tourism, anti-tourism, sustainable tourism, responsible tourism and many other forms of outdoor-oriented, non-mass tourism. These two views of what nature tourism includes and overlap, agree, but also contradict themselves. To better understand, and conclude, what nature tourism is (for the purpose of this essay) we must understand the three relations that can occur between the natural setting and the visitor which are: in, about and for the environment. So any tourism based in a natural setting and experienced in, about or for the environment will be considered 'nature tourism'.

Tourist motivation can be defined "as the global integrating network of biological and cultural forces which gives value and direction to travel choices, behaviour and experience". The general motives underlined by research of why nature tourism is the fastest growing segment internationally in tourism are: widespread changing environmental attitude, development of environmental education, development of environmental mass media. Pearce, Morrison and Rutledge (1998) present ten trends which represent important issues of content in describing tourist motives, we can mention four which are related to nature tourism motivation: motive to experience the environment, motive to rest and relax in pleasant settings, motive to pursue special interests and skills (scuba- diving, fishing), and motive to be healthy and fit.

These motives are good starting points to discuss motivation of nature tourism, but some appear to be just social changes or reasons that have affected in some way the motives of the tourist. These motives do not give us clues in how to identify human motivation towards travel, for that reason it cannot be applied to further studies. So it is necessary to undertake an analysis of travel motivation theories.

When assessing a theory of tourist motivation and deciding if it is good for our purpose we must identify seven requirements: it functions as a true theory, it appeals to different users, it is easy to communicate, it suggests ways to measure motivation, it allows for many motives, it is dynamic and, it accounts for intrinsic and extrinsic motivation. This essay will not review all theories of motivation and afterwards decide if they are pertinent to our purpose, which is to understand the motivation of nature tourism. The scope of this essay will only include theories, which have been reviewed and might have relevance to our purpose. In the reviewing process of motivation theories applied to nature tourism we searched for the seven requirements proposed by Pearce, Morrison and Rutledge (1998), and also took into consideration if they were applicable to understand nature tourism motivation.

People who live in cities, for example, are motivated to travel as tourists to wilderness areas because they need to escape from an artificial, monotonous environment. Gray's travel-motivation theory, although an oversimplification of motivation as noted by Mansfeld (1992), gives us two motives which can help explain why people go to natural settings. The first motive is the desire to go from a known to an unknown place, called in Gray's theory 'wanderlust'.

Secondly, a place "which can provide the traveller with specific facilities that do not exist in his or her own place of residence", referred in Gray's theory as 'sunlust'. It appears that the wanderlust-sunlust motives do help us understand why nature tourists search for settings which are different from the city-work-home routine and that enable the nature tourist to participate in activities in unknown territory and that are possible in those natural settings and not at home.

The problem with this theory is that it "represents a confusion between person-specific motivations and resort-specific attributes". For this same reason we will not consider 'Push & Pull' factors as relevant to the study of motivation. For this reason Gray's model only partially might help us understand what motivates a person to participate in nature tourism. Several other theories such as Crompton's nine motives and Iso-Ahola personal-interpersonal motives also work under these 'Push and Pull' factors which means that they focus not only in the intrinsic motivation to travel to natural settings, but also in the characteristics and benefits these settings might appear to offer (pull factors) to satisfy a need. For this reason of not focusing purely on the motivation of tourists, we will not consider them relevant to understand nature tourism motivation.

An interesting finding, while not considered a theory, is the one by Krippendorf after analyzing eight theories of travel motivation found in the literature on tourism. Through his research he saw a common place in these theories. "Firstly, travel is motivated by 'going away from' rather than 'going towards' something; secondly travellers' motives and behaviour are markedly self-oriented". So it seems that the pull factors are not so important, hence the benefits offered by the natural settings and their operators are of second importance in deciding to travel. There is more power in the intrinsic motive of self-indulgence and personal care, physically and psychologically, and by the so called 'escape' motive, than by pull factors considered in the mentioned motivation theories. So if this 'Push and Pull' approach does not succeed in understanding motivation maybe we can try another approach, for example focusing in factors that influence motivation such as 'needs'. Pearce presents a hierarchy of travel motives based on

Maslow's theory of motivation combined with the idea of a career ladder. "The career ladder emphasizes that people have a range of motives for seeking out holiday experiences". The travel career ladder with its different levels allows for many motives, it is dynamic and to sum up it covers the seven requirements presented before. On the other hand analyzing the different levels, especially the relationship needs, self-esteem/development needs, and fulfillment needs presents possible clues to understand the motivation of nature tourism.

By comparing the needs described in different levels of the career ladder such as 'need for achievement', for example, and then consider nature tourism activities like hiking, tramping and mountaineering where the tourist proves its competence and if successful achieves a goal, it can be concluded that the travel career ladder is a helpful theory to understand nature tourism motivation. Another comparison can be drawn from the self- esteem needs level. The "need for mastery, control and competence" can be a motivation for a nature tourism activity such as scuba diving. Where mastery is required to undergo the activity successfully and safely, as well as competence, and control is basic in case of extreme scenarios underwater conditions. So can the 'Travel Career Ladder' be the most appropriate theory to understand nature tourism motivation? If we consider the vast use of Maslow's Theory and sometimes overestimated usefulness considering it only concentrates in needs as the only driving forces to understand motivation, as well as its origin from a study of neurotic people, the answer is no. "Maslow's theory of needs largely ignores more recent developments in motivation theory" and only concentrates on needs it is a work considered a partial theory, which "tend[s] to concentrate in one particular aspect of motivation".

Travel motivation cannot be understood by concentrating on one of the factors as mentioned before in the case of needs. It requires a complete knowledge of "the processes whereby these needs are transformed into motivated behaviour and, in particular, of the way in which people's expectations give motivated behaviour its direction". Witt and Wright (1992) present a very complete and interesting "Expectancy Theory" applied to tourist motivation, based on Vroom's theory of work motivation. It is a theory that finally is able to include all the concepts involved in the motivation process by creating a theoretical framework. It includes the needs which are important to understand motivation, but also the "decision making involved in choosing whether to go on holiday". Together with this it is able to consider 'push and pull' factors, as well as reasons of travel. In conclusion the expectancy theory provides a framework for the analysis of tourist motivation. With all this good points taken into consideration the expectancy theory fails one of the requirements set by Pearce, Morrison and Rutledge (1998) when deciding on a good motivation theory and that requirement is it must be "easy to communicate". This is concluded as well by Witt and Wright when they say "the complexity of expectancy theory also makes it difficult to use the model to predict individual behaviour", and so complex that they suggest using the framework in training travel advisers to ask the proper questions to deliver the information best suited for a customer.

Taking into account the positive attributes of this framework, as well as the negative, let us use the framework to understand nature tourism motivation. Vroom proposes two equations; the first can be used to understand the motivation of travel or not to travel and the second formula to know why a tourist has chosen a certain destination. For our purpose we will concentrate on the first equation, which states that an individual's behaviour is determined by his/her belief that the attractiveness and valence of an outcome (a type of holiday taken) is useful to attain another outcome (e.g.., relaxation, spiritual growth, knowledge) with greater attractiveness and valence. In other words the need of a person will be searched for depending on the value attached to that need, maybe Maslow's hierarchy of needs is useful here, and its attractiveness, through the lived experience of the instrumental outcome considered as a chosen holiday. The belief that going to a natural setting to experience the environment is seen as an outcome with certain intrinsic value and attractiveness, but above all useful (instrumental) to attain physical and psychological recovery from stress. This framework includes important variables to understand motivation: needs, values, and beliefs. The equation is also able to tell us that a tourist to natural setting does not go only to have an encounter with nature, but also to achieve a further self-indulgent goal. Vroom's Expectancy Theory has proven its value, but there is another interesting concept to consider such as intention influencing behaviour, that according to Ajzen and Fishbein (1980) is influenced by attitudes and subjective norms. This model was called the 'Theory of Reasoned Action'. Ten years later they updated their model including 'perceived behavioral control' as another element influencing intention, calling this new model 'Theory of Planned Behaviour'. According to this theory changing beliefs will produce a change in behaviour, but this might not be enough if attitudes and/or subjective norms do not change. Attitudes "can be viewed as enduring general evaluations of people".

Subjective norms are what we expect other people will think of us if we carried out a certain action, in other words social pressure. The model states that beliefs influence attitudes and the perception of subjective norms, at the same time these attitudes and subjective norms influence intention, and intention determines behaviour.

How does this model become useful to understand nature tourism motivation? It becomes relevant and useful if we relate it to the New Environmental Paradigm and also to the general motives presented at the beginning of essay of why nature tourism has become so popular. The New Environmental Paradigm presents a new set of beliefs and values, including the desirability of restricting growth, of protecting the integrity of ecosystems, and of securing more harmonious relationships between man and nature. Relating the Theory of Reasoned Action with the New Environmental Paradigm can be a clue to understand how this change of beliefs in society are affecting the motivation of people in their travel habits resulting in a desire to visit natural areas. The general motives presented by Lindberg, Wood and Engeldrum (1998): widespread changing environmental attitude, development of environmental education, and development of environmental mass media, seem more like reasons rather than motives, but are good reasons to understand this shift to a New Environmental Paradigm. If we include this new paradigm as a new set of beliefs rising in our post-modern world, which are influencing, according to Theory of Reasoned Action, the attitudes and subjective norms then we can understand why the intention of practicing nature tourism has become such an important trend worldwide.

Through the combination of the New Environmental Paradigm and the Theory of Reasoned Action we have found a framework that includes several components of how behaviour is constructed together with actual contemporary trends in environmental beliefs. It also succeeds in covering all the requirements set beforehand to consider a theory a good travel motivation theory. For these reasons we can conclude that these combinations of perspectives are useful to understand nature tourism motivation. Another conclusion to this approach of combining the theory and the paradigm can be that motivation, while it is an intrinsic process, when influenced by beliefs and these beliefs are a product of a social shared Environmental Paradigm then motivation becomes a socio-psychological process, influenced by external factors. The revision of different theories under a scheme of requirements to find a proper one, we have come across a needs-oriented theory (Travel Career Ladder), we have disregarded any push and pull factors-based models, interpreted an all-inclusive framework of motivation (Expectancy Theory), and ended with a simple but comprehensive interpretation of the motivation of nature tourism through the complementation of the New Environmental Paradigm and the Theory of Reasoned Action. In conclusion we can say that a proper revision of travel motivation theories can help us understand what motivation is, and what elements must be considered to understand it, and then interpret the different findings to understand the motivation of a certain type of tourist. One important consideration is that when investigating what motivates a person to travel in a certain type of way we must concentrate on finding the intrinsic motivation while not distracting our attention to the "pull factors" of a specific destination. On the other hand we must say, as found while combining the Theory of Reasoned Action and the New Environmental Paradigm, that the trend of nature tourism becoming more popular can be better understood through a socio-psychological perspective, taking into account the influence of external factors, such as a new set of beliefs constructed by our post-modern western society. It is then proved that the behavioral perspective might not be enough and a psycho-sociological perspective gives us a better understanding.

Tourism Marketing

The marketing mix-the 4 Ps-target audience-segmentation-objectives-evaluation. These and other terms are all used in the process of "marketing." In tourism and tourism related industries, success means understanding this process.

This bulletin is designed for those in the tourism industry who may not be completely familiar with marketing or who may simply wish to refresh their basic marketing skills. Covered will be important concepts used in marketing, the relationship of marketing to tourism, and a process for developing a marketing plan for tourism/recreation businesses and/or communities.

It will be impossible to cover in detail all the aspects of marketing within the scope of this bulletin. There are, however, other bulletins in this series that will provide more in-depth information on the different components of a marketing plan.

What is Marketing

People hold a variety of misconceptions about marketing. Most common is its confusion with selling and advertising. Selling and advertising are actually types of promotion which is only a component of marketing.

Marketing involves much more, including product/service development, place (location and distribution), and pricing. It requires information about people, especially those interested in what you have to offer (your "market"), such as what they like, where they buy and how much they spend. Its role is to match the right product or service with the right market or audience. Marketing, as you will see, is an art and a science.

According to the American Marketing Association, marketing is "the process of planning and executing the conception, pricing, promotion, and distribution of ideas, goods, and services to create exchanges that satisfy individual and organizational objectives." Simply stated it is creating and promoting a product (ideas, goods or services) that satisfies a customer's need or desire and is available at a desirable price and place. Modern marketing is a way of doing business, heavily based on the "marketing concept" which holds that businesses and organizations should:

(1) design their products/services to meet customer needs and wants;

(2) focus on those people most likely to buy their product rather than the entire mass market; and

(3) develop marketing efforts that fit into their overall business objectives.

By adopting this concept you not only provide your customers with better products, you will avoid wasting valuable time and money developing and promoting a product or service nobody wants.

Recreation and Tourism Marketing

Earlier it was mentioned that a product can be "ideas, goods, or services." Since tourism is primarily a service based industry, the principal products provided by recreation/tourism (R/T) businesses are recreational experiences and hospitality. These are intangible products and more difficult to market than tangible products such as automobiles. The intangible nature of services makes quality control difficult but crucial. It also makes it more difficult for potential customers to evaluate and compare service offerings. In addition, instead of moving the product to the customer, the customer must travel to the product (area/community). Travel is a significant portion of the time and money spent in association with recreational and tourism experiences and is a major factor in people's decisions on whether or not to visit your business or community.

As an industry, tourism has many components comprising the overall "travel experience." Along with transportation, it includes such things as accommodations, food and beverage services, shops, entertainment, aesthetics and special events. It is rare for one business to provide the variety of activities or facilities tourists need or desire. This adds to the difficulty of maintaining and controlling the quality of the experience. To overcome this hurdle, tourism related businesses, agencies, and organizations need to work together to package and promote tourism opportunities in their areas and align their efforts to assure consistency in product quality.

The Marketing Plan

One of the most important steps a business or community can take to improve the effectiveness and efficiency of their marketing efforts is to develop a written marketing plan. This plan will guide their marketing decisions and assist them in allocating marketing resources such as money and personnel time. The plan should include:

(1) the overall business objectives—what you want to accomplish;

(2) an assessment of the market environment—what factors may affect your marketing efforts;

(3) a business/community profile—what resources are available,

(4) market identification (segmentation)—the specific groups or clientele most interested in your product;

(5) the marketing objectives for each segment;

(6) the marketing strategies (or mixes) for different markets you target—the best combination of the 4 Ps (product, price, place, promotion) for each segment;

(7) an implementation plan—how to "make it work;"

(8) the marketing budget-how much you have to spend; and

(9) a method for evaluation and change.

A framework which can be used to develop a marketing plan. Each component will be briefly discussed in the remainder of the bulletin. For more information regarding different components of the plan be sure to consult other bulletins in this series.

Overall Business Objectives

Businesses, agencies, and communities should develop overall objectives and regularly monitor their progress. The objectives should provide guidance for all decisions including finances, personnel and marketing. They should be quantitative and measurable statements of what the business or community wants to accomplish over a specified period of time. Business objectives are often stated in terms of sales, profits, market shares and/or occupancy rates. Communities frequently establish objectives relating to such things as increasing the number of tourists, developing or changing their image, facility and activity development, cooperation among tourism related businesses and increasing length of stay and local expenditures. It is important that the objectives be reasonable given the market conditions and the firm's or organization's resources. Establish a few reasonable objectives instead of a long, unrealistic "wish list." This is especially true for new businesses or communities which do not have much experience in tourism development and/or marketing.

Market Environment Analysis

The next step in developing a marketing plan is to assess the impact of environmental factors (such as economic, social and political) on present and future markets. Changes in these factors can create marketing opportunities as well as problems.

Demographic and Lifestyle Trends

Changing demographics and lifestyles are having a major impact on R/T participation. An assessment of these trends is important to understand how they will likely affect your business or community. Some of the important trends that bear watching:

(1) population growth and movement;

(2) rural community growth compared to metropolitan areas;

(3) number of adult women employed outside the home;

(4) the number of households is growing, especially non family and single parent households, but family size is decreasing;

(5) the impact of two wage earner households on real family income;

(6) the number of retired persons with the financial ability to travel;

(7) better health to an older age; and

(8) continued aging of the population (we are becoming a middle aged society).

Economic Conditions

Overall economic conditions can have significant impacts on recreation and tourism markets. A marketing strategy that is effective during periods of low unemployment rates may have to be significantly adjusted if unemployment increases. Businesses and communities should monitor and assess the likely impact of factors such as unemployment rates, real family income, rate of inflation, credit availability, terms and interest rates. Consideration should also be given to the prices of complementary products, such as lodging, gasoline and recreation equipment.

Laws and Government Actions

As a complex industry, tourism is significantly affected both positively and negatively by laws and by actions of governmental agencies. For instance, rulings on such things as liability issues or decisions regarding building and health codes may change or possibly prevent the construction of a proposed facility. If a public facility changes the prices of its services, this could affect the service offerings of associated private businesses. These actions may have both positive and negative effects on the marketing efforts of the business and community. To avoid wasting valuable resources it is important that R/T businesses, agencies, and communities continually monitor and evaluate governmental actions.

Technology

Technological developments are increasing rapidly. New recreation products, such as all-terrain vehicles and wind surfers, provide new ways for people to satisfy their recreational preferences. New production technologies and materials offer recreation and tourism businesses ways to reduce costs and improve the quality of their products/services. Advances in telecommunications have and will continue to create new promotional opportunities. Technological innovations, in relation to jobs and the home, have resulted in increased leisure time for many people.

Competition

Businesses and communities must identify and analyze existing and potential competitors. The objective of the analysis is to determine the strengths and weaknesses of the competition's marketing strategies. The analysis should include the competition's:

(1) product/service features and quality;

(2) location relative to different geographic markets;

(3) promotional themes and messages;

(4) prices; and

(5) type of customer they are attracting.

Business and Community Profiles

Too many communities attempt to market themselves as tourist destinations without accurate information about their resources (facilities, services, staff), image (projected vs. Actual), and how well their customers are satisfied. Without this information, it is difficult to make other decisions in the planning process. Included should be such things as recreational and entertainment facilities, cultural and historic sites, overnight accommodations, restaurants, shopping opportunities, special events and activities, staff size, and transportation. Each item of the "inventory" should also be assessed in terms of quality and availability.

Market Segmentation (Identification)

Recreation and tourism businesses and communities often make the mistake of attempting to be all things to all people. It is difficult, and risky, to develop marketing strategies for the mass market.

Strategies designed for the "average" customer often result in unappealing products, prices, and promotional messages. For example, it would be difficult to develop a campground that would be equally attractive to recreational vehicle campers and backpackers or promote a property to serve both snow mobilers and nature oriented cross country skiers.

Marketing is strongly based on market segmentation and target marketing. Market segmentation is the process of:

(1) taking existing and/or potential customers/visitors (market) and categorizing them into groups with similar preferences referred to as "market segments;"

(2) selecting the most promising segments as "target markets;" and

(3) designing "marketing mixes," or strategies (combination of the 4 Ps), which satisfy the special needs, desires and behaviour of the target markets.

There is no unique or best way to segment markets, but ways in which customers can be grouped are:

(1) location of residence—instate, out-of-state, local;

(2) demographics—age, income, family status, education;

(3) equipment ownership/use—RV's, sailboats, canoes, tents, snowmobiles;

(4) important product attributes—price, quality, quantity; and

(5) lifestyle attributes—activities, interests, opinions.

To be useful, the segment identification process should result in segments that suggest marketing efforts that will be effective in attracting them and at least one segment large enough to justify specialized marketing efforts. After segments have been identified, the business or community must select the "target markets," those segments which offer them the greatest opportunity. When determining target markets, consideration should be given to:

(1) existing and future sales potential of each segment;

(2) the amount and strength of competition for each segment;

(3) the ability to offer a marketing mix which will be successful in attracting each segment;

(4) the cost of servicing each segment; and

(5) each segment's contribution to accomplishing overall business/community objectives. It is often wiser to target smaller segments that are presently not being served, or served inadequately, than to go after larger segments for which there is a great deal of competition.

Marketing Objectives for each Segment

Marketing objectives which contribute to the accomplishment of the overall business objectives should be established for each target market. Objectives serve a number of functions including:

(1) guidance for developing marketing mixes for different target markets;

(2) information for allocating the marketing budget between target markets;

(3) a basis for objectively evaluating the effectiveness of the marketing mixes (setting standards); and

(4) a framework for integrating the different marketing mixes into the overall marketing plan.

The target market objectives should:

(1) be expressed in quantitative terms;

(2) be measurable;

(3) specify the target market; and

(4) indicate the time period in which the objective is to be accomplished.

For example, increase the number of overnight stays by people from the Chicago market over the next two years by five percent.

Remember, rank objectives by priority and carefully evaluate them to ensure that they are reasonable given the strength of the competition and resources available for marketing.

Marketing Strategy (Mix)

The marketing strategy, or mix, should be viewed as a package of offerings designed to attract and serve the customer or visitor. Recreation and tourism businesses and communities should develop both external and internal marketing mixes for different target markets.

External Mix

The external marketing mix includes product/service, price, place/location, and promotion.

Product

Earlier we said the principal products that recreation and tourism businesses provide are recreational experiences and hospitality. The factors that create a quality recreational experience often differ among people. A quality experience for one skier might include an uncrowded, steep slope. To another it might be a good restaurant and a chance to socialize. Decisions on what facilities, programs and services to provide should be based on the needs and desires of the target market(s). They should not be based on the preferences of the owner/manager or necessarily on what the competition is providing.

Recognize that a recreational/tourism experience includes five elements: trip planning and anticipation; travel to the site/area; the experience at the site; travel back home; and recollection. Businesses should look for ways to enhance the quality of the overall experience during all phases of the trip. This could be accomplished by providing trip planning packages which include maps, attractions en route and on site, and information regarding lodging, food and quality souvenirs and mementos.

Recreation and tourism businesses should also view their service/product in generic terms. Thinking of products/services in this manner helps focus more attention on the experiences desired by customers and also the facilities, programs and services that will produce those experiences. For example, campgrounds are the business of providing recreational "lodging" not just campsites to park an RV or set up a tent. Marinas should provide recreational "boating" experiences, not just slippage.

Location and Accessibility—Place

Too many tourism businesses and communities fail to recognize their role in improving travel to and from their areas. They focus instead on servicing the customer once they arrive at the site/community. A bad experience getting to or leaving an R/T site can adversely affect a person's travel experience. Ways to help prevent this include:

(1) providing directions and maps;

(2) providing estimates of travel time and distances from different market areas;

(3) recommending direct and scenic travel routes;

(4) identifying attractions and support facilities along different travel routes; and

(5) informing potential customers of alternative travel methods to the area such as airlines and railroads.

Potential businesses should also carefully assess alternative locations for:

(1) distance and accessibility to target markets;
(2) location of competitors with respect to target markets;
(3) modes of travel serving the area; and
(4) other attractions and activities that might induce travel to the area.

Pricing Price is one of the most important and visible elements of the marketing mix. When setting prices it is important to take into consideration all of the following:

(1) business and target market objectives;
(2) the full cost of producing, delivering and promoting the product;
(3) the willingness of the target market to pay for the product or service you provide;
(4) prices charged by competitors offering a similar product/service to the same target market(s);
(5) the availability and prices of substitute products/services;
(6) the economic climate (local and national); and
(7) the possibility of stimulating high profit products/services (such as boats) by offering related services (such as maintenance) at or below cost.

When establishing prices, R/T businesses should give attention to pricing strategies which may encourage off season and non-peak period sales, longer stays, group business, and the sale of package plans (combination of room, meals, and recreational facilities). For additional information on pricing, see Extension bulletin E-1999.

Promotion

Promotion provides target audiences with accurate and timely information to help them decide whether to visit your community or business. The information should be of importance and practical use to the potential or existing visitor and also accurate. Misrepresentation often leads to dissatisfied customers and poor recommendations. Don't make claims you cannot live up to. Developing a promotional campaign is not a science with hard and fast rules. Making decisions regarding which type or combination of promotion types to use (personal selling, advertising, sales promotions, or publicity) is not always easy. If, however, you follow a logical process and do the necessary research, chances for success will be improved. It will be necessary to make decisions regarding:

(1) Target audience—the group you are aiming at;

(2) Image—that which your community or business wants to create or reinforce;

(3) Objectives—those of the promotional campaign;

(4) Budget—the amount of money available for your promotion;

(5) Timing—when and how often should your promotions appear;

(6) Media—which methods (television, radio, newspaper, magazine) will most effectively and efficiently communicate your message to the target audience; and

(7) Evaluation—how can the effectiveness of the promotional campaign be determined.

More detailed information on tourism promotion is contained in Extension bulletins E-1939, E-1957, and E-2005.

Internal Mix

As stated, marketing services such as recreation and tourism differ from marketing tangible products. Recreation and tourism businesses must direct as much attention at marketing to customers on site as they do to attracting them. In this respect, internal marketing is important because dissatisfied customers can effectively cancel out an otherwise effective marketing strategy.

The success of internal marketing is dependent on creating an atmosphere in which employees desire to give good service and sell the business/community to visitors. To create such an atmosphere requires the following four important elements:

(1) Hospitality and Guest Relations—An organization wide emphasis on hospitality and guest relations, including a customer oriented attitude on the part of the owners and

managers as well as the employees. If the owner/manager is not customer sensitive, it is unlikely the lower paid employees will be.

(2) Quality Control—A program which focuses on improving both the technical quality (the standards associated with what the customer receives) and the functional quality (the standards associated with how the customer receives the service). All employees who come into contact with customers should receive hospitality training.

(3) Personal Selling—Training the staff in the selling aspects of the property (business) or community. This also includes rewarding them for their efforts. By being informed about the marketing objectives, and their role in accomplishing those objectives, they can help increase sales.

(4) Employee Morale—Programs and incentives aimed at maintaining employee morale. The incentives can be both monetary and non-monetary.

A customer oriented atmosphere usually results in customers that are more satisfied, do less complaining and are more pleasant to serve. This helps build employee morale, their desire to provide good service and their efficiency.

Marketing Budget

Successful marketing requires that sufficient money and personnel time be made available to implement activities comprising the marketing strategy. A marketing budget is a financial plan which shows the total amount to be spent on marketing during different times of the year and how it is to be allocated among alternative activities. Separate marketing budgets should be developed for each marketing mix strategy. The separate budgets should then be aggregated to develop an overall marketing budget. If the total amount is too great it will be necessary to modify the overall objectives and the target market objectives, narrow down or drop target markets, or adjust marketing mixes. The final budget should be realistic given your objectives. When deciding on a marketing budget, consideration should be given to the job that needs to be done as defined by the objectives. Basing marketing budgets on some percent of sales or what the competition spends usually leads to over spending or under spending. Decisions should also be based on the \costs, projected revenues, and desired profitability of different activities, not just costs alone. Successful marketing activities will generate additional revenues which can be projected based on the marketing objectives (such as increase off season stay by 5%).

Although budgets should be viewed as flexible plans, every effort should be made to adhere to them. Revisions in the budget should only be made after careful consideration of the likely impact of the change on the marketing mix and accomplishment of your objectives.

Implementation

Many well designed marketing plans fail because they are poorly executed. Businesses, agencies, and communities can increase the likelihood of successful implementation if they:

(1) identify specific tasks which must be accomplished;

(2) assign people or departments specific responsibility for different tasks;

(3) provide employees with information on the marketing plan (rationale, objectives, strategies);

(4) develop time lines and deadlines;

(5) adhere as much as possible to the budget; and

(6) regularly monitor and evaluate progress.

Evaluation

It is important that marketing efforts be continually evaluated. This will improve the effectiveness of marketing strategies by quickly identifying differences between actual results and expected performance and determining likely reasons for the success or failure to realize objectives.

A framework for evaluation would include:

(1) determining which elements of the different marketing mixes are most important to evaluate.——It is rarely possible or cost effective to evaluate all elements;

(2) establishing performance standards to compare against

actual results.—Marketing objectives, if properly formulated, should serve as performance standards;

(3) development of formal and informal methods for collecting data on actual results.—There are many ways different elements of the marketing mix can be evaluated. For example, promotions can be evaluated with money off coupons. Special information request forms, telephone numbers to call or post office box numbers to write to can identify the area the request is coming from. Also, formal (written) and informal (face-to-face) surveys can be used to determine the promotional material the customer used in planning the trip;

(4) comparison of results with objectives;

(5) determination of needed change(s).

Conclusion

Customer satisfaction in tourism is greatly influenced by the way in which the service (hospitality) is delivered and the physical appearance and personality of the business. It is critical that these elements be communicated in the best possible manner to convince people to come and experience what your business or community has to offer.

Equally important is the ability to generate repeat business because of your efforts. Thus, marketing becomes the method to reach potential visitors. It is a vital part of tourism management and can be done effectively and well, with sophistication and tact, or it can be done poorly in a loud, crass and intrusive manner. Hopefully, this bulletin has given you the basics for the former rather than the latter. Remember that to do an effective job at marketing:

(1) adopt a strong customer orientation which includes regular research and assessment of their needs, wants and attitudes;

(2) allocate sufficient resources and time to marketing;

(3) assign formal responsibility for marketing to one person or department; and

(4) develop and regularly update a marketing plan.

Information Supply in Tourism Management

Operators in tourism management, compared to other management sectors, are confronted with a vast field of complex aims, requiring different plans of action. The special working requirements of the services sector are a result of its business peculiarities. Problems instrategic, and frequently operational planning, are characterized by their complexity, often being intermingled, non-transparent, individualistically dynamic and requiring the achievement of multiple goals. The vast amount of information or complex weighting of the different sectors can present an insurmountable problem for human resources. As are sult there are high expectations of decision-makers' trouble-shooting abilities.

In order to solve complex problems, decision-makers need to have a factual knowledge of the industry (declarative knowledge) and the methodology used (procedural knowledge). The wealth of knowledge is drawn from two pools; that obtained from the "storage" of already existing experiences, and by generating knowledge in the respective field. Com-bining these two pools creates an arena for problem solving.

Declarative Knowledge – Decision Basis in Tourism Planning

Currently, information gains more and more importance, leading legitimately to the development of a fourth economic sector – the information sector. Information also plays a vital role in tourism for entrepreneurs and managers who spend the whole day involved in information processing. In the tourism industry there is no lack of market research data, on the contrary, there is a rather uncontrolled growth of various data sources, each having different survey purposes and survey designs. Tourism surveys of national and international market research institutes are published in ever shorter intervals and the level of itemization of market data increases rapidly. Information collected by these means has indicated data which can be organized into the following groups:

1. Information on markets and environment,
2. Information on customer behaviour,
3. Information on competition in the industry, and

4. Internal information for executive boards.

The first three information groups are predominantly non-discretionary from a manager's point of view as the information can very rarely be directly influenced by an individual company. Information from these groups are similar in nature and scope for most sectors represented in the tourism industry (hotel trade, restaurant trade, tour operators, travel agents, common carriers, pressure groups, etc.). In the fourth group however, there is a larger scope for variety. Due to high costs for primary market research many tourism managers abandon market research in general. Even the larger businesses and tourism organizations lack market research departments and employees rarely work exclusively on market research items. This results again in an inconsistent development of marketing aims and strategies, as businesses as often as not grope in the dark for their direction.

In Europe the most frequent or highly recognized of the commissioned tourism studies are either publicly financed, directly by national or local authorities, or indirectly by government agencies. This method of procuring market research, is important and often a condition for its development, as the expensive primary studies cannot be financed by the numerous small or medium-scale businesses. The resulting obligation to pass on information, created by the above mentioned research financing, has lead to a wider search-inregional tourism organizations, and other bodies representing tourism-to find means of successfully sharing and communicating information.

Traditional data resources in tourism market research are reports, records and statistics which may be presented either in printed format or are electronically driven (CD-ROM). Computer-based information systems (databases) are currently a rarity, but usually can be found either in connection with the official statistical data of a country or a region or international institutions. The information available by this method is rarely used since it ignores the special information requirements of the end-user (managers), or is simply inaccessible due to high fees, complicated application procedures or is simply not user friendly.

The lack of practical relevance, of these information systems, can be explained by their bias toward representing the economic interest of the sponsors and data collectors and/or by the universal requirements the systems have to meet in the collection, storage and search of statistical data from other industries. Market research results are mainly available in print and they can be obtained either in bookshops, online or directly from the author. From the consumer's perspective this way of passing on secondary information has a number of dis- advantages:

- Due to the complex design of market research reports the surveyed data is not up to date any more.
- Data from different sources cannot be easily compared especially if it has been surveyed for different purposes.
- Information contained in reports is often of limited relevance for the particular problem.
- Presentation of data is either not detailed enough, not significant enough, or supplementary information is missing which prevents a faultless interpretation of results.
- Often only very specific data from a more comprehensive study is required and thus the cost-benefit-ratio becomes unattractive.

There is usually an overabundance of available information leaving managers to cope with determining which is the best source. Often the entrepreneur has to rely on external consultants and market research specialists resulting in additional costs.

Procedural Knowledge – Decision Basis in Tourism Planning

"The big problem with management science models is that managers practically never used them." More than 20 years ago John Little described the discrepancy between the scientific development of planning instruments, models, level of itemization and the fact that, when available, the knowledge gathered is rarely put into practice. This is caused by the numerous, often poorly documented assumptions of model architects, which was denoted as model plutonism by Hans Albert. As a response to this problem Little suggested that the manager is included in the model. He postulated in his article on the Decision Calculus, aniline models with the following features: robustness, ease of control, simplicity, completeness of relevant detail and suitability for communication.

The communication problem is of vital importance in the every day life of managers' daily events. It is still common practice to employ various levels of change rather than continue- ally observe the changes in market share and volume. Many entrepreneurs do not even know terms such as market segmentation or market positioning and they do not regard them as essential. They keep on looking for measures to expand seasonal business but lack knowledge of methods that will measure their success. Corporate planning only takes place if external financing is required and supporting documents have to be submitted to the lender. Heuristic forecasting methods are hardly ever used, accordingly quantitative methods are never used. Models of strategic market plan- ningportfolio analyses and analyses of the lifestyle of a product-employed in other in- dustries are hardly ever used in tourism management. The grounds for the poor employment of methodological processes in tourism management can be divided into two groups; technological development and insufficient training. Issues related to the technological development of existing information processing and transmission systems are:

- Data required for the application of tourism models is either not up-to-date or unsuitable.
- Standard software is not able to support the relatively complex tasks in tourism management.
- Specially developed software is too expensive for single tourism businesses. Issues related to the insufficient training of tourism managers are:
- Managers have little knowledge of existing methods or available data.
- Managers are confronted with various data sources and different results and they do not know how to cope with this situation.
- Managers do not know which data sources and models are suitable.

The Transmission of Market Research Data in the Internet

Due to the vital role of tourism in many countries and regions in Europe a number of programs concerning tourism promotion have been installed. Government and private tourism organizations have been established in order to strengthen a tourism destination. Usually the aim is to increase the added value of a region. The major tasks of these bodies are:

- to provide consumers with information about the destination,
- to coordinate and implement sales promotion measures,
- tourism advertising,
- support in sales and distribution, and
- to coordinate and implement market research projects.

For most of their tasks (except the coordination and implementation of market research projects) these tourism promoting bodies provide efficient methods. The actual effect of the last item mentioned has been lost in the past due to inefficient instruments relating to the transmission and utilization of declarative and procedural knowledge. Now with the development of cheaper hard- and software many tourism organizations are reconsidering their promotion policy.

In almost all industries systems are being developed in order to support investment and marketing planning. Also the tourism industry has de- veloped decision support systems and the most important applications are: (1) systems supporting marketing decisions in national tourism organizations, (2) travel counselling systems for shipping clerks, (3) systems supporting regional planning regarding the optimal selection of locations in which to invest (4) systems providing tourism portfolio analyses, (5) simulation tools for forecasting travel behaviour in certain regions. In Austria in 1982 the Austrian Society of Applied Research in Tourism (ASART) started a project aiming at the development of a marketing information system for the national tourism organization in Austria (Austrian National Tourist Office). The first version of the tourism marketing information system (TourMIS) consisted of a database installed in a host system of the Scientific Computer Centre Vienna and an optimization programme for the advertising budget of the Austrian National Tourist Office. Though the programmes were adapted in 1991 in favour of PC-software, and hence became accessible for a greater number of people (mainly employees of tourism organizations in the federal provinces), the area-wide information supply for top managers in the tourism industry did not begin until 1999 when the internet version was introduced.

Tourism Marketing Information System

The major aim of Tour MIS is an optimal information supply and decision support for the tourism industry. The first step is to provide aniline tourism survey data, as well as evaluation programmes to transform data into precious management information. Tour-MIS predominantly comprises:

1. A database containing tourism market research data (declarative knowledge),
2. Various program modules (method-base, procedural knowledge) converting acknowledged methods/models into simple surfaces, and
3. Various administrative programmes which assist the maintenance of the data- base and track and control the information search behaviour of users.

The internet supports the transport and presentation of animated and unanimated pictures, sound and video recordings and text and numerical data and is expandable. A high- performance SQL-database and a functionally designed user interface for Tour MIS based on hypertext and Perl permits the development of interactive applications.

The programme modules contained in the method-base are developed according to the specific requirements of tourism managers. The internet offers a number of advantages against the old PC-solution. Since changes in the database have immediate worldwide effect the speed of information transmission can be reduced to the availability of the information source. For example, Tour MIS makes the monthly projections of Statistics Austria available within only a few seconds to all regional managers of the Austrian National Tourist Office regardless of whether they are located in New York, Sydney, Tokyo or Madrid. Anybody provided with access to the internet and entitled to use Tour MIS may access data and information, make calculations or simulations send or receive data – without tiresome postal procedures, danger of loss, delays and costs. All these advantages have led to a significan expansion in the number of users.

Conditions for the use of the System

In the beginning Tour MIS was provided with strict access control and used to be only accessible to certain users. In this respect the application did differ from traditional internet offers. However, the present concept is also not an Intranet. Unlike the Intranet which supports internal information management systems Tour MIS is not owned by a certain organization but is open to all authorized tourism organizations, societies, tourism consultants, companies, tourism training centres, pressure groups, etc. in Austria and abroad. By covering the maintenance costs, a consortium of 12 of the most important initiators of market research projects in Austria (Austrian National Tourist Office, nine provincial tour- ism organizations, the two special interest associations for Hotel Trade and Restaurant

Trade of the Federal Chamber of Commerce, Federal Ministry for Economic Affairs and Labour Tourism and Recreational Commerce Section) guarantee the continuous updating of the comprehensive database. Since 2000 this initiative has provided the Austrian tourism industry with free access to overall data and functions (with some exceptions) of Tour MIS. The necessary hardware resources are situated at the Institute for Tourism and Leisure Studies at the University of Economics and Business Administration in Vienna where a major part of the necessary maintenance work is carried out.

The Tour MIS Database

In the beginning Tour MIS contained data that was strongly influenced by the internal interests of its commissioner, the Austrian National Tourist Office. In this respect international tourism statistical data, empirical tourism studies and economic indicators for the most important markets of origin for the Austrian tourism industry have been collected in Tour MIS. The PC-version, developed in the early nineties, contained more than 10,000 time series. The periodicity of information was generally based on annual data, however the most significant time series have also

the average duration of stay, the seasonality, market shares, guest-mix structure, and, in connection with the capacity statistics, the occupancy rate. Tour MIS presently offers official tourism statistics only at the provincial basis which nevertheless requires maintenance work of 11,700 data sets per month. The necessary data transfer from the host system of Statistic Austria (ISIS) to Tour MIS takes place automatically each time after the arrival of new data segments and in accordance with various maintenance routines.

The information supply of Tour MIS users takes place by means of predominate tables and reports created for the user in real time operations. The content and design of tables or reports plays an important role in the user's perception of the system's usefulness and usability. Only if the information supply meets the users' needs will the system achieve its aim of providing a high-performance usage of market data and improve the information supply in tourism management.

Source Feature Evaluation Period Update Data

Statistic Austria bed nights, arrivals, capacity (suppliers and beds) 50 countries of origin (mar- kets), 13 types of accommodation – for Austria and her 9 provinces since 1960 monthly secondary data in time series format

Austrian Guest Survey 250 variables incl. intention to revisit, guest satisfaction, type of travel, means of transport, duration of stay, travel motive, expenses, selection of accommodation, activities, net income of the household, profession, education, etc. 16 countries of origin (markets) – for Austria and her 9 provinces since 1991 each third year primary data ETC (European Travel Commission) bed nights, arrivals, capacities (beds) 21 countries of origin (markets) – for 33 destinations (countries) in Europe since 1990 annually secondary data in time series format ECT (European Cities' Tourism) bed nights, arrivals, capacities (beds) 21 countries of origin (markets) – for 80 European cities since 1983 annually secondary data in time series format

Number of visitations in Austrian attractions (Austrian National Tourist Office) number of visits for 240 Austrian attractions federal provinces of Austria since 1998 annually secondary data in time series format Austrian Hotel and Restaurant Panel 60 variables incl. net product, fixed and working assets equity and debt capital,, cash flow, profitability-ures, etc. location, size, category and type of business. Since 1982 annually primary data.

- no particular database knowledge is required by the user,
- the data transformations and calculations implemented in the method-base of Tour MIS allow for adequate problem reporting, and
- the user interface refers to a familiar technical terminology.

Especially for the requirements of the managers in the provincial tourism organizations. The table compares the seasonal results of one federal province (Carinthia) with the results of all other federal provinces in Austria.. The comparison with the developments in other (competitive) destinations permits an evaluation of the market share development in Carinthia.

The analysis in indicates for example that Carinthia could defend its position regarding the three most important markets (Germany, Netherlands, Italy), shown in the increase of market shares, despite the fact that Carinthia experienced a severe loss in bed-nights. On the other hand an apparent success regarding the increased demand of American guests (+ 7,7%) has to be put into perspective since the other federal provinces outperformed Carinthia in this segment. Due to the comparative analysis and a simple and informative presentation of the statistics (using sorting features and different colors to distinguish between market share gains (green) and losses (red)) the data material is upgraded. The analysis presented in may be used for historical or current data, for each Austrian province, based either on arrivals or bednights for each of the 13 different accommodation types.

Competitive Analysis for Austrian Regions

The opportunities for implementing tools which use official tourism statistics for bench-marking analyses, the implementation of early warning systems and forecasting tourism trends is obvious. Due to the refinancing interests of data collection authorities and the lack of financial resources in the tourism industry, however, the data analysis for smaller tourism regions or report communities has been prevented in the past. This factor must be regretted since it can be assumed that the evaluation of key success factors in tourism mar- keting will significantly improve when they are measured in smaller regional units. Also tourism managers, especially those operating on a regional level, usually have only very little influence in the organization of nationwide surveys. Therefore, many of the statistical series are based on administrative regions that are not always congruent with actual regional use and by tourists and subsequent flows.

Number of Visitations in Austrian Attractions

The collection of statistical data on leisure-time activities and especially the measurement of visitor arrivals in attractions is a rather complex project. It is rarely executed internationally on a systematic or continuous basis. The major problems lie in the delimitation of the study object and the methods of measurement. Since the early 90's the Austrian National Tourist Office has collected and distributed information on the visitation numbers in Austrian attractions. In close collaboration with the nine provincial tourism organizations a list of 240 Austrian attractions is checked for completeness and updated on an annual basis.

Number of Visitations in Austrian Attractions

Since 2001 this maintenance procedure is carried out online in Tour MIS. Here the market research specialists at the respective provincial tourism organizations enter their information into the system. Due to the newness of the database the reporting facilities are still very limited. The present tables either provide simple time series for a single attraction or list all attractions for one or more federal province(s) arranged according to frequency of visits.

Austrian Guest Survey

Since 1988 alternating each third year a comprehensive visitor survey in Austria has been carried out. The Austrian Guest Survey is one of the most important sources of information in tourism market research. It provides vital information on guest profiles, customer satisfaction, information and booking behaviour, type of travel, destination, means of transport, accommodation, activities, visitor expenditures and other current topics. The Austrian Guest Survey is financed and coordinated by a consortium of authorities responsible for tourism promotion in Austria (Austrian National

Tourist Office and nine provincial tourism organizations), the Chamber of Commerce and the Federal Ministry for Economic Affairs and Labour (Tourism and Recreational Commerce Section). Since the Austrian Guest Survey is a primary study it presents some features which complicate the information diffusion in Tour MIS compared to the above mentioned secondary data sources. The main reasons for these additional difficulties are:

(1) the much wider scope of the study,

(2) the required data analyses are more demanding, and

(3) interpretation possibilities are limited by the sample size and characteristics.

The Austrian Guest Survey has more than 200 features which are partially modified for each survey. Considering the scope of the study and that only descriptive evaluation is possible the Austrian Guest Survey offers more than 1 million findings per survey. Traditional forms of report (market research report, press releases etc.) cover just a small part of the real investigation and evaluation potential. Thus important questions managers would raise remain unanswered although theoretically the answers exist.

Data of primary analyses are available unprocessed (disaggregated data format). Regarding the Austrian Guest Survey there are 10,000 interviews per survey, all of the features being available in quantitative form. However, information processing requires the application of analytical methods ranging from calculating simple mean values to complicated data mining procedures. The necessary methodological knowledge has to be obtained from statistics experts who create costs which, in most cases, cannot be covered by the tourism industry. Therefore, due to a lack of know-how or lacking financial support, many questions managers raise remain unanswered although data actually would be available. Contrary to a census, as found in official statistics, sample surveys do not integrate all elements of the whole picture into the study. The major aim in statistics is to draw reliable conclusions regarding to the totality from a limited number of elements. The previously mentioned evaluation procedures take more effort and interpretation depends on the features of the sample (sample size and sampling technique).

Query – Austrian Guest Survey

To know whether a study result may be regarded reliable requires expert know-how. On the other hand, sometimes, statisticians have not enough technical knowledge to evaluate the fault tolerance for certain problems in the tourism industry. Thus information processing by means of electronic media becomes very interesting for primary surveys. The challenge is to combine expert know-how from two different fields: statistics and tourism. The aim is to create an arena for practitioners allowing them to access all possible evaluations concerning a data item, without considering the necessary procedures of analysis.

Tour MIS offers help in the selection of simple, descriptive evaluation methods. Depending on the level of measurement of the features selected by the user the appropriate evaluation method is applied:

Automatic Selection of Analyzing Methods

In addition the user may select only a certain part of the overall data set for evaluation (i.e. data of a certain province or market). In order to prevent interpretation errors due to unreliability of results, those values based on a small sample are only indicated after informing the user about the problem.

The analysis takes place in real time. Tour MIS provides the facilities to evaluate more than one survey, at the same time offering two alternatives: longitudinal and cross section analyses. The first application informs the tourism manager about changes in the guest behaviour over a specified period of time. Query support is provided by offering only variables surveyed unmodified over the overall selected period of time (i.e. the standard questionnaire programme). The latter application increases the sample size (for 4 surveys more than 45,000 interviews) which makes answers to detailed questions possible (assuming a particular time invariance, of course). This function permits for example reliable results about the share of side expenses of Italian guests in the federal province of Salzburg during a particular season.

Comparison of Hotel and Restaurant Groups

The database supports regional planners and tourism managers in their decisions as well as managers in the hospitality industry.

The results of the past 10 years of a project which has been executed by the Austrian Society of Applied Research in Tourism and commissioned by the Austrian Hotel and Restaurant Association situated within the Austrian Federal Chamber of Commerce are presented in Tour MIS. In this project operating data and annual financial statements for hotels and restaurants in Austria are compared on an annual basis. Information collected directly from the businesses with a high level of itemization is supplemented with comprehensive, compressed data stored at cooperative industry related organizations such as the Wirts chafts för derungs institute der Austrian Federal Economic Chamberund Tourism us bank and BÜRGES Förder ungsbank of the Austrian Federal Ministry of Economic Affair and Labour. In connection with the design and evaluation of continually repeated surveys a number of new approaches for the diagnosis and comparison of industry groups are developed. Tour MIS presently provides the following applications:

- Industry information for more than 1,300 hotels and restaurants per year since 1991.
- Various functions supporting key ratio analyses in the hotel and restaurant industry.
- The chance for hotel and restaurant managers to participate online in the most significant hotel and restaurant panel survey in Austria.

Information about more than 50 different key ratios is provided in the form of arithmetic mean and median values for 30 distinguished industry groups. Within the industry groups additional evaluations for businesses of excellent profitability (best practice enter- prises) are available.

For the hotel and restaurant panel database Tour MIS users are provided with the following query and analyzing facilities:

- Evaluation of a key ratio for all industry groups referring to a certain year.
- Comparison of all key ratios for a particular industry group.
- Development of a key ratio uncovering the main industry developments.

- Benchmarking analysis for a particular hotel or restaurant (only provided when managers are actively participating in the study).

The quality of information based on the results of the survey is strongly influenced by the number of participating businesses. Due to the chance for interaction in the internet the first results may be obtained straight after entering business data. In this context the problem of how to prevent participants from entering incorrect data occurs. Tour MIS offers a number of plausibility controls during data entry and records data in a second, temporary database. At regular intervals experts determine which records are qualified to be stored in the general database.

Analysis of the user Behaviour of Tour MIS

How do we know that we have successfully implemented a system? Researchers have not really agreed on an indicator for successful implementation. One appealing approach is a cost-benefit study. In this evaluation, one totals the costs of developing a system and compares them with the benefits resulting form the system. In theory, this sounds like a good indicator of success, but in practice it is difficult to provide meaningful estimates. Obtaining the cost side of the ratio is not too much of a problem if adequate records are kept during the development of the system. However, an evaluation of the benefits of a computer-based information system is difficult. How can the value of improved information processing be measured? With transactions processing and some operational control systems, it is usually possible to show tangible savings. For example, many transactions systems have resulted in increased productivity in processing paperwork without a proportional increase in cost. Operational control systems, such as those used to control inventories in large hotels and restaurants, may reduce inventory balances, saving storage and investment costs while maintaining existing service levels.

For systems that aid a decision maker, it is much more difficult to estimate the benefits.

For a marketing information system, like Tour MIS, use of the system is voluntary. A manager or other user receives a report but does not have to use the information on it or

1. Council of the European Union, Council Directive 95/97/EEC of 23 November 1995 on the collection of statistical information in the field of tourism, Official Journal. L291 of 6 December 1995, p. 1.
2. Commission of the European Communities Report to the Council, the European Parliament, the

Economic and Social Committee and the Committee of Regions on the Application of the Directive of the Council 95/97/EEC on the compilation of statistical data in the field of tourism, 17 January 2001, p. 3 even read the report. In particular systems that provide aniline retrieval of information from a database can be classified as voluntary since the use of such a system is frequently at the discretion of the user. For this type of system where use is voluntary, it is generally accepted that high levels of use is a sign of successful implementation. In this case the economic or personal success of its users is indirectly measured by the frequency of usage. Several authors have shown that the frequency of usage is determined by the perceived usefulness (textual component) and the ease of use (technical component).

The acceptance of Tour MIS can be determined by means of constantly updated and aniline available access statistics. Contrary to other internet applications the accesses to websites is not counted but the number of virtually answered queries is. Results of the Tour MIS statistics are therefore not influenced by website characteristics (number of graphics or distortions due to the application of window techniques), but do represent the 'genuine user acceptance'. In addition, the comprehensive protocol system permits the analysis of que- ries broken down into various user groups, information sources and the type of query.

The community of Tour MIS users has continually developed. In 1998 there were only 50 registered users at the Austrian National Tourist Office and at the end of 2001 more than 1,000 registered Tour MIS users have been counted. The distribution of user groups indicates that Tour MIS is not only favoured by tourism managers (44.6%), but also by employees, students and pupils of education and research institutes (31.6% of all queries) and other non-tourism professionals or private persons (23.8%). The distribution of various user groups is present. The average number of queries per user in 2001 and therefore indicates the frequency of use for a specific Tour MIS user group. The employees of provincial tourism organizations use Tour- MIS most (92 queries per user) due to the comprehensive data material available on the federal provinces. The students, as the largest user group, show a relatively low number due to only temporal interest (for a seminar paper or a diploma thesis they need access to data material only once). The number of accommodation providers and F&B managers using the system is, considering the number of existing businesses, very low. A reason for this is probably that the most interesting information source for this user group (the Austrian hotel and restaurant panel database) is a relatively new data set that is simply not known by the managers. Overall, 34.538 queries have been processed in 2001, signifying an increase of 35.5% in comparison to the previous year (25,492 queries).

About half of all queries are made regarding the official tourism statistics in Austria. The industry appears to be very interested in the development of the major markets of origin and accommodation types in the federal provinces (on average approx. 50 queries per day). Regarding the official statistics for Austria most queries are made in connection with in- formation concerning monthly statistics (20% of all queries). The international data sources ECT and ETC gained 18.7% respectively and they rank behind the official Austrian statistics. The significant increase of queries regarding these two international data sources as well as the tendency towards English queries, however, indicate a growing international interest in Tour MIS.

The assessment of demand of information certainly needs a more detailed investigation than simply monitoring the current use of market research resources. However, in Tour- MIS 'demand of information' not only refers to the principal (statistical) sources, but also to the sort of data transformations (analysis) and formats of automatically generated reports available to the users. The functional characteristics and the design of the system have always been developed in close collaboration with the affected managers. For instance, concerning the development of the decision support tools part of the international data sources in the system, the developers have met more than 20 times in form of working group meetings and seminars with representatives (CEOs and research directors) of European Cities Tourism and the European Travel Commission. The involvement of the managers in the design and operation of the information system resulted in favourable user attitudes and perceptions of the information system and led to higher levels of use. In the be- ginning only a few members were able and willing to actively contribute to this project by entering their data on a regular basis. Today, more than 100 managers working in different tourism destination marketing organizations, based in more than 30 different European countries, and speaking more than 15 different languages, are obviously convinced by the significance of the project and the value of the system as they regularly and voluntarily enter their data into the system.

Conclusions

Generally speaking tourism managers benefit from access to the internet in two ways: the internet provides the opportunity to communicate and serves as a platform for new distribution channels. The present article does not deal with new distribution channels and new booking systems in the tourism industry. This undoubtedly important topic has been discussed in an number of publications and symposia. The present article introduced Tour MIS, an aniline accessible decision support tool for tourism and hospitality management which has been successfully used by more than 1,000 users for three years. According to Ritchie and Ritchie for the development of an industry supported destination marketing information system, information must be both generally accessible and widely advertised so that managers are aware of the benefits it offers. In lieu of a more preferable cost-benefit analysis, the success of Tour MIS was analyzed by studying actual system use observed from various log files generated by the system. The merits of this form of evaluation lie in the objectivity of the findings, the cost-effective procedure, and the comparability of the estimates when the analysis are performed on a regular basis.

The major reason for the poor application of management science models and methodologies in tourism management is the insufficient education of practitioners and the inadequacy of problem solving features of standard software solutions. The development of simple, affordable (shareware) programs, downloadable for every tourism manager, is the first step into a new era of dialogue between research and practice. Within a short time, for internal diagnosis, forecasts and simulations on the net there will be high-performance computer languages available which are now being developed by major international soft- ware producers.

Technological progress will also offer benefits for the electronic transmission of tourism market research data. Interdisciplinary research projects will be challenged with tourism research, research in statistics and commercial information technology. For example there are still a number of problems to be solved in order to be able to jointly use ecoscopic and demoscopic tourism data within a marketing information system. These combination options require a constant standardization of information sources as well as new approaches towards the methodological processing of data gained from various studies. Another vital research initiative will be the development of information systems about themselves? Optimizing the knowledge presentation of 'service quality in information services' has been neglected in the past. By applying and accepting decision support systems the significance of this field of research will increase. Another important factor will be the role system imminent? Protocol presentations play, which are continually improved. Thus data on the user behaviour offers not only information on necessary improvements in the data processing of tourism market research results, but also on the future focus of tourism market research. The sudden explosion of data and the growing need for information challenges basic re- search as far as data reduction and decision support methods are concerned. Therefore existing concepts for qualitative forecasts and market reaction models and their calibration options in a marketing information system have to be reconsidered. In this respect projects which aim at a systematic and regular compilation of experiences experts made with regard to various technical subjects (i.e. short-term development of singular markets of origin) are considered to be promising. It is their aim to provide an improved evaluation of future market developments and eventually to integrate the findings into the strategic planning of national and regional tourism organizations and businesses. Another necessary development regards already existing data collections and the processing of the

European cities' statistics. In this respect this author has observed many shortcomings relating to the international comparability of the data. The improved communication possibilities provided by the new medium stimulates critical discussions and behavioural learning among all participants. Within European Cities Tourism, among other things, new initiatives to evaluate one city's major competitors have been released due to the managers' increased awareness of the importance of this problem.

The trend towards globalization in research, where the internet plays a vital role, refers also to tourism research. To those critics who refer to the internet as uncontrolled growing, complicated and in its applications too playful, supporters used to point out that one day smart and profitable applications would be found. That is where we stand now. The new areas of responsibility regional and national tourism managers are confronted with today, not only suggest shortcomings in education but also promise new opportunities for the next manager generations to acquire status.

Bibliography

Carl H. : *Internet Distribution of European Travel and Tourism Services*, Research Centre of Bornholm, Denmark, 1999.

Cukier, J. : *Tourism Employment in Bali: Trends and Implications*, London: Thompson, 1996.

Donald E. : *Public Personnel Management: Contexts and Strategies*, Upper Saddle River, NJ: Prentice Hall, 1998.

Douglas C: *Practical Tourism Forecasting*, Oxford, Butterworth Heinemann, 1996.

Eckel, Peter J.: *College & University Foodservice Management Standards*, Westport, AVI Pub. Company, 1985.

Foster, Douglas: *Travel and Tourism Management*, London, Macmillan Educational, 1985.

Ghimire, Krishna: *The Native Tourist*: Mass Tourism within Developing Regions, London, Earthscan, 2001.

Graham M S: *Language of Tourism*, The, Wallingford, CAB International, 1996.

Ireland, Lewis: *Quality Management for Projects and Programs*, Upper Darby, PMI, 1991.

Jennings, Gayle: *Tourism Research*, Chichester, Wiley, 2001.

Karski, A: *Urban Tourism* - A Key to Urban Regeneration?, 1990.

Klein, S. : *Information & Communication Technologies in Tourism*, Springer-Verlag, Wien-New York, 2000.

Kotler, Philip: *Marketing for Hospitality and Tourism*: New Jersey, Prentice-Hall, 1998.

Labarge, Margaret Wade: *Medieval Travellers: The Rich and Restless*, London, Hamish Hamilton, 1982.

Larkham, P J: *Building a New Heritage: Tourism, Culture & Identity in the New Europe*, London, Routledge,1994.

Leivadi, S: *Sociology of Tourism, The: Theoretical And Empirical Investigations,* London, Retailed, 1996.

Lewis, Robert C.: *Cases in Hospitality Marketing and Management,* New York, John Wiley, 1997.

Lucas, Rosemary E.: *Managing Employee Relations in the Hotel and Catering Industry,* London, Cassell, 1995.

Morrell, J. : *Employment in Tourism,* London: British Tourist Authority, 1985.

Nancy N.: *Choosing a Career in Hotels, Motels, and Resorts,* New York, Rosen Pub. Group, 1997.

Pearce, Douglas: *Tourism Today: A Geographical Analysis,* Harlow, Longman, 1995.

Peters, M: *International Tourism,* London, Hutchinson, 1969.

Richards, G. : *Tourism in Central and Eastern Europe: Educating for Quality,* Tilberg, Tilberg University Press, 1996.

Rocco, M.: *An Introduction to Hospitality Today,* Orlando, Educational Institute, 1998.

Rosenzweig, J. E.: *Organisation and Management,* New York, McGraw Hill International, 1963.

Scottish Tourist Board: *Visitor Attractions: A Development Guide,* Edinburgh, Scottish Tourist Board, 1991.

Sharma Sunil : *Planning and Development of Tourism and Hospitality,* Rajat Pub, Delhi, 2007.

Slinn, Judy A: *Tourism: Management of Facilities,* London, Pitman: M & E, 1993.

Smith, G. : *International Tourism and Hospitality Careers through Education and Training,* CHRIE Annual Conference, Washington DC, 1996.

Swarbrooke, J.: *Marketing Tourism, Hospitality and Leisure in Europe,* London, International Thomson Business Press, 1996.

Thomas, F.: *Introduction to Management in the Hospitality Industry,* New York, Wiley, 1995.

Vallette, J.: *The International Trade in Wastes: A Greenpeace Inventory,* Washington, Greenpeace, 1989.

Walden, Richard: *Genetic Transformation in Plants,* England, Open University Press, 1988.

Index